I0225337

CONTROLLING AND PREVENTING
DISEASE

CONTROLLING AND PREVENTING

DISEASE

THE ROLE OF WATER AND ENVIRONMENTAL SANITATION INTERVENTIONS

Erik Rottier and Margaret Ince

Water, Engineering and Development Centre
Loughborough University
2003

Water, Engineering and Development Centre,
Loughborough University,
Leicestershire, LE11 3TU, UK

© WEDC, Loughborough University, 2003

ISBN: 9780906055908

A reference copy of this publication is also available online at:
http://www.lboro.ac.uk/wedc/publications/cpd.htm

Rottier, E. and Ince M.E. (2003)
Controlling and Preventing Disease:
The role of water and environmental sanitation interventions

All rights reserved. No part of this publication may be reprinted or reproduced or utilized
in any form or by any electronic, mechanical, or other means, now known or hereafter
invented, including photocopying and recording, or in any information storage or retrieval
system, without the written permission of the publishers.

A catalogue record for this book is available from the British Library.

WEDC (The Water, Engineering and Development Centre) at Loughborough University in
the UK is one of the world's leading institutions concerned with education, training, research
and consultancy for the planning, provision and management of physical infrastructure for
development in low- and middleincome countries.

This edition is reprinted and distributed by Practical Action Publishing.
Since 1974, Practical Action Publishing has published and disseminated books and
information in support of international development work throughout the world. Practical
Action Publishing trades only in support of its parent charity objectives and any profits are
covenanted back to Practical Action (Charity Reg. No. 247257, Group VAT Registration No.
880 9924 76).

All reasonable precautions have been taken by the WEDC, Loughborough University to
verify the information contained in this publication. However, WEDC, Loughborough
University does not necessarily endorse the technologies presented in this document. The
published material is being distributed without warranty of any kind, either expressed or
implied. The responsibility for the interpretation and use of the material lies with the reader.
In no event shall the WEDC, Loughborough University be liable for damages as a result of
their use.

Editorial contributions: Kimberly Clarke and Rod Shaw
Designed and produced at WEDC
Layout: Karen Betts
Illustrations: Ken Chatterton

Contents

Chapter 1

Introduction

Improving health is one of the main goals of water and environmental sanitation interventions. Despite this, many aid and development workers working in the field of water and environmental sanitation have only a limited knowledge of the infections they try to prevent. Although the relevant information does exist, it is often scattered in specialised literature and rarely finds its way into the field.

This manual addresses this problem by presenting information to aid and development workers on these infections in relation to the interventions that these workers control: water supply, sanitation, drainage, solid waste management, and vector control.

1.1   Definitions of commonly used terms in this manual

Water supply is the means by which people are provided with water for domestic use. This is water used for drinking, cooking, washing, and other domestic activities like watering gardens or water for domestic animals.

Sanitation refers to all aspects of excreta disposal (human and animal, faeces and urine). It includes sanitary structures (e.g. latrines); material needed for the proper operation and use of the structures (e.g. water, soap); and the human behaviour and attitudes relating to excreta and its disposal.

Environmental sanitation means *drainage* (how unwanted water is disposed of); *solid waste management* (how refuse is dealt with); and *vector control* (measures taken to reduce the risks of disease posed by vectors).

Water and environmental sanitation means water supply, sanitation, drainage, solid waste management, and vector control. These are called the *components* of water and environmental sanitation projects. These components have physical aspects (e.g. latrines), as well as behavioural aspects (e.g. keeping latrines clean). Water and environmental sanitation is often shortened to *WES* in this manual.

Infection usually means the entry and development of organisms (e.g. virus, bacterium) in a host (human or animal) (Benenson, 1995). In this manual we use the word *infection* for the development in a host of an organism(s) whose transmission and/or prevention are influenced by WES.

Disease is a broad term normally used for any malfunction of the body resulting from a cause other than injury. An infection is only a communicable or infectious disease if it results in illness. Although, strictly speaking, it is not correct to use disease and infection synonymously (most infections covered in this manual can result in infection without symptoms), we have done so here to improve readability.

Please note: Throughout this manual, Dracontiasis is referred to as Guinea-worm, the commonly used name for the disease.

1.2   Who this manual is for

This manual has been produced primarily for non-medical aid and development workers working in water and environmental sanitation at field level. Nevertheless, anyone working in WES, or in the prevention of infections related to WES, may find this book useful.

Aid and development workers operating at various stages of the project cycle will find this manual useful. Whether you need to assess the health risks in an existing situation; write, or assess, a project proposal; or implement an intervention, you will find relevant information in this book. You do not need to have extensive knowledge, of or experience in WES or in disease to be able to use this manual.

1.3   Scope of the manual

This manual covers infections that occur in all developing countries, and will be useful for both emergency and longer term development projects. It can be used in both urban and rural situations, and with settled as well as displaced populations such as internally displaced people and refugees.

The various components of WES up to the level at which aid and development workers in the field usually work are covered. We focus on appropriate technology options. The specific health problems related to industries, mines, large hospitals, abattoirs, or sewage treatment plants are not addressed.

Although housing plays an important role in the prevention of disease, housing issues have not been addressed here as the improvement of housing will not usually be the responsibility of the WES specialist.

1.4   Structure of the manual

While some readers will want to study subjects in depth, many fieldworkers need relevant, concise information which is accessible, and easy to work through. This manual, therefore, provides information in two ways and has two parts.

Part 1 is comprised of information in chapters as summarised in Section 1.4.1 below. Part 2 is comprised of annexes: information in list and tabular form as outlined in Section 1.4.2.

1.4.1   Part 1

Chapter 2: Disease and disease transmission
This chapter looks at how the infections related to WES are transmitted. The elements of the transmission cycle of disease are presented, along with important related issues. In addition, this chapter categorises the infections linked to WES into groups with similar transmission cycles.

Chapter 3: Disease in the population
In this chapter we introduce some basic concepts about the dynamics of disease in a population, and examine endemic and epidemic occurrence of disease, epidemiology, and mortality and morbidity rates.

Chapter 4: Water and environmental sanitation projects
Chapter 4 looks at the background to WES projects. We consider why these projects are necessary, and what they try to achieve. The WES project cycle is also described. In addition, several issues relating to the impact and sustainability of interventions are presented. The chapter ends with an examination of the link between health, poverty, and development.

Chapters 5 to 8
In these chapters we introduce the components of WES – domestic water supply, sanitation, drainage, and solid waste management – along with the health issues associated with each component.

We do not specifically look at vector control here, as this subject would be too vast to cover adequately. The role that water supply, sanitation, drainage, and solid waste play in vector control is, of course, important, and this is covered in the relevant chapters. Although we do not cover vector control in its own chapter, we have included all vector-borne diseases of importance in Annexe 1, and Annexe 3 presents summary tables on both vector-borne infections and vectors and their control.

1.4.2   Part 2

Annexe 1: Properties of infections related to WES
In this annexe we list all the common infections related to WES with their properties relevant to WES specialists. We cover over 85 infections in a standard format.

Annexe 2: Occurence, transmission and control of infections related to WES (excluding vector-borne infections)
Annexe 2 presents information on the occurrence of infections, whether it has animal vectors, and measures of control in the form of tables. Vector-borne diseases are covered in Annexe 3.

Annexe 3: Vector-borne infections: their vectors and control
In this annexe we present tables which link infections to vectors, vectors to properties, and vectors to methods of control.

Annexe 4: The chlorination of drinking water
Here we look at how to determine the demand of chlorine in water, and how to calculate how much chlorine to add to large water volumes.

Annexe 5: Sizing pits for latrines and determining their infiltration capacity
This annexe explains how to size the pit for a latrine, and how much liquid the pit can cope with.

Annexe 6: Designing a simple drainage system for stormwater
Here we present a method for estimating how much stormwater a catchment area will produce, and how to size a drain which has to cope with this flow.

Annexe 7: Minimum standards in emergencies
In this annexe we present the basic needs of healthy people to survive, and the minimum standards of WES service that have to be provided to people in an emergency situation.

1.5   How to use the manual

To understand better the issues relating to disease transmission, the dynamics of disease in the population, and WES projects and WES components, read Chapters 2 to 7 from start to end. Many readers, however, will not be in a position to read through the text in this way, so the manual has also been designed to be used as a reference book, with information listed in the table of contents and the index.

The manual is also structured to allow the reader to extract information by disease, by project, or by the components of WES.

The diseases
Information on individual infections is presented in Annexe 1.

More than 85 infections are covered in 60 individual sections. All sections have the same format, although some less relevant or less important infections are only summarised. Readers can find important information on each disease, such as distribution of the infection, severity of the disease, how transmission occurs, whether the infection is a risk in a disaster and preventative measures.

This information is important to know how to reduce an existing problem, or how to prevent the infection from becoming a problem in the future.

Annexes 2 and 3 present summary information on different infections. This allows the reader to verify quickly whether preventative measures are likely to be effective against specific diseases, and to associate different infections with specific preventative measures.

If a more general perspective on disease transmission is required, or information on the dynamics of disease in the population, Chapters 2 and 3 will be useful. In addition, these chapters will give more background information on issues raised in the other sections on diseases.

The WES project
Chapter 4 is an introduction to WES projects, and presents the issues that should be considered to improve impact and sustainability.

Chapters 5, 6, 7, and 8 briefly present some issues other than health which are associated with components of WES and which should be taken into consideration when making a project proposal.

The components of WES
Readers who want general information on water supply, sanitation, drainage, solid waste management, or vector control can find this in Chapters 5, 6, 7 and 8 and Annexes 3, 4, 5, 6, and 7. In these chapters, the issues related to health are presented, which will be useful for people who have to assess the health risks in an area, who want to know whether certain components would be effective in reducing the health risk, or who have to assess whether a proposed component would be the most effective measure. In these chapters and annexes we look at the

practical aspects relating to the components which will help workers who have to plan, design, or implement interventions, or who have to assess whether existing structures or services are adequate.

Although this book has not been designed as as technical manual, technical information important to the proper functioning of WES components is included to avoid the comon frustration experienced by readers of such texts: 'They tell us what to do, but not how to do it!'. The technical information is not complete, but may be useful, for example, to address rapidly specific problems that arise in an emergency such as the chlorination of drinking-water, the design of sanitary structures, or the removal of stormwater from a refugee camp. In addition, an annexe has been included which presents the priorities and minimum standards of WES in emergencies in summary form.

Chapter 2

Disease and disease transmission

An enormous variety of organisms exist, including some which can survive and even develop in the body of people or animals. If the organism can cause infection, it is an infectious agent. In this manual infectious agents which cause infection and illness are called pathogens. Diseases caused by pathogens, or the toxins they produce, are communicable or infectious diseases [45]. In this manual these will be called disease and infection.

This chapter presents the transmission cycle of disease with its different elements, and categorises the different infections related to WES.

2.1   Introduction to the transmission cycle of disease

To be able to persist or live on, pathogens must be able to leave an infected host, survive transmission in the environment, enter a susceptible person or animal, and develop and/or multiply in the newly infected host.

The transmission of pathogens from current to future host follows a repeating cycle. This cycle can be simple, with a direct transmission from current to future host, or complex, where transmission occurs through (multiple) intermediate hosts or vectors.

This cycle is called the transmission cycle of disease, or transmission cycle. The transmission cycle has different elements:

- The pathogen: the organism causing the infection
- The host: the infected person or animal 'carrying' the pathogen
- The exit: the method the pathogen uses to leave the body of the host
- Transmission: how the pathogen is transferred from host to susceptible person or animal, which can include developmental stages in the environment, in intermediate hosts, or in vectors

- The environment: the environment in which transmission of the pathogen takes place.
- The entry: the method the pathogen uses to enter the body of the susceptible person or animal
- The susceptible person or animal: the potential future host who is receptive to the pathogen

To understand why infections occur in a particular situation, and to know how to prevent them, the transmission cycles of these infections must be understood. The rest of this chapter looks at the elements of the transmission cycle in more detail.

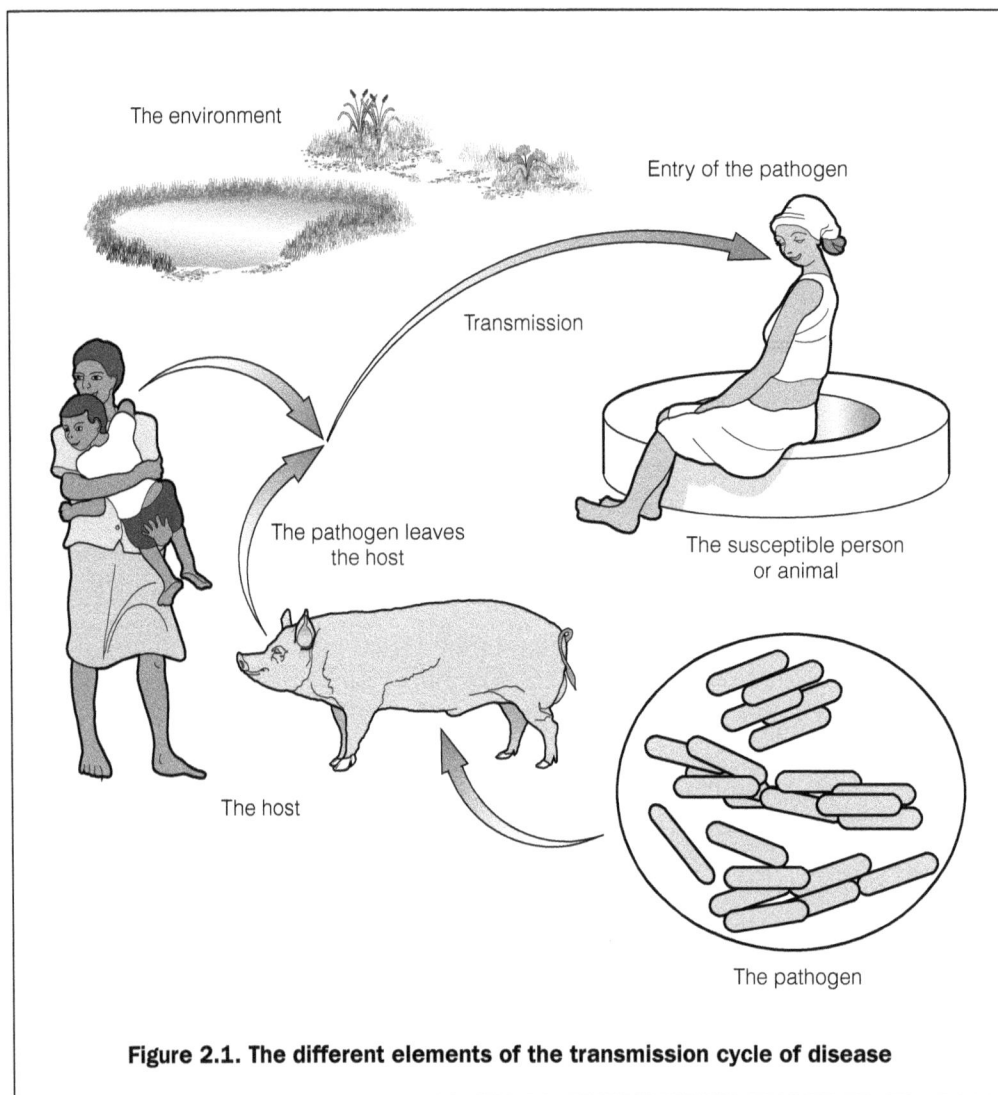

The environment

Entry of the pathogen

Transmission

The pathogen leaves the host

The susceptible person or animal

The host

The pathogen

Figure 2.1. The different elements of the transmission cycle of disease

2.2 The pathogen

The pathogen is the organism that causes the infection.* Specific pathogens cause specific infections. Cholera is caused by the bacterium *Vibrio cholerae*, for example, and Leishmaniasis is caused by different species (spp.) of the protozoa *Leishmania*.

Specific infections also have specific transmission cycles. To be able to react appropriately to health problems in a population, the specific infection causing the problems must be known. Identification of the infection will usually be done by medical personnel.

Different categories of pathogens can infect humans. The pathogens causing the diseases covered in this manual include viruses, bacteria, rickettsiae, fungi, protozoa, and helminths (worms). All pathogens go through a lifecycle, which takes the organism from reproducing adult to reproducing adult. This cycle includes phases of growth, consolidation, change of structure, multiplication/reproduction, spread, and infection of a new host. The combination of these phases is called the development of the pathogen.

Two terms are commonly used to describe pathogens leaving the host through faeces or urine: latency and persistence.

After excretion, a latent pathogen must develop in the environment or intermediate host before a susceptible person or animal can be infected. During the latent period the pathogen is not infectious. A non-latent pathogen does not need to go through a development, and can cause infection directly after being excreted.

Persistency describes how long a pathogen can survive in the environment. A persistent pathogen remains viable for a long period outside the host (perhaps months), while a non-persistent pathogen remains viable for only a limited period [6] (days, or weeks).

Active immunity is the resistance the person or animal develops against the pathogen after overcoming infection or through immunisation (vaccination).[45]. Depending on the pathogen, the effectiveness of active immunity often decreases over time.

---

* It is important to realise that not all infections will result in disease. While a pathogen may cause illness in one person, it may be killed or cause asymptomatic infection in another.

Usually immunity only develops against the specific pathogen that caused the infection. If there are different types (serotypes or strains) of the same pathogen (e.g. in dengue fever and scrub typhus), immunity will often only develop against the particular type which caused the infection. The person or animal can still develop the illness when infected with another serotype or strain of the pathogen[3].

Table 2.1 presents the different categories of pathogenic organisms with some of their characteristics, including latency, persistence, and immunity. The information is general, and exceptions can occur.

2.3 The host

The host is the person or animal infected by the pathogen. The importance of the host in the transmission cycle is its roles as both reservoir and source of pathogens.

There are two types of host: definitive and intermediate host. The definitive host is the person or animal infected with the adult, or sexual, form of the pathogen. In the infections covered here, people are usually the definitive host. To keep things simple the definitive host is called just 'the host'.

The intermediate host is an animal or person infected by a larval, or asexual, form of the pathogen[3]. Cysticercosis and hydatid disease are the only infections covered here for which people are the intermediate host. Where intermediate host is meant, this term is used. Of the infections covered here, only helminths have both definitive and intermediate hosts. All other pathogens only have definitive hosts, although vectors function technically as intermediate hosts for protozoa.

Zoonosis: transmission from animal to person

Some pathogens are specific to humans, others to animals. Many pathogens are less specific and can infect both people and animals. Infections that can naturally be transmitted from animal to person are called zoonoses [3]. Zoonoses are very common; over half of the infections covered in this manual are zoonoses. Many of these infections normally occur in an animal cycle, with people being infected by chance.

The problem with zoonoses is that a continuous reservoir of pathogens exists outside humans. Even if all human infections were cured and transmission to people stopped, the presence of an animal reservoir would remain a continuous risk to people.

Table 2.1. Categories of pathogenic organisms and their characteristics

Pathogen	Description	Latency	Persistence	Additional information
Virus	Particles invade living cells. The pathogen needs structures in these cells to reproduce. [45]	The pathogens are non-latent.	Viruses can survive for months in tropical temperatures. [28]	Where vector-borne, transmission to offspring is possible [3]. The immunity is often long-lasting. [73]
Rickettsiae	Organisms resemble bacteria. [45]. However, similar to viruses, the pathogen needs to develop inside the cells of the host. [2]	n/a	n/a	Transmission of the pathogen to the offspring of the vector occurs. [73]. The immunity is usually long-lasting. [3]
Bacteria	Bacteria are single cell organisms. They are considered more primitive than animal or plant cells. [45]	The pathogens are non-latent.	Persists up to several weeks. [16,73]. Can multiply outside the host. [3]	The immunity developed is often incomplete or short-lived. [3]
Fungi	A group of organisms which include yeast, moulds, and mushrooms. [45]	n/a	n/a	The duration of the immunity is variable. [3]
Protozoa	Protozoa area single cell organisms. [45]	The pathogens are non-latent.	Forms a resistant cyst which can survive for months. [3,44]	The immunity is only maintained by repeated infections or vaccinations. [73]
Helminths (worms)	Helminths are worms (roundworms, flukes or tapeworms) [45]. Often male and female must meet in host to reproduce, and sometimes they multiply in intermediate hosts.	The pathogen is latent. It often has a complex lifecycle with a development in the environment or intermediate hosts. [73]	The pathogen is persistent and some may survive for years in the environment. [3, 16]	Usually no immunity is built up against the pathogen. [3]

n/a: Not applicable as the pathogens are not excreta-related.

Prevention of zoonoses often includes control of animal hosts. This is possible by reducing the number of hosts (e.g. controlling rats), immunising domestic animals, or avoiding unnecessary contact with host animals.

Carriers: hosts without obvious illness

A person or animal who develops an illness is an obvious example of a host. It is very common, however,for infections to occur without the disease developing. The person or animal infected can potentially spread the pathogen, but does not show clear symptoms [8]. The symptoms may be mild, or may be completely absent.

These hosts are called carriers, or asymptomatic carriers. Table 2.2 shows some infections that are frequently mild or asymptomatic. The host can be infectious for a short period in transient carriers, or over a prolonged period in a chronic carrier [3]. Incubating carriers have been infected and can spread the pathogen, but do not yet show the symptoms of the illness. Convalescent carriers continue to spread the pathogen even though they have recovered from illness.

In many infections carriers play an important role in transmitting the pathogen. It is usually not possible to identify asymptomatic carriers [73], and unless the family and other close contacts of the sick person or even the whole population can be treated, carriers will remain a threat to the health of those surrounding them.

Table 2.2. Examples of infections with asymptomatic carriers	
Infection	*Asymptomatic infections*
Bacillary dysentery	common [3]
Cholera (El Tor)	only 1 in 30-50 infections develops illness [16]
Giardiasis	1 in 2-4 infections develops illness [44]
Polio	very common
Typhoid fever	very common [73]
Schistosomiasis	very common [16]
Hookworm	very common
Yellow fever	common [3]
Japanese Encephalitis	only 1 in 1,000 infections develops illness [44]
Filariasis	very common
Malaria	common [3]
River blindness	common [2]
Plague	common during epidemics [73]

Other reservoirs of pathogens

Besides hosts, there are several other pathogen reservoirs that can play a role in the transmission of disease. Some pathogens are very resistant, and can survive in the environment for considerable time. Though this will normally be an exception, roundworm eggs can remain viable in soil for years [3].

Intermediate hosts may be important reservoirs of pathogens, and several helminths can even multiply in the intermediate host.

Vectors are usually infectious for life, and several pathogens can be transmitted to the offspring of the vector over several generations [2]. A soft tick, for example, can survive for more than five years and can pass to its offspring the pathogen which causes tick-borne relapsing fever [73].

Some pathogens can live their entire lifecycle outside the host. These include threadworm and several faecal-oral bacteria which cause bacillary dysentery, (para)typhoid, and salmonellosis [3].

Animal hosts, asymptomatic carriers, and other potential reservoirs of pathogens can be important sources of infection, and this must be taken into account when trying to control disease. The whole population at risk may have to be treated, or animal hosts controlled. With several diseases these preventive measures will have to be maintained over a long period before a reduction in the occurrence of the infection will be noticeable.

2.4 Transmission of disease

To survive as a species, pathogens must infect new people or animals. To do this, they must leave the body of the host, find their way to a new susceptible person or animal, and enter the body of that person or animal. As the exit, transmission, and entry of the pathogens are closely associated, we will cover them together.

Water and environmental sanitation interventions that aim to improve the health of a population usually try to reduce the risk of transmission of infection. To do this appropriately, the WES specialist needs to be familiar with the pathogens' transmission route(s). It is this understanding that enables the specialist to determine which control measures will be most effective in a particular situation.

As many infections are linked to WES, it is useful to categorise the different diseases.

For a water and sanitation specialist the most useful categorisation is based on the transmission cycles of the infections. Generally speaking, diseases with similar transmission cycles can be controlled by similar preventive measures, and will occur in similar environments.

The infections are categorised and their transmission routes described at the same time. More information on the transmission routes and potentially effective preventive measures of specific diseases can be found in Annexe 1.

Some terms relating to the transmission or classification of infections are defined here:

Food-borne infections: infections which can be transmitted through eating food containing the pathogen.

Vector-borne infections: infections transmitted through vectors. We use vector-borne infections only for infections with a *biological vector*, that is a vector in which the pathogen goes through a development before further transmission is possible (e.g. mosquitoes, tsetse fly, body louse). We do not classify as vector-borne those infections which are transmitted by *mechanical vectors*, that is the animal is only a vehicle for transporting the pathogen (e.g. domestic flies, cockroaches).

Water-borne infections: infections which can be transmitted through drinking-water which contains the pathogen.

Water-washed infections: infections caused by pathogens whose transmission can be prevented by improving personal hygiene.

Infections can have either direct or indirect transmission routes.

2.4.1   Infections with direct transmission

A pathogen with a direct transmission route can infect a susceptible person or animal immediately after leaving the host. The pathogen does not need to develop in the environment, in an intermediate host, or in a vector.

In faecal pathogens these are the non-latent infectious agents.

This group contains three disease-groups: faecal-oral infections, leptospirosis, and infections spread through direct contact.

2.4.1.1 *Faecal-oral infections*

These pathogens leave the host through faeces, and enter the susceptible person or animal through ingestion. Transmission occurs mainly through direct contact with contaminated fingers; food contaminated directly with excreta, contaminated hands, domestic flies, soil, or water; contaminated drinking-water; or contaminated soil. Faecal-oral infections are food-borne, water-borne, and water-washed. As faecal-oral infections are transmitted directly, any route that will take matter polluted with faeces directly or indirectly to somebody's mouth could potentially transmit the pathogen. Figure 2.2 shows some common transmission routes of faecal-oral infections.

Some of these infections have mainly animal hosts, while others are limited to humans. Faecal-oral infections include diarrhoeal diseases such as cholera and bacillary dysentery, typhoid, hepatitis A, and poliomyelitis.

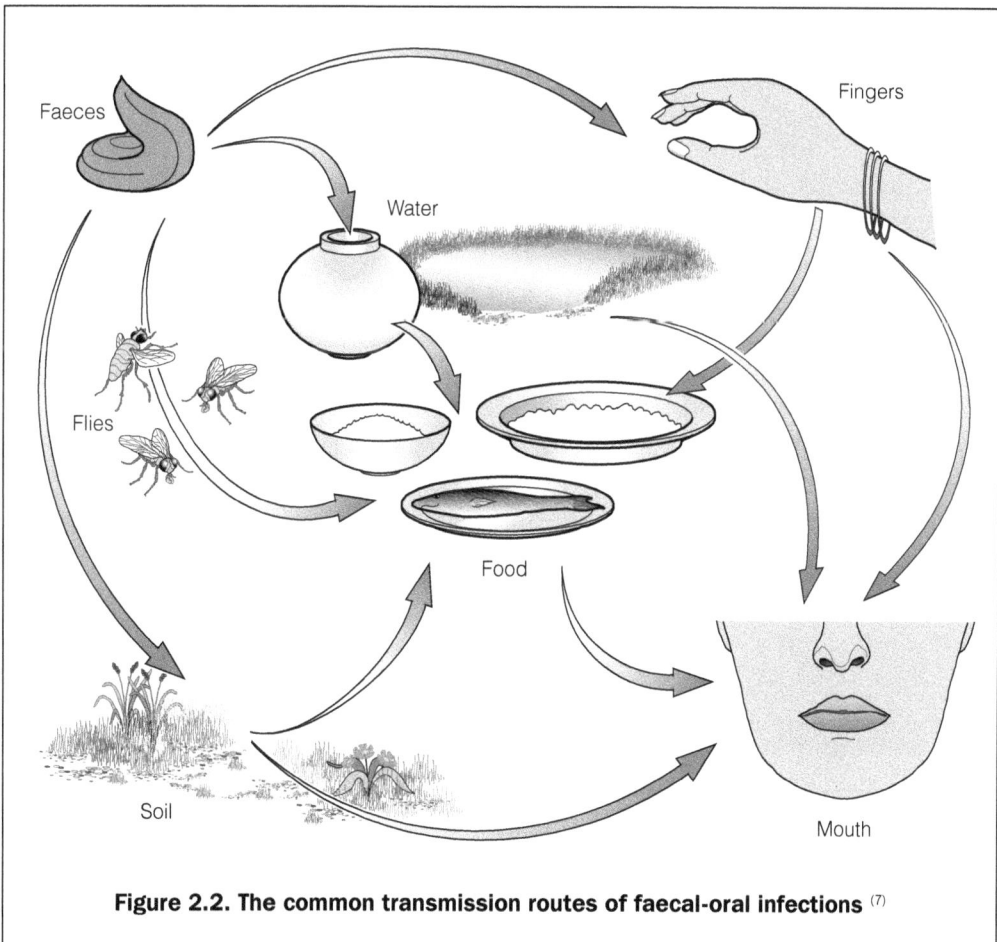

Figure 2.2. The common transmission routes of faecal-oral infections [7]

2.4.1.2 *Leptospirosis*

The main reservoir of leptospirosis is normally rats, though many other animals can potentially transmit the infection. The pathogen leaves the animal host through urine. People are usually infected through direct skin contact with water, moist soil, or vegetation contaminated with urine from infected animals. Other ways of transmission are direct contact with body tissues of infected animals or ingesting food contaminated with urine. Transmission from person to person is rare [3].

2.4.1.3 *Infections of direct contact*

All the diseases covered in this manual that fall into this category are infections which affect the skin or eyes. Pathogens are present on the skin or in the discharges of affected body parts or eyes. The pathogens are transmitted directly through contaminated hands, clothes, domestic flies, or any other contaminated material.

The pathogen enters the body through skin or mucous membranes such as the eyes. These infections are associated with poor personal hygiene and are water-washed.

Few of these infections have animal hosts. The diseases in this category include conjunctivitis, trachoma, yaws, and scabies.

2.4.2 Infections with indirect transmission

A pathogen with an indirect transmission route must go through a development phase outside the host before it can infect a new susceptible person or animal. This development will take place in a specific intermediate host, vector, or type of environment.

This need to go through a particular organism or environment gives the transmission route a focus, which preventive measures can target, for example by vector control or improved food preparation.

In the faecal pathogens these are the latent infectious agents.

The disease-groups with indirect transmission are soil-transmitted helminths, water-based helminths, beef/pork tapeworm infection, Guinea-worm infection, and vector-borne infections.

2.4.2.1 Soil-transmitted helminths

These worms leave the body through faeces as eggs or larvae. After excretion they have to develop in soil. They can be further divided based on how the pathogen enters the human body.

Entrance by penetration of the skin: the pathogen enters the body through skin which is in direct contact with contaminated soil. This is the method used by hookworms and threadworms.

Entrance by ingestion: if either contaminated soil, or food or hands contaminated with polluted soil come into contact with the mouth, the pathogen can be transmitted. These infections can be food-borne and water-washed. This method is used by roundworms and whipworms.

The infections covered here do not have animal hosts. Figure 2.3 presents the transmission routes of the soil-transmitted helminths.

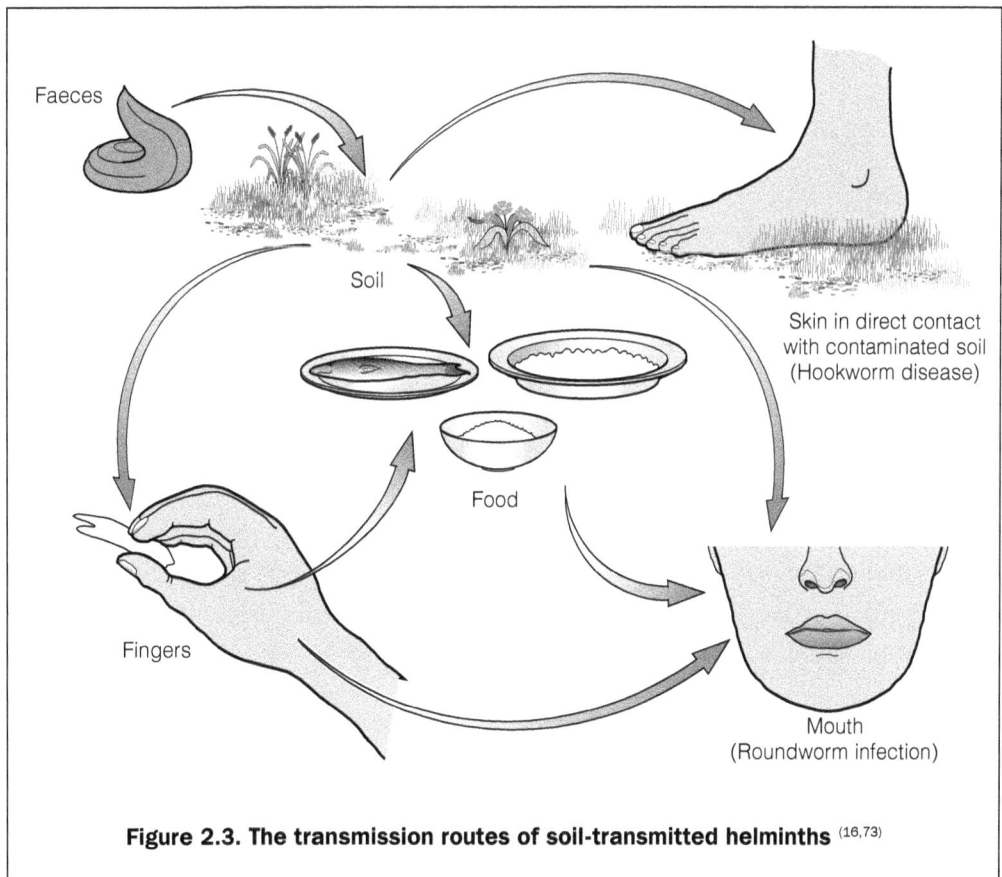

Figure 2.3. The transmission routes of soil-transmitted helminths [16,73]

2.4.2.2 Water-based helminths

These pathogens leave the body through excreta. The infectious agents must develop in intermediate hosts living in freshwater. The transmission of these infections is therefore only possible if excreta containing the pathogens reaches fresh surface water in which there are suitable intermediate host(s). Based on transmission cycle, this category can be sub-divided in two groups:

Schistosomiasis. After excretion, the pathogen infects a freshwater snail, in which it develops and multiplies. The snail releases the pathogens into the water, and people are infected when these pathogens penetrate skin which is in direct contact with infected freshwater. Only one type of schistosomiasis (which occurs only in Asia) has an important reservoir in an animal host; all other types have people as the only host of importance.

Water-based helminths with two water-based intermediate hosts. The first intermediate host is a freshwater snail or copepod. The second intermediate host is a freshwater plant, fish, or crabs/crayfish. The intermediate hosts are specific to the pathogen. These infections are food-borne and people become infected when they eat the second intermediate host without properly cooking it. All these infections affect both animals and people. These diseases include opisthorchiasis, clonorchiasis, and lung fluke disease.

The transmission routes of the water-based helminths are presented in Figure 2.4.

2.4.2.3 Beef/pig tapeworm infection

The pathogens leave the person through faeces. The excreted eggs then have to be ingested by either cattle or pigs. Once the pathogen is ingested by the animal, it will develop in the body of the cow or pig. The infections are food-borne and people become infected when they eat undercooked beef or pork containing the pathogen. People are the only hosts to the infection.

A dangerous complication called cysticercosis is possible when people ingest the eggs of the pig tapeworm. The pathogen will form cysts throughout the person's body. Transmission of this infection is like faecal-oral infections.

2.4.2.4 Guinea-worm

In this infection the pathogen, a large worm, creates a blister on the person's skin, which erupts when it comes into contact with water, releasing the worm's larvae. These larvae then infect a copepod (*Cyclops*), in which it develops. The disease is water-borne. People become infected by drinking water containing *Cyclops,* and

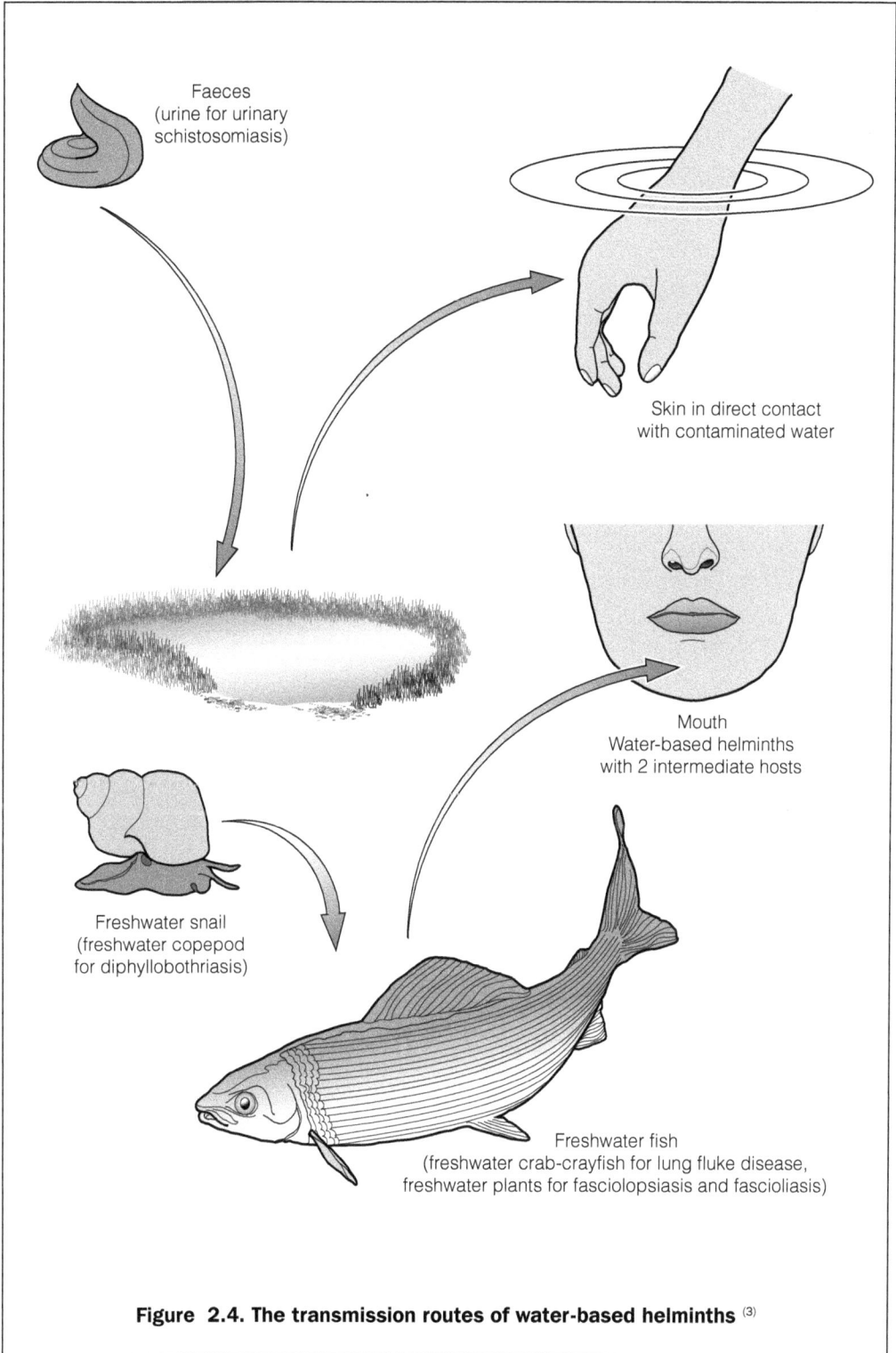

Figure 2.4. The transmission routes of water-based helminths [3]

Faeces
(urine for urinary
schistosomiasis)

Skin in direct contact
with contaminated water

Mouth
Water-based helminths
with 2 intermediate hosts

Freshwater snail
(freshwater copepod
for diphyllobothriasis)

Freshwater fish
(freshwater crab-crayfish for lung fluke disease,
freshwater plants for fasciolopsiasis and fascioliasis)

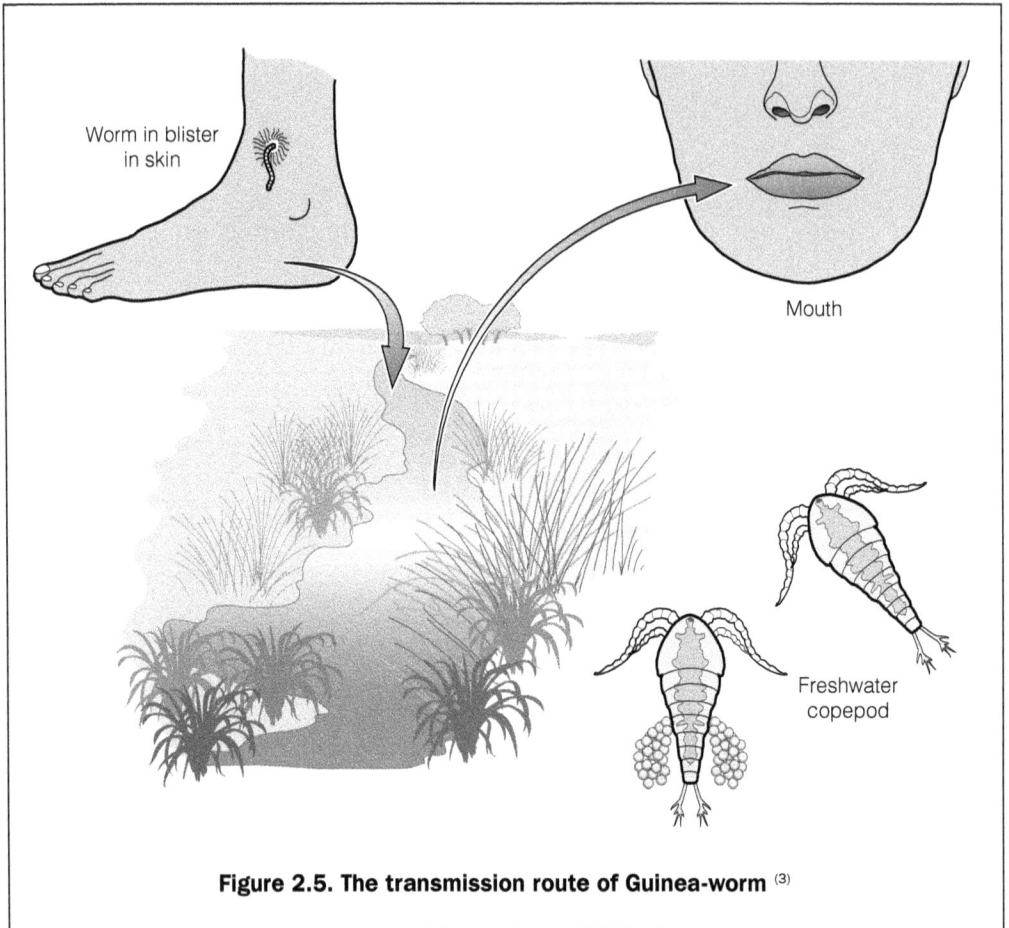

Figure 2.5. The transmission route of Guinea-worm [3]

are the only host to this infection. Figure 2.5 shows the transmission route of Guinea-worm.

2.4.2.5   *Vector-borne diseases*

These infections are transmitted by vectors. Vectors are arthropods (insects, ticks, or mites) which can transmit infections from host to future host [73]. The pathogen exists in the blood or skin of the host. The vector becomes infected when it feeds on a host. The pathogen develops and multiplies inside the vector, which then becomes infectious. People are usually infected through the bite of an infectious vector, though other ways of entry are possible. With several vector-borne diseases animal hosts are important reservoirs. Vector-borne diseases include yellow fever, malaria, sleeping sickness, plague, epidemic louse-borne typhus fever, and louse-borne relapsing fever.

2.5 The environment

The environment is everything that surrounds the pathogen in its transmission from host to susceptible person or animal. Obviously the environment is a vast subject, and we can only look at some of the more important environmental factors here.

Interventions which involve WES will often modify the environment to try to reduce the transmission risk.

The environmental factors that we will look at here are climate, landscape, human surroundings, and human behaviour. Environmental factors are often associated, for example higher altitudes result in lower temperatures, landscapes are formed by the climate.

2.5.1 The climate

The climate and its seasonal changes play an important role in disease transmission. The presence of vectors and intermediate hosts often depends on rain and temperature.

The climatological requirements of the vector or intermediate hosts can predict whether an infection is likely to be a problem in an area. Malaria, for example, will normally not occur in temperatures below 16°C and infection is thus unlikely at altitudes above 2,000 metres.

In general, direct sunlight, a dry environment, and high temperatures will reduce the survival times of pathogens in the environment.

Conditions may not be suitable to transmission year round, and many infections are seasonal, occurring when the environment is favourable to transmission. Mosquito-borne infections, like malaria and yellow fever, are linked to the rainy season [16,44]. The occurrence of diarrhoeal diseases often increases with the first rains after the dry season, as faecal pollution is washed into rivers. Ponds which disappear in the dry season may in the wet season contain water with snails that will transmit schistosomiasis [73].

The climate influences human behaviour. In cold climates people will crowd together and wear more clothing. If this is combined with poor personal hygiene the the body-louse, vector of louse-borne typhus fever and louse-borne relapsing fever, can thrive.

In warmer climates children are also likely to play in surface water, where they can be infected with schistosomiasis.

2.5.2   The landscape

The landscape consists of the larger physical structures in the environment. These structures are usually natural, but can be man-made. They include mountains, deserts, rivers, jungle, artificial water reservoirs, and deforested areas. Aspects of the landscape that would influence disease transmission most are the micro-climate, the presence of water, and types of vegetation.

Man-made modifications of the landscape often increase the risk of disease transmission by creating a habitat favourable to vectors or intermediate hosts. Large artificial water reservoirs frequently increase the occurrence of malaria and schistosomiasis [6], for example, and introducing irrigation schemes can increase the occurrence of schistosomiasis [15].

Although the WES specialist working in the field must recognise the risk-factors linked to the landscape, he or she will normally not be able to modify the landscape to reduce the risks of disease transmission.

2.5.3   The human surroundings

Landscape and human surroundings are closely linked, and it is difficult to divide the two clearly. The difference is one of scale; while the landscape normally cannot be modified or improved by individual people, individuals can modify the human surroundings.

Although the landscape will normally be similar for all people living in an area, the human surroundings may be very different for people living in the same region, village, or even household. Many infections are linked to specific circum-stances, and people with specific occupations, socio-economic status, gender, or religion may be far more at risk than others. While the father of an African family may be exposed to leptospirosis and plague because he works in sugarcane fields and regularly traps rats, the mother may be exposed to sleeping sickness as she goes to the river to wash clothes, and the children may be exposed to schisto-somiasis while playing in the local pond.

The human surroundings are created by a combination of natural elements and how people have modified these elements.

People adapt their surroundings to their needs. If these adaptations are well done, they can help to prevent the transmission of disease. In practise they often encourage the transmission of disease, however, as people do not have the space, motivation, understanding, time, energy, or financial or material means to do them properly.

In relation to the WES aspects, human surroundings are concerned with water supply, proper handling of excreta, removal of unwanted water, adequate management of solid waste, and control of vectors or intermediate hosts through modification of the environment or change in behaviour.

Waste products like excreta, wastewater, and refuse are disposed of in the human surroundings. These wastes must be properly managed to prevent them becoming a health risk.

The WES specialist working in the field will have to know what aspects of the human surroundings increase the risk of disease transmission. This will enable him or her to determine which aspects play an important role in the transmission of disease in a specific situation. Based on this, an intervention can be planned which will reduce the health risks to the population. More on the health risks relating to the human surroundings, and the components from WES interventions can be found in Chapter 5.

2.5.4 Human behaviour

People behave in a certain way because they believe that they are making the most of their lives. Human behaviour is complex. It is influenced by culture, for example religion, attitudes, and traditional beliefs; by social position, such as gender or age; by availability of means, for example money, energy, time, or material; and by politics.

One type of handpump may be acceptable in one culture, but unacceptable in another. One type of latrine may be preferred by men, while women or children might prefer another. People may not accept things from a government they despise, or from an insulting development worker.

Having access to a safe water supply, or technically adequate sanitation, does not automatically mean people will use them [25]. If people do not regard structures as acceptable, appropriate, or as an improvement to their quality of life, they will not be used, or will not be used to their full potential.

Interventions that have only focused on structural improvements have often given poor results in controlling infections. Studies in disease prevention indicate that the most important factor in reducing the transmission of diseases related to WES is hygiene improvements resulting from changes in behaviour [13]. Changing human behaviour in relation to WES should therefore be one of the priorities of the WES specialist.

The specialist will have to identify existing behaviour, attitudes, and behaviour concerning WES and their causes. This will form a base from which health and hygiene promotion can be introduced. All interventions should look at human behaviour, and where needed, reinforce existing positive behaviour while trying to modify behaviour that favours disease transmission.

2.6 The future host

The success of a pathogen in infecting a person will depend on:

- the infectious dose of the pathogen, and the number of infectious agents which manage to enter the potential new host (this applies mainly to faecal-oral infections); and
- whether the pathogen can overcome the barriers of the host.

These two factors are now considered in more detail.

2.6.1 The infectious dose

The infectious dose is the number of pathogens which have to enter the body of a susceptible person to cause infection. Although this figure should not be seen as exact, it does give an indication of how easily an infection can occur.

The infectious dose is normally only used for faecal-oral infections. As every larva of a helminth can become an adult worm, worms have a very low infectious dose.

Table 2.3 gives the infectious doses of several faecal-oral infections.

Infections with a low infectious dose are more likely to be spread by direct person-to-person contact than infections with a high infectious dose. Measures such as improving drinking-water quality, or reducing the concentration of pathogens in surface water (for exampleby treating sewage), are more likely to have effect on infections with high infectious doses than on those with low ones [73]. Intuitively one would say that flies are more likely to transmit infections with a low infectious dose, but this is complicated by the fact that several bacteria can multiply in food, and thus reach the infectious dose in this way.

Table 2.3. Examples of infective doses of faecal-oral diseases	
Disease	**Infectious dose (in number of pathogens)**
Bacillary dysentery (shigellosis) [16]	10 to 100
Giardiasis [16]	10 to 100
Rotaviral enteritis [16]	100 to 10,000
Cholera [73]	Usually 10^6 to 10^8
Typhoid [73]	10^3 to 10^9

2.6.2 The barriers of the body against pathogens

The body has a range of mechanisms that prevent a pathogen from causing infection.

The skin and mucous membranes have anti-microbial substances, and the stomach is acid to act as the first barriers against pathogens. Low acidity in the stomach or an open wound (e.g. insect bite, cut, abrasion) can make this barrier ineffective.

The next barriers are mechanisms that react to the pathogen, and try to counter its development. These barriers are not specific to the pathogen, and the body does not need to have been in contact with the pathogen for them to be effective. These mechanisms are the host's resistance against pathogens [41]. Resistance is lowered if someone is suffering from other infections [73], or is malnourished, stressed, or fatigued [41]. Women have a higher risk of infection when pregnant [73].

An individual's immune system may have experienced a pathogen through an earlier infection or immunisation (vaccination) with inactivated pathogens. When the pathogens enter the person's body, their immune system will recognise the pathogen and make antibodies which will attack the pathogen. This is called active immunity [45]. The effectiveness of active immunity depends on the pathogen, and the length of time since the body has been in contact with the pathogen. Active immunity is effective only against that particular pathogen. The effectiveness against bacteria and viruses usually lasts for years [3].

Passive immunity is created by introducing foreign antibodies into the body. An unborn baby receives antibodies from the mother through the placenta, which will protect it for some time after birth. Vaccination with antibodies is another way of creating passive immunity [73]. The foreign antibodies will slowly disappear from the body, and passive immunity will usually only last days or months [3].

A person or animal who lacks effective barriers (has a poor resistance and/or a low immunity) against a pathogen is susceptible to this infectious agent [45].

Two important practical points define the susceptibility of a population:

- A population that is weakened because of poor nutrition or a high occurrence of disease, fatigue, or stress has an increased risk of disease.
- When a pathogen is very common in a population, or the population is immunised, most people will have some form of immunity against it. In this case the disease will attack mainly children. If the same pathogen is introduced into a population which has low immunity, there is a risk of an outbreak (an epidemic) which can attack all ages.

2.6.3 The infection over time

When a pathogen is introduced in sufficient numbers, and overcomes the resistance and immune system of a person or animal, infection will follow. The time between entrance of pathogen and appearance of the first signs of disease or symptoms is called the incubation period. As mentioned earlier, not all infections will result in disease, and for many infections asymptomatic carriers are common.

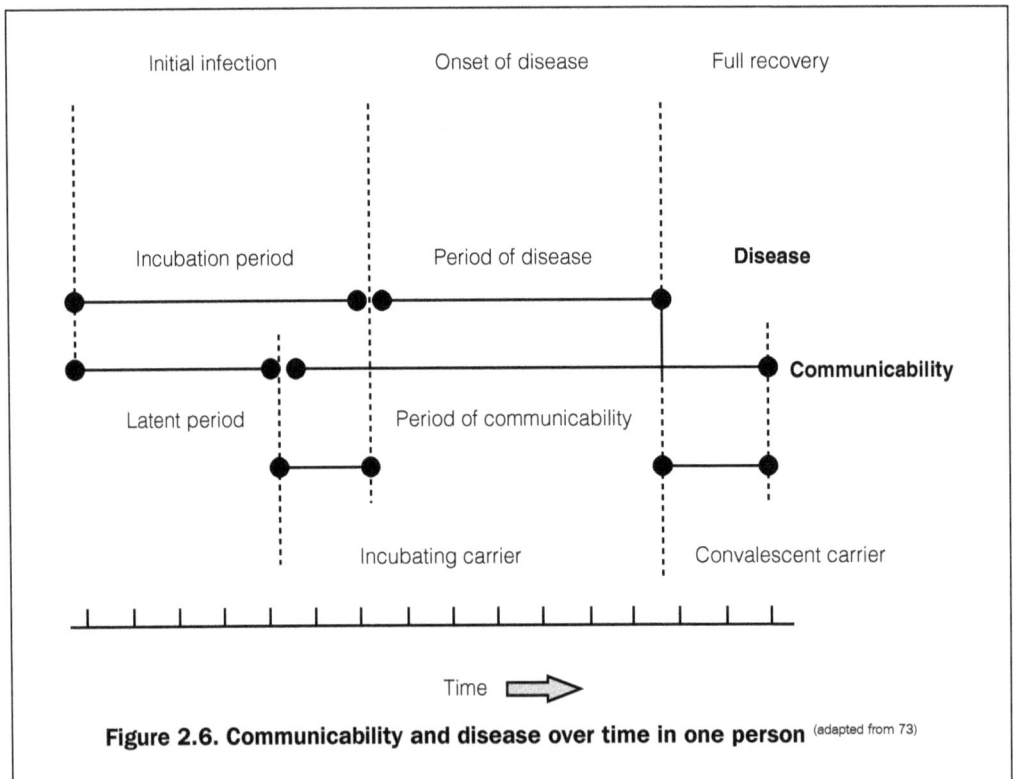

Figure 2.6. Communicability and disease over time in one person (adapted from 73)

The period of communicability is the period in which the host is infectious, or the period in which pathogens are shed in the environment. The time between entrance of pathogen and the onset of communicability is the latent period. This is shown on a timeline in Figure 2.6.

In some infections the period of communicability starts before illness is apparent. Hosts who can transmit the pathogen before showing symptoms are called incubating carriers. If the period of communicability extends beyond the end of the illness, the hosts are called convalescent carriers.

Chapter 3

Disease in the population

This chapter introduces the dynamics of communicable disease in a population. We look at immunity, endemic and epidemic occurrence of disease, some epidemiological concepts, and we considermortality and morbidity rates in a population in both stable and emergency situations.

Immunity in the population

Immunity plays a crucial role in the dynamics of disease transmission. The more people are immune, the less likely it is that a pathogen will find a susceptible person. If enough people are immune, the chance of the pathogen causing an infection becomes so small that transmission stops, even though there are still susceptible people. This is called herd immunity [41]. With poliomyelitis, for example, if 80 to 85 per cent of the entire population is immune, the virus will disappear [50]. A population can lose its herd immunity through births, migration of susceptible people into the population, or waning immunity in the population over time. Figure 3.1 presents a model of immunity in the population.

Two important points can be deduced from Figure 3.1:

- The immunity in a population is the result of people either overcoming the infection or being immunised (vaccinated).

- The susceptibility of the population in an area increases through the influx of non-immune people, birth, and from people losing their immunity (through time or another reason, such as HIV infection).

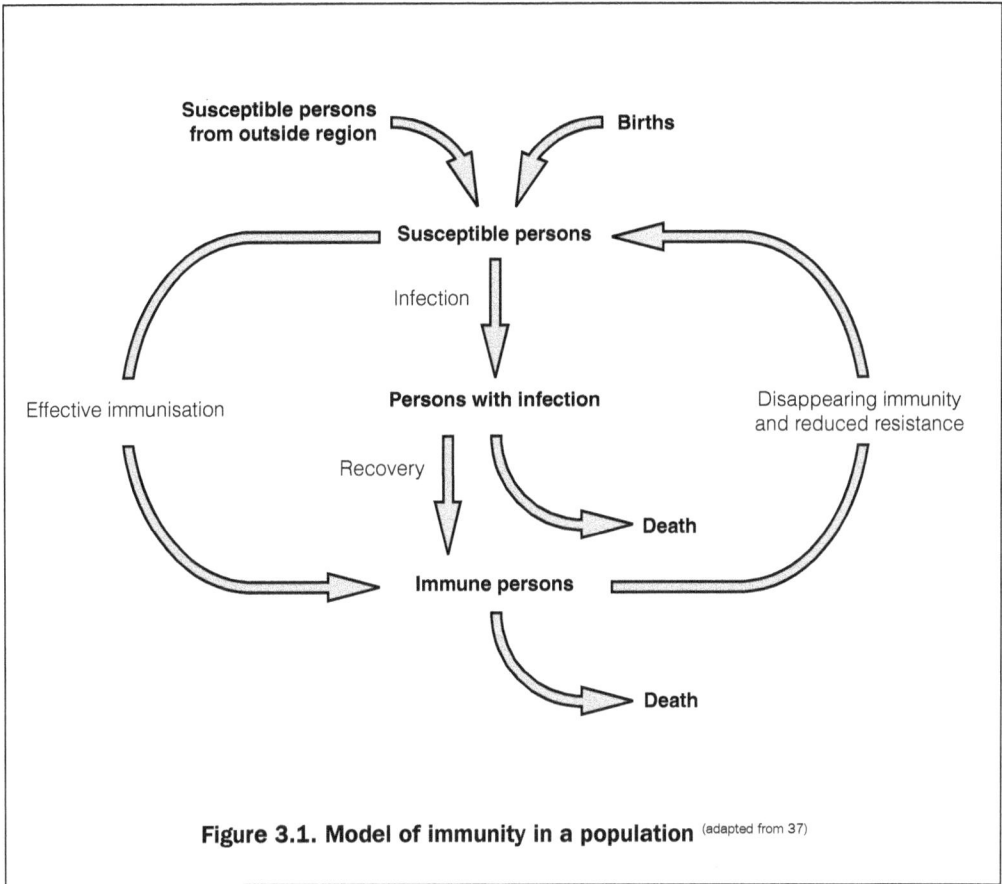

Figure 3.1. Model of immunity in a population (adapted from 37)

3.1 Endemic and epidemic occurrence of disease

The occurrence of an infection in a population is determined by many factors, including the pathogen, its persistence and/or latency, whether it has a high or low infectious dose, whether it can multiply outside the host, and whether it infects both humans and animals or only humans. It depends on hosts, how many pathogens they shed, and whether their behaviour favours transmission. It depends on the environment in which transmission occurs, its climate, and its human physical environment, which may favour direct transmission, vectors, or intermediate hosts. It depends on potential new hosts and their behaviour, resistance, and immunity against the infection. (These factors were covered in Chapter 2.)

These factors can either favour, or oppose, the transmission of the pathogen from a host to a potential new host. Favouring and opposing factors balance each other. Three situations are possible:

- The opposing factors are stronger than the favouring factors: the infection disappears or does not occur. This situation is what we try to achieve.
- The opposing and favouring factors are in balance: there is a continuous presence and transmission of the infection in the population. The disease is endemic.
- The opposing factors are weaker than those that favour transmission: the occurrence of the infection increases in the population. If the occurrence is clearly more than normally expected, then the infection is epidemic.

This balancing between the opposing and favouring factors is a dynamic process that can easily alter with changes in the pathogen, hosts, environment, or potential new hosts.

Communicable diseases are usually either absent, endemic, or epidemic in a population (although sporadic or imported cases can occur). Most infections can be both endemic and epidemic, but only some can cause explosive, severe epidemics. Even though epidemics can be dramatic, endemic disease is often worse for the population [51].

In health programmes it is the eradication of frequent, severe, and preventable or controllable infections that should receive priority [71].

3.1.1 Endemic occurrence of disease

An infection is endemic when it is always present in a population [3]. How often the infection occurs depends on the factors mentioned in Section 3.1, but seasonal fluctuations of infections are also common.

When an infection is common and results in long-lasting immunity, disease will usually occur in childhood, as adults will have built up immunity. If the infection is highly endemic, it is unlikely that an epidemic will occur, unless several subtypes of pathogens can cause the same disease and the population is immune against only one of these, which can happen with dengue fever, for example [3].

Disease is often unevenly distributed in a population. Depending on people's occupation, environment, and behaviour, some may be more exposed to pathogens than others. Children may be more at risk because of their behaviour (e.g. schistosomiasis caused by playing in water) [16]; the poor may be more at risk because of the conditions in which they live (e.g. poor housing resulting in Chagas disease [73]); people with certain occupations or living in specific locations may be more exposed (e.g. farmers or sewage workers would come in contact more easily with leptospirosis). It is important to identify the people who are most at risk, and why to know who to target and what preventive measures to take.

3.1.2   Epidemic occurrence of disease

An epidemic, or outbreak, occurs if there are clearly more cases of an infection than would be expected in a given area over a given period of time or season [71].

Outbreaks can occur if the following features are combined [10]:

- a pathogen must be introduced or be present in the area;
- the environment must be favourable to transmission; and
- there must be enough susceptible people in the population.

There is a large risk of an outbreak when:

- infected people enter a non-immune population, in an environment favourable to transmission (e.g. infected refugees or migrants enter a non-endemic area);
- susceptible people move into an endemic area (e.g. non-immune refugees or migrants enter an endemic area; people enter an area where a zoonosis occurs in an animal population [79]);
- the population has lost its resistance or immunity, and the pathogen is reintroduced (e.g. people's immunity has diminished over time; babies have been born; or people are suffering from disease or malnutrition [73]); and
- the environment has changed, and has become more favourable to transmission (e.g. construction of a dam has produced an environment favourable to mosquitoes (a malaria vector) or snails (the intermediate host of schistosomiasis)).

An outbreak can become an emergency if the infection is severe, if the society is disrupted because of the number of cases occurring, or if medical infrastructure is unable to cope because of lack of personnel, material, or organisational skills [10].

The most severe epidemics are those caused by infections which are easily transmitted, have short incubation periods [71], and have a potentially severe outcome. The main iInfections that cause severe outbreaks are diarrhoeal diseases (e.g. cholera, bacillary dysentery), yellow fever, malaria, epidemic louse-borne typhus fever, and louse-borne relapsing fever, but other infections can cause emergencies too.

Most of the infections covered in this manual can cause epidemics which impact hard on society or individuals. They will not normally cause emergencies though, as they develop slowly, are less serious, or people have high levels of immunity. Where an infection is endemic it is impossible to give a threshold level that marks the beginning of an epidemic, as this depends on what is 'normal' in a given population, in that area, in that season. Where cholera is not endemic, one case of locally acquired cholera will be declared an epidemic [10]. Where cholera is endemic, two new cases in a week would not necessarily cause concern. An epidemic would be confirmed if more cases occur than occurred in the same season in the recent past [55]. Table 3.1 presents the epidemic threshold level for several diseases.

As with endemic occurrence of disease, outbreaks may be limited to specific groups of the population. Analysis of outbreaks are covered in the next section.

Table 3.1. Threshold levels of epidemics [10]		
Infection	*In a non-endemic population*	*In an endemic population*
Salmonellosis	A group of cases with one common source of infection.	
Cholera	One locally infected confirmed case [a]	A 'significant' increase over what is normal in that season
Yellow fever	One confirmed case in a non-immune population with a presence of vectors	A 'significant' increase in the number of cases over a 'limited time'
Mosquito-borne arboviral encephalitis	A group of cases in a non-immune population (the first case is a warning)	A 'significant' increase in the number of cases caused by that specific pathogen over a 'limited time'
Malaria	A group of cases occurring in a specific area	Rare
Plague	One confirmed case	A cluster of cases caused by domestic rodents or respiratory transmission or an epidemic in rodents
Epidemic louse-borne typhus fever	One confirmed case in a louse-infested, non-immune population	A 'significant' increase in the number of cases over a 'limited time'

[a] A 'confirmed case' is an infection confirmed by laboratory tests.

3.2 Introduction to epidemiology

Epidemiology is the study of the distribution, occurrence, and causes of a disease in a population to improve the existing health situation [54]. Epidemiology covers endemic as well as epidemic occurrence of disease, and the approach taken to both is similar.

A full epidemiological study will consist of four phases [71]:

1. An assessment of the distribution and frequency of a disease in a population.
2. Determining and analysing the causes of the disease.
3. Conducting an intervention to try to reduce the occurrence of the infection.
4. Evaluating the effectiveness of the intervention.

Conducting a full and methodical epidemiological inquiry is complex, and should remain the domain of an epidemiologist, but an intuitive form of epidemiology is already used by WES specialists. Identifying poor personal hygiene, caused by lack of water, as a cause of trachoma or diarrhoea, and installing a water supply to improve water availability, is intuitive epidemiology. Although intuitive epidemiology does not have the scientific rigour of classic epidemiology, it is more practical for fieldworkers.

The following sections will help water and sanitation specialists to take this intuitive approach to disease prevention.

3.2.1 Data collection

Epidemiology is about information. The mortality and morbidity rates of those diseases which are an important health problem will have to be collected from local medical staff or authorities, or from medical agencies working in the area. The rates may not be very accurate, but for a WES specialist accuracy is not essential. Collect the monthly or weekly incidence rates of diseases related to WES, going back for some years if possible (i.e. the number of new cases occurring in a population per unit of time [3]).

The incidence rates, combined with a questionnaire or survey on the background and the environment of the cases, should answer the following questions:

- What infection is being investigated?
- Who is affected? What are their characteristics: socio-economic background (e.g. income level), occupation (e.g. agricultural workers), age, sex, ethnic group, specific behaviour (e.g. use of one specific source of water) or other characteristic (e.g. HIV infected)?

- Where does the disease occur (place of exposure)? What is the geographical distribution (e.g. altitude) and the environment (e.g. slums, swamps, forests, poor sanitation).
- When does the disease occur? Is there a season (e.g. wet season, when many vectors are present), a specific occasion (e.g. one week after a feast, or visit to a town, or a strong increase of the disease in years after the construction of a dam) [71]?

Being aware of the risk factors which can cause transmission will help to identify relevant information. More detailed information about risk factors concerning WES can be found in Chapter 5.

The local risk factors that cause transmission will have to be identified by surveying the environment and human behaviour. It is also important to look at local attitudes and beliefs regarding the disease and its prevention, as these could affect potential interventions. The survey will also have to assess the risk the infection poses, and the capacity of the local authorities to deal with the existing situation or with a potential outbreak. Then the relative importance of the different risk factors will have to be determined.

While endemic occurrence will usually exist in a relatively static situation, an epidemic is always the result of some kind of change which favours transmission. Either a pathogen is introduced into a susceptible population, the population has become more susceptible, or the environment has changed in a way which favours transmission. This change should be identified.

In an outbreak, the primary transmission, or the way the initial cases are infected, may be different from the secondary transmission, or the way the pathogens are transferred from the initial cases to new cases [8]. An outbreak of typhoid fever may originate with infected drinking-water, while secondary transmission may occur through infected food handlers. Similarly, with endemic diseases not all cases need to be infected in the same way.

Once the local risk factors are identified and their importance assessed, the potential effects of eliminating or controlling these factors has to be estimated. By combining this information with what is known about local limitations and resources, it is possible to come up with an indication of what type of intervention would be appropriate in a particular place. When an outbreak results in an emergency, all feasible measures that could potentially reduce transmission should be taken.

This analysis will usually be enough to choose an intervention for endemic and epidemic diseases. Trying to analyse an outbreak can be more complex, as the process is more dynamic. The following aids can help analyse an outbreak.

3.2.2 Aids in analysing an outbreak

The minimum requirement to follow and analyse an outbreak is up-to-date information. A sufficient number of competent and motivated medical staff must be present to identify cases, and reliable and regular reports on cases must be collected at a central point.

It is usually qualified medical personnel who will analyse an outbreak, but the WES specialist has to understand some of the basic aids that can be used, with a questionnaire or survey, to assess the risks and extent of the outbreak, and the possible sources of the epidemic.

3.2.2.1   The spot map: mapping the outbreak

A 'spot map' is a map on which the location of the cases is marked. The spot map shows both the distribution and trend of the outbreak, and potential sources of infection [55]. It also indicates which villages or neighbourhoods are most at risk of further transmission. If possible, the map should show where people became infected to help locate the source of infection. If the infection is easily spread from person to person, it may be useful to map where the cases live or work to predict where there is the greatest risk of secondary transmission.

3.2.2.2   The epidemic incidence curve: following the outbreak in time

During an outbreak an 'epidemic incidence curve' should be drawn. It is a graph that plots the number of new cases day by day, or week by week. The curve can then be extrapolated to show when the initial infection occurred. Looking at the whereabouts and activities of the initial cases will help to pinpoint the cause of the infection.

The curve can highlight a trend and the nature of the outbreak [71].

The point-source or common-source outbreak

A point-source outbreak is caused by a particular incident that infects a group of people almost simultaneously. It is typical of water-borne and food-borne outbreaks, or outbreaks caused by handling infected material [55]. This type of outbreak could be caused by contaminated food served at a feast, for example, or travellers drinking from a contaminated stream. By plotting the incidence curve of an outbreak of a known disease, the approximate time of primary infection can be determined. The first cases that appear are the ones with the shortest incubation period; the last ones are those with the maximum incubation period. Going back in time for the length of the incubation period indicates when infection occurred. By looking at where the people were and what they were doing at that time, the source of infection can be identified [73].

Figure 3.2 shows a point-source outbreak of diarrhoea in a village. The first cases of diarrhoea appear on the morning of 16 July. The diarrhoea is identified as salmonellosis. As the incubation period of salmonellosis is between six hours and three days [3], people were probably infected on the evening of 15 July. A survey shows that on the evening of the 15th all the known cases attended a funeral. At this funeral food was served, and the majority of those who ate meat have fallen ill, while those who did not have no problems. In this case it is probable that the meat served at the funeral was the source of infection.

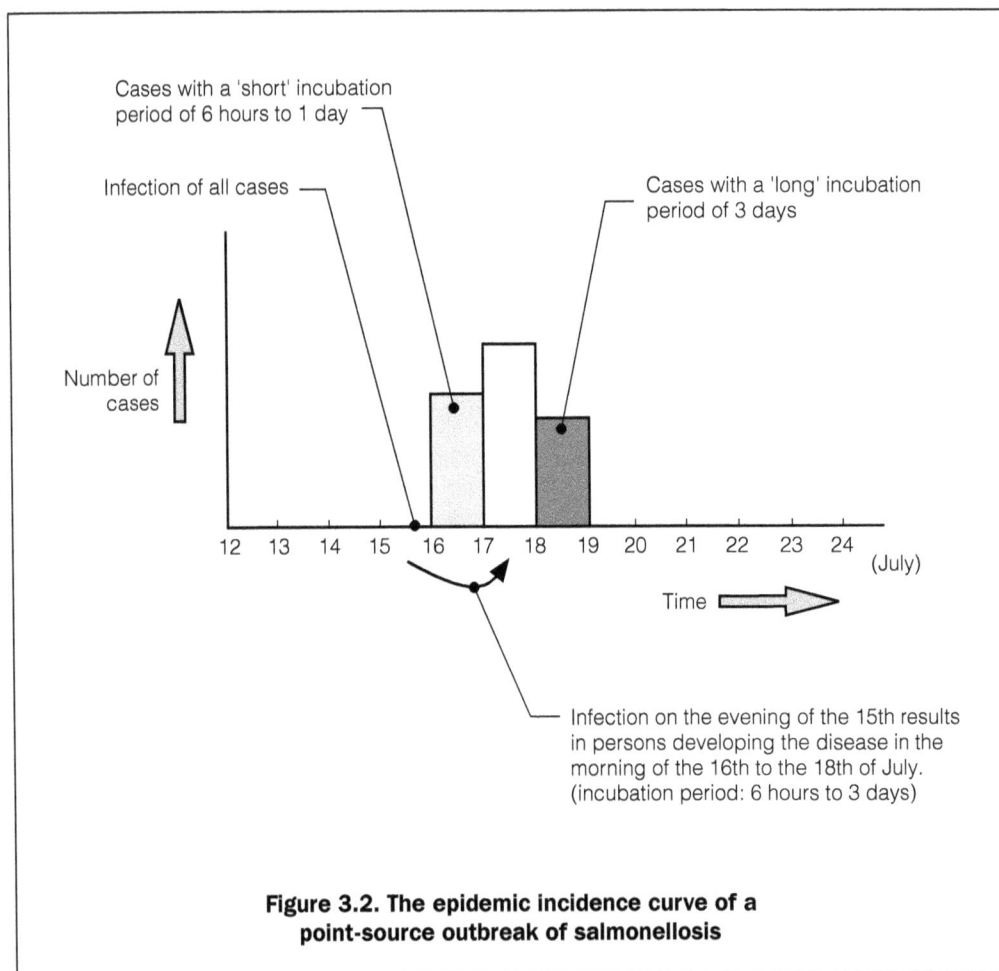

Figure 3.2. The epidemic incidence curve of a point-source outbreak of salmonellosis

The extended point-source outbreak

These outbreaks are caused by specific sources that have infected people over a period of time. The onset is comparable to a point-source outbreak, but cases continue to appear over a longer period [71]. This type of outbreak could be caused by sewage leaking into a water supply system, for example.

The process of finding the source of infection is similar to that with the point-source outbreak. The probable time of initial infection is determined by going back to the time the first cases appear and back further for the shortest incubation period of that infection. A survey of where the first cases occurred, and what those people were doing will normally indicate the probable cause of infection [73].

Figure 3.3 shows the epidemic incidence curve of an extended point-source outbreak of cholera. As the shortest possible incubation period of cholera is one

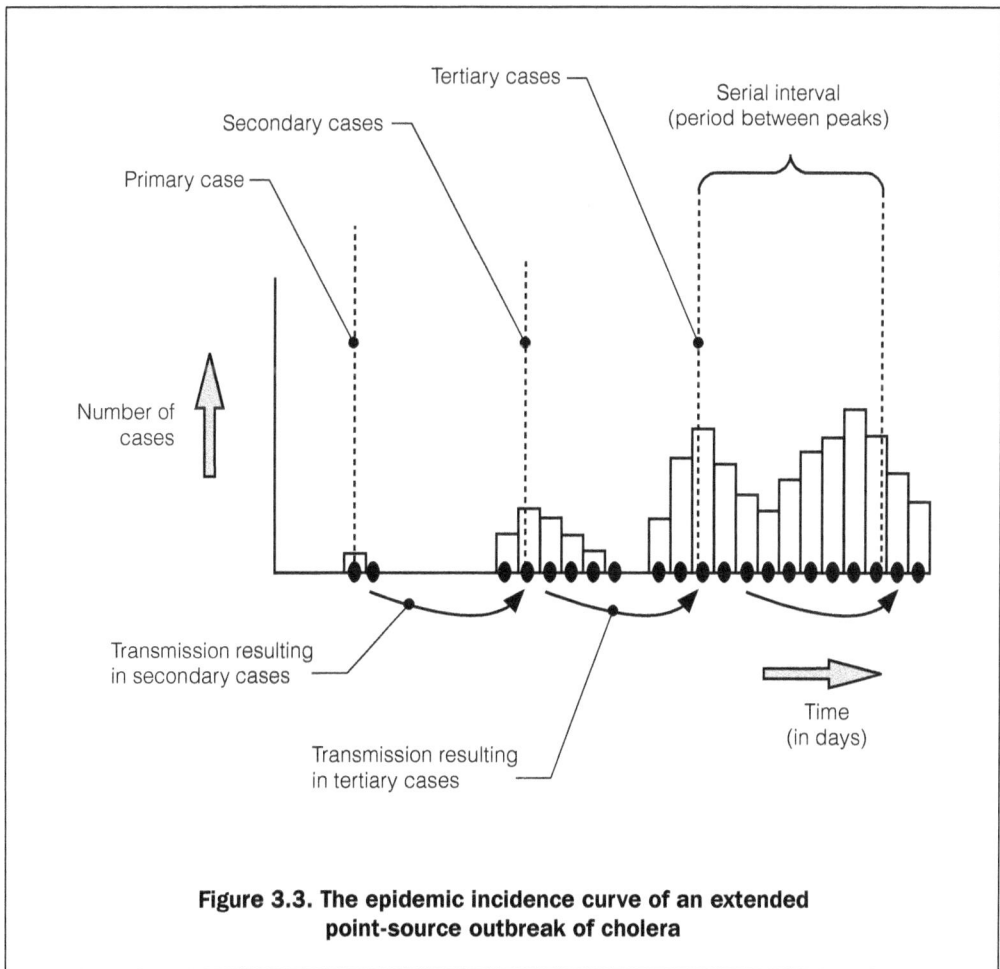

Figure 3.3. The epidemic incidence curve of an extended point-source outbreak of cholera

day, the initial infection probably occurred on 9 May. A survey shows that all the cases ate at a particular food stall on the local market. The stall was closed the evening of the 14th. Cases continued to appear until the 19 May because some of the people infected on the 14th will have had an incubation period of five days.

The propagated-source outbreak

This type of outbreak is the result of progressive transmission. One case, the primary case, will infect a cluster of cases, the secondary cases, who will infect the next cluster, the tertiary cases, and so on. Usually the onset and decline of the outbreak will be more gradual than a point-source outbreak. This type of outbreak is possible with most infections covered in this manual.

Every cluster of cases will show a peak in the incidence curve. The period between the peaks is called the 'serial interval' [73]. The serial interval will depend on the latent period, the period of communicability of the host, and the time it takes for the pathogen to develop in a vector or intermediate host. This will often be about the average incubation period, plus, if applicable, the period of development in the vector or intermediate host. The longer the latent period, the longer the period of communicability, and the longer the time the pathogen needs to develop in the vector or intermediate host, the more spread out over time the curves will be.

The number of cases that will occur will depend on how effective transmission is. The presence of risk factors such as overcrowding, behaviour which favours transmission, a large susceptible population, or an environment favourable to vectors or intermediate hosts, will increase the number of cases [55,71].

Figure 3.4 is an example of a propagated-source outbreak. This is a theoretical example of an infection that has an incubation period of seven to 10 days and period of communicability of two days.

3.2.2.3   Limitations of the spot map and the epidemic incidence curves

The spot map and epidemic incidence curves have several limitations:

- The reported rates always lag at least one incubation period behind the actual situation of the infection. The cases identified now were infected one incubation period earlier. People infected since then are developing the infection, but do not show any symptoms yet (even if transmission were to stop abruptly, new cases would continue to appear for the length of the incubation period). Delay is also likely because of communication problems between the field and the central registration point.

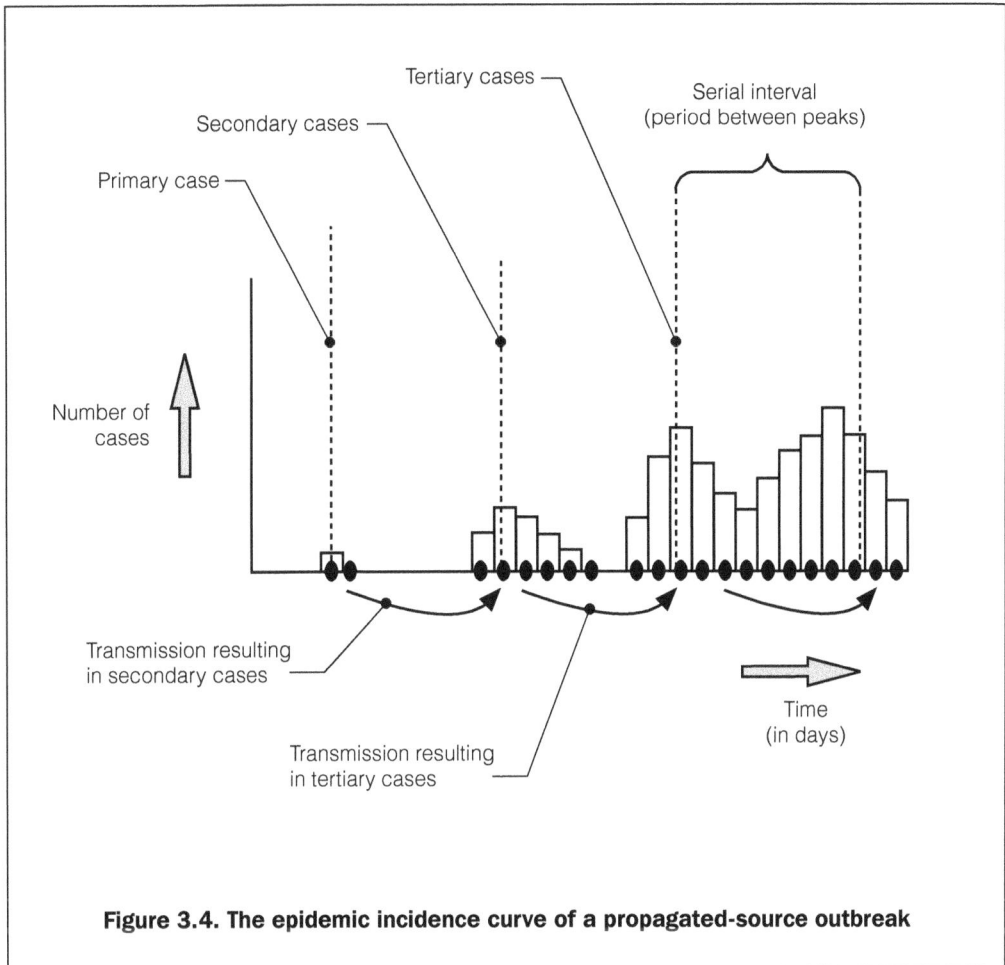

Figure 3.4. The epidemic incidence curve of a propagated-source outbreak

- Reliable and up-to-date information identifying the infection and recording cases is vital. Problems in identifying or reporting cases make analysing an outbreak difficult.
- Normally only symptomatic cases will be registered, and asymptomatic infections will not be identified. This means that you may only be seeing the tip of the iceberg.
- The epidemic incidence curves only indicate when the initial infection probably occurred. The actual cause of the outbreak must be identified by people in the field assessing the cases and their environment.
- When cases infected by primary transmission spread the pathogen to others, they may do so through a different route than the one that infected them. With secondary transmission every new case becomes a potential new source of infection for others, behaving as little (extended) point-source outbreaks them-

selves. The incidence curve may be the result of an accumulation of these many little outbreaks. Cases can often transmit the infection over long periods of time, which will 'smear out' the distinct peaks in a propagated-source outbreak, so the epidemic incidence curves found in practise will not rarely look like the neat models shown here.

3.3 Mortality and morbidity rates in a population

The mortality and morbidity rates of infections are an indication of health problems in a population. Combined with an environmental assessment, the rates of important infections will help to identify health risks relating to WES. The importance of a disease will depend on:

- its frequency in the population (i.e how common it is, or how big is the risk of an epidemic); and
- its severity (i.e. whether the infection causes disability or death) [71];

Seasonal rates are important in identifying seasonal health risks and potential epidemics.

3.3.1 Mortality rates in a stable population

Table 3.2 presents the Crude Mortality Rate (CMR) and the Infant Mortality Rate (IMR) common to a stable population. The CMR is the total number of deaths in the population due to disease, injury, and malnutrition. The IMR is the total number of deaths in children under the age of one year per total births.

The figures for poor communities are not threshold levels, but give an idea of what to expect. The rates for these communities are not acceptable at these levels, and should be brought down, preferably to the CMR of developed communities.

Table 3.2. Mortality rates in a stable population		
	Situation	*Mortality rates*
Crude Mortality Rate (CMR)	Developed communities	10 deaths/1,000/year [71] (0.3 deaths/10,000/day)
	Poor communities	18-25 deaths/1,000/year [11,47] (± 0.6 deaths/10,000/day)
Infant Mortality Rate (IMR)	Poor communities	60-150 inf.deaths/1,000births/year [71] (± 3 deaths/10,000/day)

It is not possible to give 'acceptable' incidence rates for specific diseases in a population, as this will depend heavily on the local situation, but the figures should be lower than the ones presented in Table 3.4. In practise the rates will have to be compared with the feasibility of reducing morbidity by improving the situation through an intervention.

3.3.2 Mortality and morbidity rates in emergency situations

In an emergency situation the CMR is the most practical indicator of the health status of a population. As long as the CMR in a population is more than 1 death/10,000/day the situation remains an emergency [47]. Mortality rates in the initial phases of an emergency can be much higher than this [11,47]. Table 3.3 presents figures of what would be acceptable upper threshold levels in the post-emergency phase in camps for displaced people or refugees.

Table 3.3. Threshold levels of Crude Mortality Rate and Infant Mortality Rate in camps	
	Mortality rates
Crude Mortality Rate	1 death/10,000/day
Infant Mortality Rate	± 2.5 deaths/10,000/day

Even though it is difficult to give concrete figures on incidence rates of diseases, Table 3.4 gives an indication of acceptable rates in camps for displaced people or refugees.

Table 3.4. Indicative acceptable incidence rates and specific mortality rates in camps for displaced persons or refugees [72]		
	Incidence rate (in cases/10,000/week)	**Mortality rate** (in deaths/10,000/week)
Diarrhoea total	60	
Acute watery diarrhoea	50	1
Bloody diarrhoea	20	
Cholera	Every suspected case must be reacted upon	
Fever of unknown origin	100	0.5
Malaria	20	
Skin infections	40	-
Eye infections	35	-

Children under five are more likely to develop disease, and incidence rates of roughly 1½ times those presented here would be acceptable in this group [72].

Chapter 4

Water and environmental sanitation projects

This chapter looks at the problems that WES projects try to address. The planning of WES interventions is considered briefly, and the project cycle is presented. Issues which will have to be considered to improve the impact and sustainability of projects are discussed, and the chapter concludes with a more global perspective of development by looking at poverty in society.

Some terms used in this chapter:

NGO: non-governmental organisation

Agency: any organisation that is implementing a project, including both national and international NGOs

Project: an intervention that tries to achieve one specific objective (e.g. to provide an adequate and sustainable water supply for 20,000 people living in particular villages) through specific activities (e.g. installing 60 handpumps)

Programme: is usually on a larger scale than a project, and has a goal which is more general (e.g. a sustained improvement of health for 40,000 people living in low-cost housing areas in Jakarta). A programme will usually have several objectives (e.g. install adequate and sustainable services for water supplies, sanitary services, hygiene promotion, and solid waste management), and is usually made up of several projects [adapted from 19,20,23].

Although this manual only covers infections linked to WES, it should be remembered that these are only part of the total health burden of people in developing countries.

4.1 The price of poor WES

Infectious diseases related to WES are very common in developing countries. It is estimated that 1 billion people are infected with roundworm [44] and the same number with hookworm [4]. A study in Lubumbashi, in the Democratic Republic of Congo, showed that more than 90 per cent of young children in poor areas were infected with malaria and/or worms [63]. Estimates in the 1980s of the number of infections that occurred worldwide in one year were: diarrhoea, up to 5 billion; malaria, around 150,000,000; trachoma, around 25,000,000 [59].

Every year an estimated 2,900,000 people die of diarrhoea [52], around 900,000 of malaria [76], and around 600,000 of typhoid fever [3]. Every year these three diseases together kill the equivalent of the population of Norway – more than 12,000 deaths per day.

Illness more often results in (temporary) disability than in death. Infections like leprosy, trachoma or filariasis are rarely fatal, but often result in permanent disfigurement, blindness, and disability [59]. DALYs (Disability-Adjusted Life Years) are a measure of the cost of disease. DALYs represent the number of years lost due to early death, and time and severity of the disability caused by the disease. Table 4.1 shows the number of DALYs lost to several important infections every year.

The developing world is paying the highest price for disease. Only 12 per cent of the suffering caused by disability and early death occurs in developed countries. In developing countries, 35 per cent of all DALYs lost are a result of communicable disease, compared to just over 4 per cent in developed countries [51].

Table 4.1. DALYs lost to disease worldwide, yearly figures (from 51 and 76)

Infection	DALYs
Diarrhoeal disease	99,600,000
Malaria	31,700,000
Roundworm infection	10,500,000
Trichuriasis	6,300,000
Schistosomiasis	4,500,000
Trachoma	3,300,000
Chagas disease	2,700,000
Leishmaniasis	2,100,000
Sleeping sickness	1,800,000
Hookworm disease	1,100,000

Disease is expensive at all levels. At a personal level illness results in suffering, loss of time and money because of disability, payment for medical care, transport to health facilities, care by a healthy person, and the need for special food. At national level disease costs because medical facilities have to be maintained, care and medication must be provided, and because part of the workforce is unable to produce.

Poor health is not the only price people pay for poor water supply and (environmental) sanitation. Often water has to be carried over long distances, taking up energy and time. In some regions over half the daily energy available to one person is needed to carry the water used by the household every day [1]. This time and energy cannot be invested in other activities like going to school, or growing vegetables for sale or consumption. Carrying heavy loads of water can result in deformities of the body and other physical problems [20,38]. Where water must be bought from vendors, it may account for a large proportion of the household's expenditure (up to 40 per cent of the income of a household is mentioned) [69]. Where (environmental) sanitation is poor, people may live or work in an unpleasant environment of bad smells, nuisance by insects or rats (which can carry disease), and unsightly conditions.

4.2 The planning of WES projects and the project cycle

The aim of WES projects and programmes is usually to improve the health and socio-economic conditions of a population [20]. Health is improved by breaking the transmission cycle of diseases present in the project area. People's socio-economic conditions are improved by helping people to gain time, energy, money, and skills in management and decision-making.

Projects and programmes are best approached in a methodical manner. This ensures that no steps are overlooked in the planning and implementation of the project. Although we will not go into much detail on how to plan and conduct projects or programmes, we will point out some important issues.

To be able to assess whether a project functions well, or has been successful, every project should have a clear goal, and a clear idea of how this goal is going to be achieved. Figure 4.1 shows how an organisational tree could be set up for a project. The objective must lead to the aim; to attain the objective, certain outputs will have to be achieved; and to realise the outputs, certain activities will have to be accomplished. In the end everything that will have to be done and achieved in the project must be included in clear and measurable form in the organisational tree, which is a simplified form of the logical framework.

Aim:
A sustainable improvement in health
and well being for 15,000 poor people in
the city of Luanda

Objective:
establishment of appropriate and sustainable
services in water supply, sanitation and hygiene
promotion for 15,000 poor people by the year 2004

Output:
construction of 120 sustainable
tapstands in a low-income housing area
by the year 2003

Output: 2   **Output: 3**

Activity:
train 10 people in repair and
maintenance of the system by
the year 2003

Activity: 2   **Activity: 3**

Figure 4.1. Example of an organisational tree for planning a project (adapted from 23)

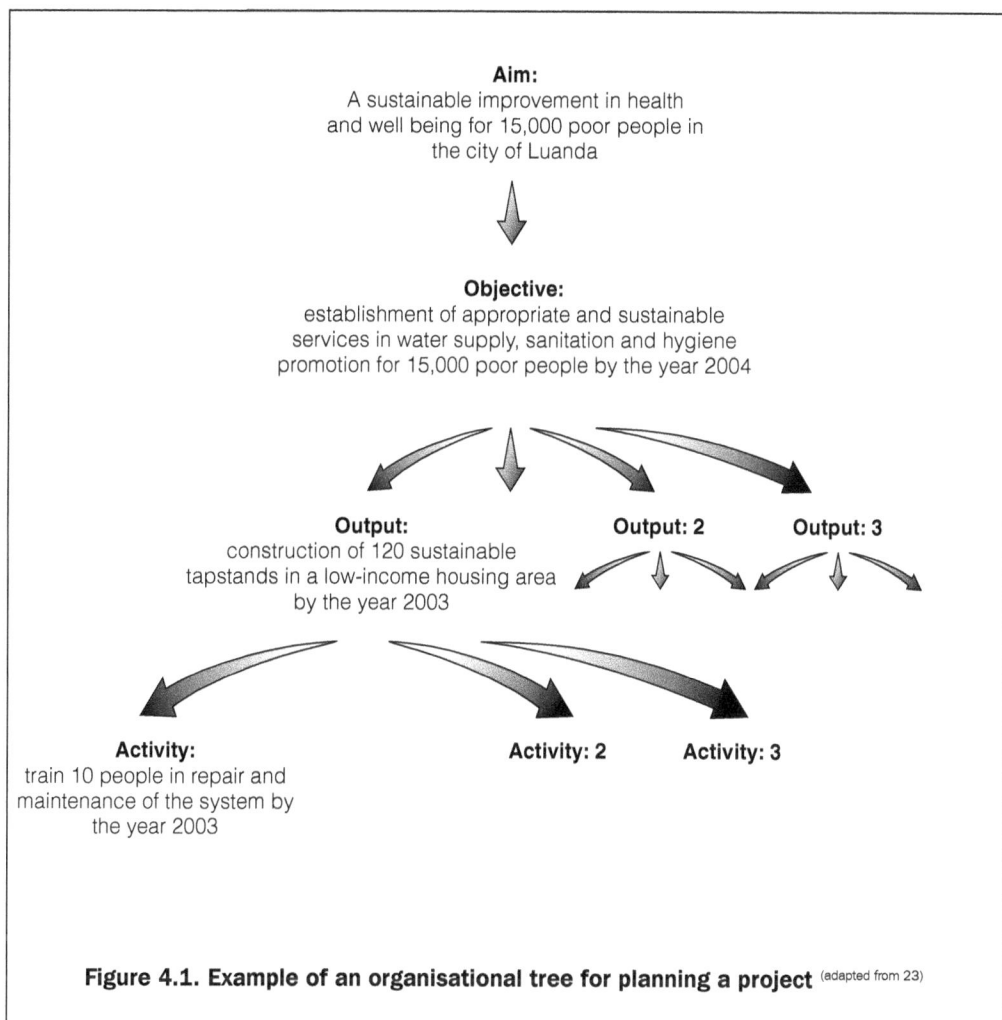

A project goes through a cycle, the project cycle, which consists of a sequence of assessment, planning, implementation and evaluation activities.

Figure 4.2 presents the steps of project cycle.

4.3   Improving impact and sustainability

Projects take place in a dynamic society with its own cultural, financial, physical/ technical, and institutional/political particularities. It is therefore difficult to predict all the short- and long-term effects of an intervention. Although it is impossible to eliminate all uncertainties, a thorough assessment of the local situation, and an intervention that is well adapted to the local situation, will improve the chances of success of a project.

(1) What is the situation?
Making contacts. Assessment of the existing situation. Evaluation of the possibility and need of intervention in the local context. Identification of current and future problems.

(2) What are the priorities?
Which problems should be dealt with first? What the local population see as priorities?

(3) What can be done?
Which problems can potentially be addressed with the available resources and the existing constraints? Are the local population (and authorities) willing and able to operate and maintain components independently?

(4) What will be done?
The agency decides with all people and structures involved on the problems that will be addressed in the project.

(5) How will it be done?
Specific activities needed to solve the problems are decided upon.

(6) What resources are needed?
What human, material and financial inputs are needed? The inputs and responsibilities of all stakeholders must be agreed upon.

(7) Proposal
A project proposal is made in co-operation with the stakeholders.

(8) Appraisal and approval
The project proposal is examined, if necessary adapted, and accepted.

(9) Implementation and operation
The actual project activities are executed. During implementation the project should be monitored.

(10) Extension or expansion
The project is adapted, prolonged, or extended.

(11) Evaluation
At the end of the project its functioning and effects are analysed.

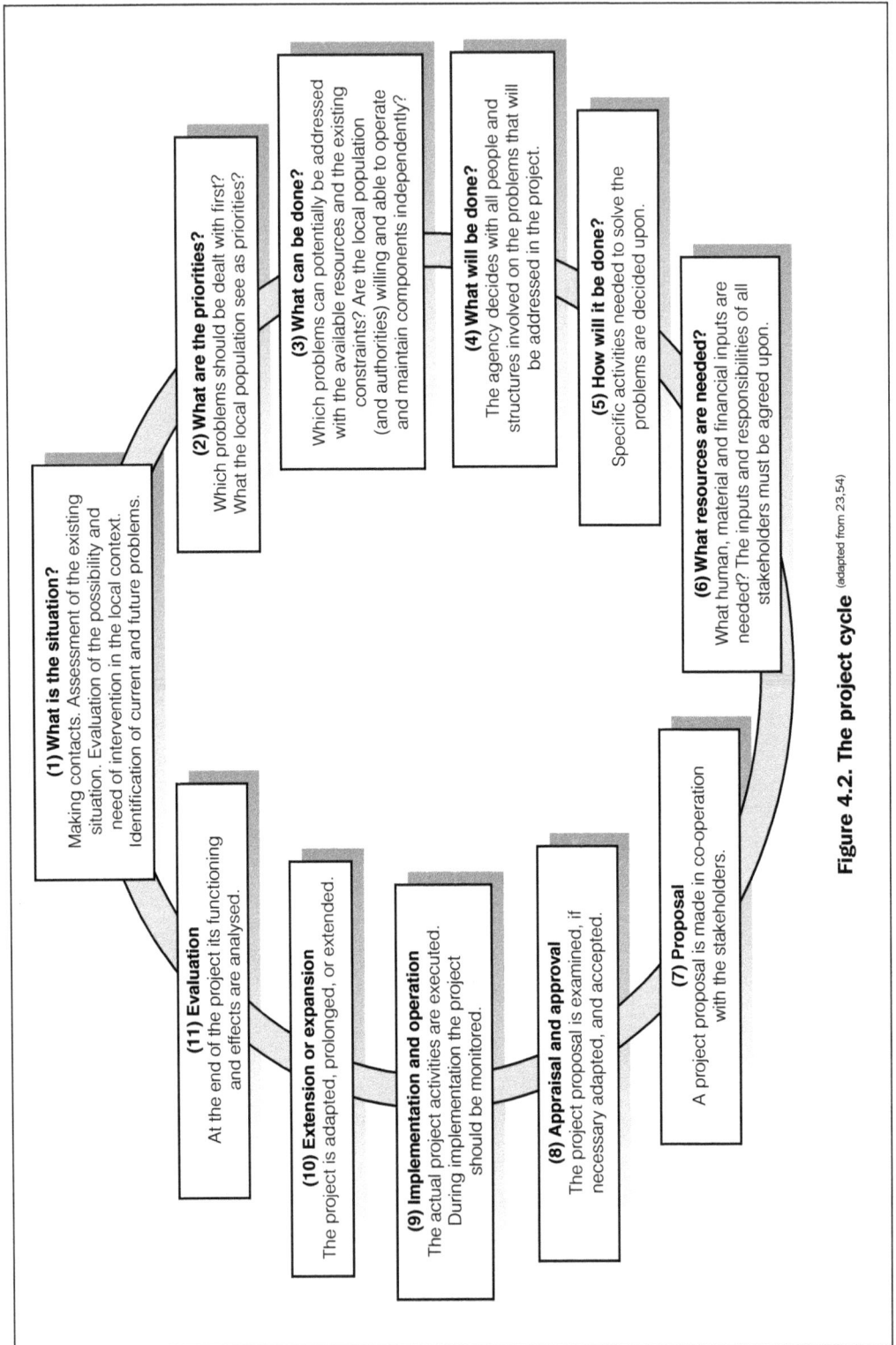

Figure 4.2. The project cycle (adapted from 23,54)

This section looks at some of the cross-cutting issues which must be addressed in the project planning phase to improve impact and sustainability.

Integral approach to projects and programmes

Most of the infections covered in this manual could be controlled by any one or several components of WES. Water supply, sanitation, drainage, solid waste management, and vector control should therefore always be combined to achieve the best overall results in disease control. Interventions that combine the different components are usually the most effective in improving the health situation [38].

Health is affected by many factors other than WES. Programmes should try to combine components of all relevant sectors (e.g. WES, medical, environmental, economic) to achieve maximum impact. Programmes are most effective when projects from different sectors are integrated [26,38].

Hygiene behaviour and health and hygiene promotion

Adequate hygiene behaviour is crucial in preventing disease. Improving infrastructure without improving behaviour will rarely result in effective disease control. The largest improvements in health have occurred where hygiene improved because of a change in behaviour [13]. Improving hygiene behaviour through health and hygiene promotion should therefore receive the same priority as structural improvements.

Changing people's behaviour is difficult and often requires prolonged education. Health and hygiene promotion must therefore be included in a project from the beginning, and will require its own time scale, material, and people with specific skills [20]. Health and hygiene promotion must be adapted to the local culture [27].

Technical aspects

Infrastructure must be designed to fulfil needs. Where the population density is high and the infiltration capacity of the soil low, a sewage system may be appropriate. In most other cases, however, sewerage will be inappropriate because it is expensive and requires demanding operation and maintenance.

Often different components of WES need to be supplied together. A water supply system should always be combined with adequate wastewater disposal; a sewage system needs a reliable piped water supply system.

Infrastructure should be adapted to local needs and capabilities. A handpump may be very convenient, but a proper hand-dug well may be more appropriate in terms of local capacity to build and maintain the structure. A brick latrine may look good, but may also be too expensive for local people. If people use corncobs to clean after defecating, a pour-flush latrine will soon be blocked.

Changes in population, or in use of the structures, have to be planned for. The number of people using the infrastructure may increase because of natural growth or migration. A latrine designed to receive only excreta may not cope with the sullage if a piped water supply is later installed. Where possible, infrastructure should be built with potential upgrading or extension in mind.

Operation and maintenance
Operation and maintenance (O&M) must be addressed early in the project. Infrastructure which functions poorly often becomes a health threat, and improvements will only last if a reliable O&M system is in place. O&M must be as easy and affordable as possible. Spare parts and other necessary materials must be affordable and easy to obtain, and responsibility for O&M should be agreed upon early in the planning of a project.

Infrastructure should be installed at family level if possible, as O&M by users is the most reliable system. To facilitate this, local construction techniques and materials should be used as much as possible. People should be offered training and adequate tools for building and O&M. The quality of construction should be as high as possible, but adapted to what is adequate and affordable to the users.

Socio-cultural aspects
Even if the population understands the importance of improved infrastructure and behaviour, there is no guarantee that the infrastructure will be used or good behaviour practised [18]. If users believe the components are inadequate, they will not respect them.

Although an outsider will never completely understand people's perceptions of adequate and inadequate, it is important to understand the issues that are relevant to the project. For this the traditional beliefs, ideas, and expectations of the people about WES must be identified and taken into account.

Societies are not homogeneous; they are made up of people of different sex, age, religion, ethnic origin, socio-economic status, occupation, and caste. Some are more vulnerable than others, particularly women, children, religious and ethnic minorities, and people who are old, disabled, or poor. These groups of people must be identified and included in the project as much as possible. As domestic WES is often the responsibility of women, they should play an important role in the planning of an intervention [23]. All components must be acceptable to all users.

If certain groups do not see the infrastructure as adequate, they will either not use it or use it incorrectly. It cannot be assumed that the agency, authorities, or communities' representatives know what type of structures are most appropriate to all users.

The accessibility of infrastructure

The presence of improved water supply or sanitation does not mean that everyone has access to it [25]. Accessibility of services depends on the time, energy, money, and security. To make infrastructure accessible it has to be present in sufficient numbers, close to where it is needed, at a price affordable to all, and where it can be used and reached safely. Using the services must be as easy and comfortable as possible.

The groups that are most at risk in a society (e.g. single women, people who are older, disabled, or poor) will often suffer most because of poor accessibility, and accessibility for these groups must be taken into account during planning.

Financial aspects

Improvements are more likely to be sustainable if the full costs of operation and maintenance can be borne by the users. How much people are able and willing to pay for the services must be determined in an open discussion between the people and the agency. Where people buy water from vendors the price they are already paying is an indication of what people are prepared to pay [15]. It is not realistic to say that all families will be willing to pay the same percentage of their income for water and sanitation. What people are willing to pay for improved services will depend on the importance of WES to them, how much they pay for the service already, what level of service is on offer, and their expectations from authorities or agency.

Where possible the initial costs of construction should be (at least partly) recuperated in the form of money, labour, or material. Again, the community's contribution must be adapted to what they are able and willing to provide. This has to be determined in discussions between the agency and the community, and by realistically assessing the availability of resources.

If there is a central regulating body (e.g. for a piped water supply or communal latrines), an adequate system of collecting fees must be installed. Where the infrastructure is at a household level, the family can cover its own maintenance and operation costs. If subsidies are offered, they should be used to make services accessible to people who would otherwise not be able to afford them. To prevent abuse, the policy for allocating subsidies must be transparent [23].

Institutional aspects

The agency does not plan and run projects on its own. It usually works with one or several governmental bodies. Other authorities or organisations will often be given the responsibility to implement the project, or operate or maintain infrastructure.

It is important to identify all the organisations that are, or could be, connected to the project. They have to be assessed on their organisational skills, capabilities, level of motivation, availability of time as well as their access to resources, transport, and materials. Transparency and accountability will be important issues. Training or help buying materials will be necessary.

The general guidelines and regulations of the country have to be followed, and the project should fit as closely as possible in the programmes, plans, or guidelines of the government or other organisations.

4.4 Health, poverty, and development

Health in a population is linked to many factors. The general environment [79], housing, legal and physical security at home and at work, education, nutrition, gender differences, access to health facilities [88] and stress [41] all play important roles in public health. Most of these factors are closely related to poverty.

The poor are usually most at risk of infection because of their degraded environment and inadequate nutrition, so they are the hardest hit when ill as they have no reserves or rights to fall back upon, have difficulty accessing medical care, and pay the most for it. Few poor people can afford to create a healthy environment with good housing, adequate water supply and (environmental) sanitation.

Disease can also be very expensive because of the direct costs (e.g. treatment, transport) and loss of income (sick people cannot work).

Poor health often leads to poverty, and poverty often leads to poor health. Once people are in this vicious circle, it is very difficult to escape. Most people in developing countries live in poverty. In 1993 it was estimated that half of the over 1.5 billion people who inhabit cities live in extreme poverty [81].

Poverty, and with it poor health, is not only crippling for individuals, it is a serious handicap to developing countries as a whole. Improving environmental hygiene, water supply, housing, education, nutrition, and health facilities is only possible if resources are available. But as a large proportion of their population already suffers from disease, these countries do not have the productive workforce needed to create these resources [1].

While general access to an adequate water supply and acceptable (environmental) sanitation are crucial to good health in a population, the only long-term solution to poor health and underdevelopment is poverty reduction. The only way the poor can afford and maintain better services (wells, piped water, improved latrines) is by increasing their income [78]. Remember this when planning a programme, and address poverty wherever possible.

Chapter 5

Domestic water supply

Domestic water supply means the source and infrastructure that provides water to households. A domestic water supply can take different forms: a stream, a spring, a hand-dug well, a borehole with handpump, a rainwater collection system, a piped water supply with tapstand or house connection, or water vendors.

Households use water for many purposes: drinking, cooking, washing hands and body, washing clothes, cleaning cooking utensils, cleaning the house, watering animals, irrigating the garden, and often for commercial activities. Different sources of water may be used for different activities, and the water sources available may change with the seasons.

There is always some kind of water source present where people live, as they could not survive without one. The source may be inadequate, however; it may be far away, difficult to reach, unsafe, or give little water, making it inaccessible or unavailable. It may give water of poor quality.

Although both problems play an important role in people's health and well-being, the availability of water is often more important than quality.

5.1 Water availability

Whether water is available or accessible to people depends on the time, energy, and/or money they have to invest to obtain it. Water from a handpump that is 25m from the but always has a long queue may be as inaccessible as water from a river 1.5km away or water that has to be bought. In addition, safety problems, such as mines or a hostile population near the water may also limit accessibility.

Issues on water availability other than health
If water availability is poor, people will lose time, energy, or money that could have been invested elsewhere. If the supply is limited, people will have to be

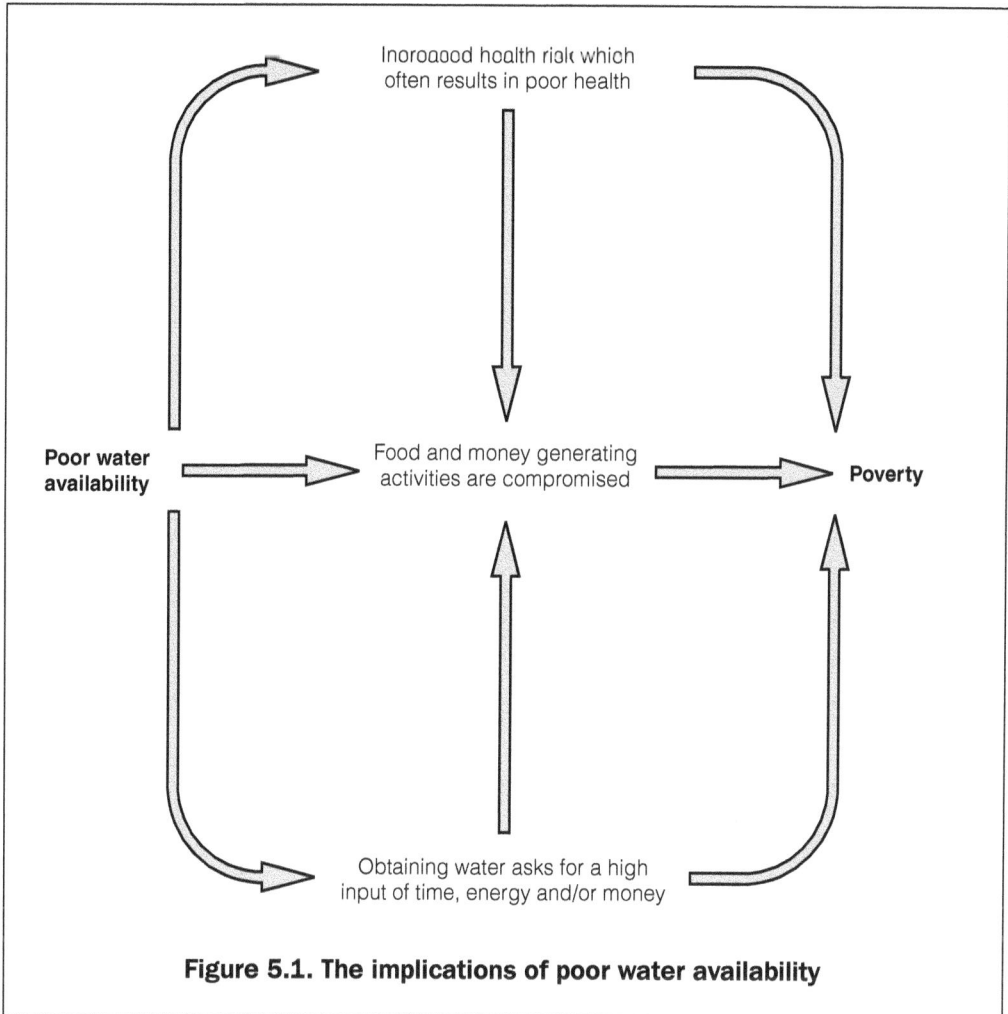

Figure 5.1. The implications of poor water availability

Diagram labels:
- Increased health risk which often results in poor health
- Poor water availability
- Food and money generating activities are compromised
- Poverty
- Obtaining water asks for a high input of time, energy and/or money

selective about what they use the water for. Figure 5.1 shows the implications of poor water availability to people.

Where water availability is insufficient, an effort should be made to improve the supply. It is important to ensure that making more water available to some does not take it away from others.

If a limited number of water sources are available, the areas around the sources may become degraded if too many people or animals use them. If unsustainable amounts of water are extracted, the environment may become degraded through falling groundwater levels or surface water sources such as rivers or streams may dry up. Be careful to ensure that short-term gain does not result in long-term loss.

5.1.1   Water availability and disease transmission

Poor personal hygiene favours disease transmission. The transmission of many infections can be prevented both by washing hands and by washing body and clothes. These infections are called the water-washed diseases.

People need access to enough water to be able to maintain good personal hygiene. Although good access to water does not automatically result in good personal hygiene, poor water availability will usually result in poor personal hygiene. Once there is enough water, health and hygiene promotion will often be needed to improve personal hygiene practises.

5.1.1.1   Handwashing

Contaminated hands can carry pathogens to where these can enter the body. Hands contaminated with faecal matter can transmit faecal-oral pathogens to food, water, or directly to the mouth. The soil-transmitted helminths that cause roundworm infection and trichuriasis can be transmitted if hands are contaminated with soil containing their eggs. Hands contaminated with the discharge from the eyes of people suffering from conjunctivitis or trachoma, or the contagious liquid from papules of people with yaws, can transmit these infections to other people through direct contact.

Washing hands after every contact that could potentially pick up the pathogen, and before doing anything that could transmit the pathogen onward, can prevent transmission. Faecal-oral infections can largely be prevented if hands are washed after defecation, after coming in contact with animals, and after contact with anything that could be contaminated with faeces. In addition, hands should be washed before preparing or handling food, and before eating.

Washing hands after contact with soil or anything contaminated with soil and before handling food can reduce the risk of transmitting helminths.

The transmission of trachoma and conjunctivitis can often be prevented by washing hands after touching a person's face or after handling material used to wipe somebody's eyes or face, and before coming into contact with another person's face or eyes. The risk of transmitting yaws can be reduced by washing hands after contact with contaminated skin or material.

Washing hands removes the pathogens as well as the dirt containing and protecting the pathogens [7]. How effective handwashing is depends mainly on how thoroughly the hands are rubbed, and for how long. Water alone is not as effective as water with a handwashing agent such as soap or ash, which are both effective in removing pathogens from hands.

The number of pathogens will be reduced significantly if the hands are rubbed with a handwashing agent for at least 10 seconds and then rinsed with water [33]. Table 5.1 shows the groups of infections associated with poor handwashing.

5.1.1.2   Hygiene of body and clothes

Several pathogens can be transmitted through infectious skin or contaminated clothes. Certain vectors of disease live on clothes, or prefer people with a poor personal hygiene. All infections that spread by direct contact can be transmitted via direct person-to-person contact through contaminated skin or clothes.

Conjunctivitis and trachoma can be transmitted through infected skin, clothes, or other contaminated material that came in contact with infectious eye discharges. Several other infections transmitted through direct contact affect the skin, and the pathogens can be spread simply through direct skin contact, including yaws, scabies, and tinea.

Body lice, the vector of louse-borne typhus, louse-borne relapsing fever, and trench fever live on people's unwashed clothes [61]. Fleas, which transmit plague and murine typhus fever prefer people with poor personal hygiene [73]. Keeping body and clothes clean will reduce the transmission risk of all these infections.

The disease groups linked to poor hygiene of body and clothes are shown in Table 5.1.

Table 5.1. Disease categories associated with poor personal health

Risk-factors related to poor personal hygiene	Faecal-oral infections	Schistosomiasis	Water-based with two intermediate hosts	Soil-transmitted helminths	Beef and pork tapeworm	Leptospirosis	Guinea-worm infection	Spread by direct contact	Vector-borne infections
Poor handwashing			(a)	(b)					
Poor hygiene of body and clothes								(c)	

(a) : the ingested soil-transmitted helminths: roundworm infection and trichuriasis
(b) : only cysticercosis
(c) : louse-borne and flea-borne infections

5.1.2 The health impact of improved water availability

Table 5.2 shows how improving the water availability and personal hygiene of people will reduce transmission of some infections.

Table 5.2. Reduction in infections associated with improved water availability and personal hygiene

Disease (group)	Reduction in occurrence	Remarks
Diarrhoea	20% [26]	increase water availability (handwashing)
Infant diarrhoea	30% [32]	wash hands with soap after defecation and before eating
Roundworm	12-37% [26]	increase water availability (handwashing)
Trachoma	30% [26]	increase water availability (washing of hands and face) [3]
Yaws	70% [29]	increase water availability (washing of body)
Louse-borne typhus/ relapsing fever	40% [29]	increase water availability (washing of clothes and body)

5.1.3 Practical issues concerning water availability

Ideally, all users should have a convenient, culturally acceptable source that provides an unlimited amount of water at an affordable price and without degrading the environment. In practise, it will rarely be possible to provide this, and a compromise will have to be made which takes into account the local social, cultural, physical, financial, and environmental constraints.

The amount of water that people need, or use, will depend on its availability and what it is used for. Factors that influence water use include the socio-economic status of the users, whether and how people have to pay for the water, whether water is easy to get, and whether water is used for special activities (e.g. irrigation of vegetable gardens, watering of animals). Table 5.3 presents figures on water needs and demands and shows the amount of water people need and how development will change water demand. Future changes in population and development level will have to be considered. Water is lost during distribution, and this will have to be taken into account when looking at how much water must be provided to a population.

In the initial phase of an emergency internally displaced people and refugees will need a minimum of three to five litres per person per day to survive, and as soon as possible this will have to be increased to 15 to 20 l/p/d to allow for water for personal hygiene [21]. In a stable situation, the minimum amount of water available to people should be 25 l/p/d [68].

Table 5.3. Water needs, demands, and losses

People (in litres/person/day (l/p/d)) [21,68]		**Institutions** (in l/p/d) [21,66,68]	
Minimum survival	3-5	Health centre, out-patients	5
Drinking and cooking needs	8-10	Health centre, in-patients	40-60
Minimum supply required	15-20	(without laundry)	
		Cholera treatment centre	60
		Therapeutic feeding centre	15-30
Livestock (in litres/animal/day) [21]		School	25
Cattle	20-40		
Donkeys, horses	10-40	**Other** [21]	
Sheep, goats	1-5	Irrigation	3-6 l/m²/day

		Water losses in supply systems	
Standpipe supply (in l/p/d) [68]		In a medium to large distribution system in reason-	
Rural, village control	45	able condition: 15-25%.	
Rural, washing, laundry on site	65	In old system with mains in poor condition: 35-55%	
Urban, no payment	70+	[68]	
		In a water trucking scheme: around 20% [21]	
Household connection (in l/p/d) [68]			
Low income, unreliable supply	50-55		
Low income, metered supply	70-90		
Low income, no payment	130+		
Middle income	180		
High income	240		

Water collection time and use

The collection time of water is a good indicator of water availability as it takes into account distance, waiting times, and to a certain extent the effort needed to obtain water. Studies have shown that people will not really restrict their water use if collection times are less than three minutes, or a distance of about 100m in easy terrain with no waiting times. Longer collection times will result in a restriction on the use of water.

Interestingly, the amount of water collected if the collection time is between three and 30 minutes remains constant. This means that if it takes eight minutes to fetch water, the amount of water used will be more or less the same as if it took 20 minutes to collect it. If collecting water takes more than 30 minutes (i.e. a distance of roughly 1km), the amount of water used decreases again [15]. Figure 5.2 plots water collection time against the quantity of water used.

The largest health benefit from an improved water supply will result if collection times are below three minutes. Although bringing the water collection time down from 25 minutes to six minutes will result in an important saving in time and energy (in itself a large benefit), but will probably not reduce water-washed infections.

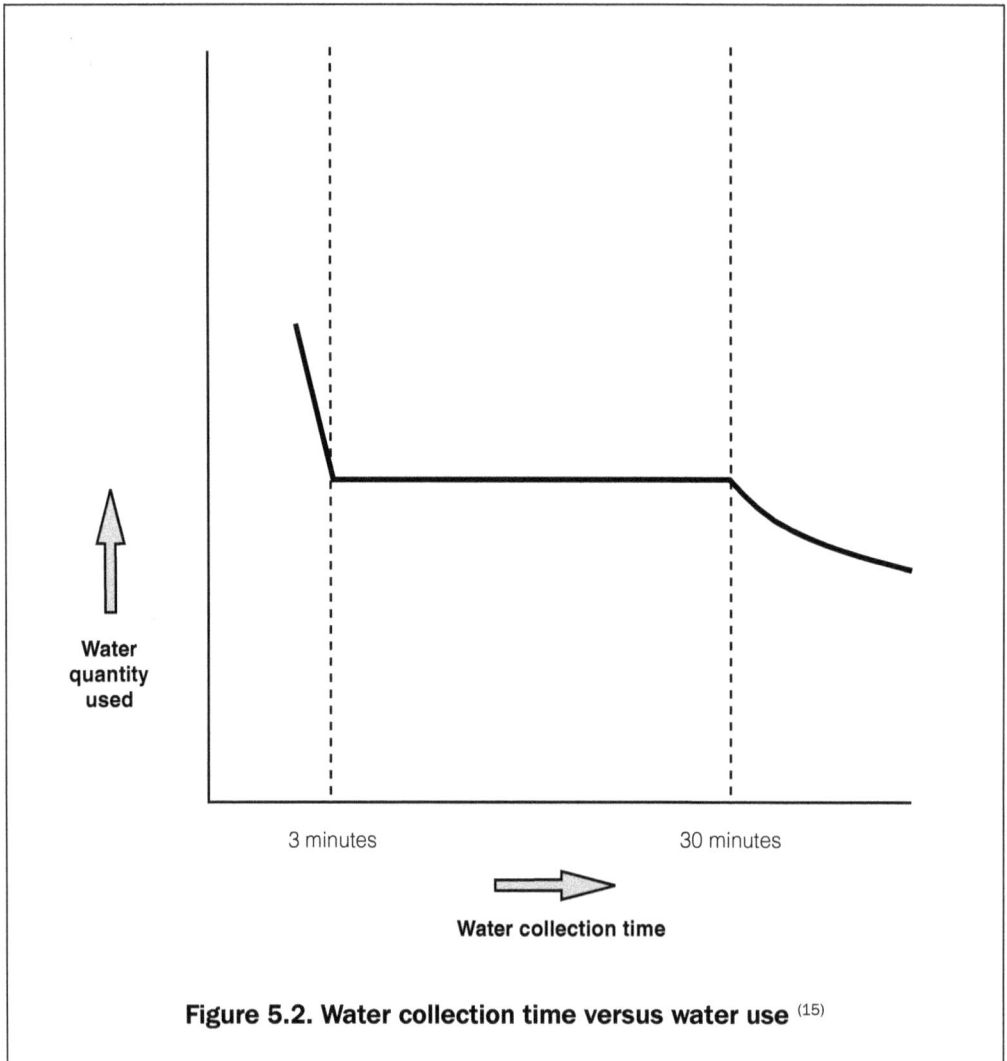

Figure 5.2. Water collection time versus water use [15]

To avoid long waiting times at the sources, their numbers and yield must be sufficient. There should be a maximum of 500 to 750 people using each functional handpump, and 200 to 250 people per tap. If tapstands with multiple taps are used, no more than six to eight taps per tapstand should be installed [47].

The minimum flow at a supply should be around 7.5 litres per minute [66]. During all seasons the sources' yield should be high enough, and seasonal changes in supply must be taken into account.

If a source has a low but constant yield it may be possible to collect the water in a reservoir (e.g. a spring box) then put a tap on the reservoir.

Storing water

Water is only available if it is at hand when needed. Unless the source is on the household plot, access to water is limited. This problem can be overcome by storing water on the plot.

Where the water supply is unreliable (e.g. harvesting rainwater, piped water with intermittent supply) storage improves availability when water is not accessible.

An additional advantage of storing water is that the water quality improves over time. If water is stored for one day over 50 per cent of the bacteria will die. Suspended solids, which can contain pathogens, will often settle out during storage. By pouring the clear water out carefully, the settled solids can be separated from the water [64].

Vessels that can be used to store water include local traditional clay pots, mortar jars, ferrocement tanks, and plastic or fibreglass vessels or tanks.

To avoid contamination vessels or reservoirs used for drinking-water should have a small opening or tap to prevent people from dipping the water out. The vessel should be covered with a clean, tight lid to keep animals, insects, and contaminated material out. If the water is not used for drinking, the way it is extracted is less important, but as *Aedes* mosquitoes – vector of yellow fever, dengue fever, and several other arboviruses and filariasis – can breed in household reservoirs no matter what their size, all water reservoirs should be covered properly.

How much water should be stored will depend on the situation. In general the less reliable the supply, the more effort needed to obtain the water, and the higher the water need, the larger the storage capacity should be. If there is a reliable, continuous piped water supply with a house connection then storage will not usually be necessary; but if people rely on rainwater storage needs may be large. Where there is a reliable source throughout the year, a storage capacity equivalent to the amount of water used in one to two days is probably adequate.

In addition to water storage vessels, households usually need vessels to transport water. These should be made so that carrying the water is as easy and comfortable as possible. The vessels should be covered with a clean cover or lid, and the water should be poured instead of dipped out.

In emergency situations it is often necessary to distribute water vessels so that people can collect and store water. The minimum for each household is two water containers of 10-20 litres for collecting water, and an additional 20 litres for household storage [66].

5.2 Water quality

Water quality includes the physical quality (e.g. turbidity), the chemical quality (e.g. content in salt), and the microbiological quality (whether it contains pathogens). Here we will only look at the microbiological quality of the water.

Water quality issues other than health

The presence of pathogens in water will not usually cause any problems other than health.

If the water is treated, polluting sludge (e.g. the sludge produced during coagulation) may be produced.

5.2.1 Water quality and disease transmission

Water can transmit pathogens directly to people in two ways. The pathogens may be water-borne and the disease is transmitted through drinking-water, or the water may contain pathogens which can penetrate the skin.

Faecally polluted drinking-water can transmit faecal-oral infections. The transmission route is direct from person (or animal) to person. These pathogens may contaminate the water at the source, but contamination may also occur during the transport, distribution, or handling of the water.

Transmission of the Guinea-worm is more complex. People infected with Guinea-worm will have a blister on their skin. If the blister comes in contact with water, it bursts and discharges the worm's larvae. These larvae can infect *Cyclops* (a water flea), inside which they develop. People become infected when they ingest *Cyclops* through drinking-water. Guinea-worm infection cannot be transmitted directly from person to person. The water will be contaminated at the source, and if the water at the source is safe, contamination at a later stage is not very likely.

If water containing a particular species of snail is contaminated with urine or faeces from infected people, schistosomiasis can be transmitted. This pathogen can penetrate the skin of people who are in direct contact with the contaminated surface water.

If water is contaminated with the urine of animals infected with leptospirosis, the pathogen can be transmitted through direct skin contact with the water. Rats are the main reservoir of leptospirosis.

Table 5.4 presents the different disease-groups linked to water of poor quality.

Table 5.4. Infections associated with poor water quality

Risk-factors related to poor water quality i Drinking-water ii Skin contact with surface water	Faecal-oral infections	Schistosomiasis	Water-based with two intermediate hosts	Soil-transmitted helminths	Beef and pork tapeworm	Leptospirosis	Guinea-worm infection	Spread by direct contact	Vector-borne infections
i Contaminated with excreta	H/A								
Contaminated by Guinea- worm						H			
ii Contaminated with excreta		H/A			A				

H: human host
A: animal host

5.2.2   The health impact of improved water quality

Contaminated drinking-water is just one of the potential transmission routes of faecal-oral infections, which can also be transmitted by food or hand-to-mouth contact. Where faecal-oral infections are endemic, and sanitation, handwashing practise, and food hygiene are poor, the majority of cases will probably not have resulted from drinking contaminated water. In contrast, where faecal-oral infections are common, and sanitation, handwashing practise and food hygiene are adequate, the role of drinking-water in the transmission of faecal-oral infections is probably important [15].

As Table 5.5 shows, improving water quality in unsanitary neighbourhoods will probably not really affect levels of (infant) diarrhoea, while improving the water quality in 'clean' neighbourhoods probably will reduce it [70]. Water quality is

Table 5.5. Reduction in infections associated with improved drinking-water quality

Disease (group)	Reduction in occurrence	Remarks
Diarrhoea	15% [26]	
Infant diarrhoea	negligible [70]	if neighbourhood sanitation is poor (open defecation in neighbourhood)
	40% [70]	if neighbourhood sanitation is good (no open defecation in neighbourhood)
Guinea-worm infection	78% [26]	

especially important in an urban or peri-urban environment, where water supplies are often at risk of pollution, and the risk of large outbreaks is higher than in a rural environment[15]. As Guinea-worm will normally only be transmitted through drinking-water, improving the drinking-water quality at the source is very effective in controlling the infection.

The quality of the water used for washing hands, body, and clothes is not really important as long as it is not heavily polluted. The risk of transmitting pathogens other than schistosomiasis [15] and leptospirosis during bathing in surface water is limited.

Animals do not need water of very high quality, but most domestic animals can be infected with faecal-oral infections, and cattle and pigs can be infected with beef and pork tapeworm, so their water quality should be as high as possible.

5.2.3   Practical issues concerning water quality

This section looks at some general points on water sources, storage and distribution, treatment, and water quality assessment in the field.

Water sources

One of the priorities in selecting a water source is quality. The quality and protection of the source is important regardless of whether the water will be treated or not. Good quality water needs less, or no, treatment; and if treatment fails there will be fewer health risks. Sources must be protected from pollution by installing adequate structures for protecting, collecting, and distributing the water. Health and hygiene promotion will probably be needed to make people aware of the importance of protecting the water source.

Water can be obtained from several different types of source.

Springs: An adequately protected spring will normally produce good quality water. Building a proper headwall, access structures, and drainage system will prevent degradation. Latrines should not be sited above the spring, and a hedge or fence should keep animals at least 10 metres away from the area above the spring. A ditch should be dug close to the fence to divert runoff. Figure 5.3 shows an example of a protected spring.

If a spring has a low yield, a spring box might be constructed to collect and store water that can then be withdrawn through a tap. The spring box should be well constructed, and all openings (e.g. man-holes, overflow pipes) should be closed securely or covered with fly screen.

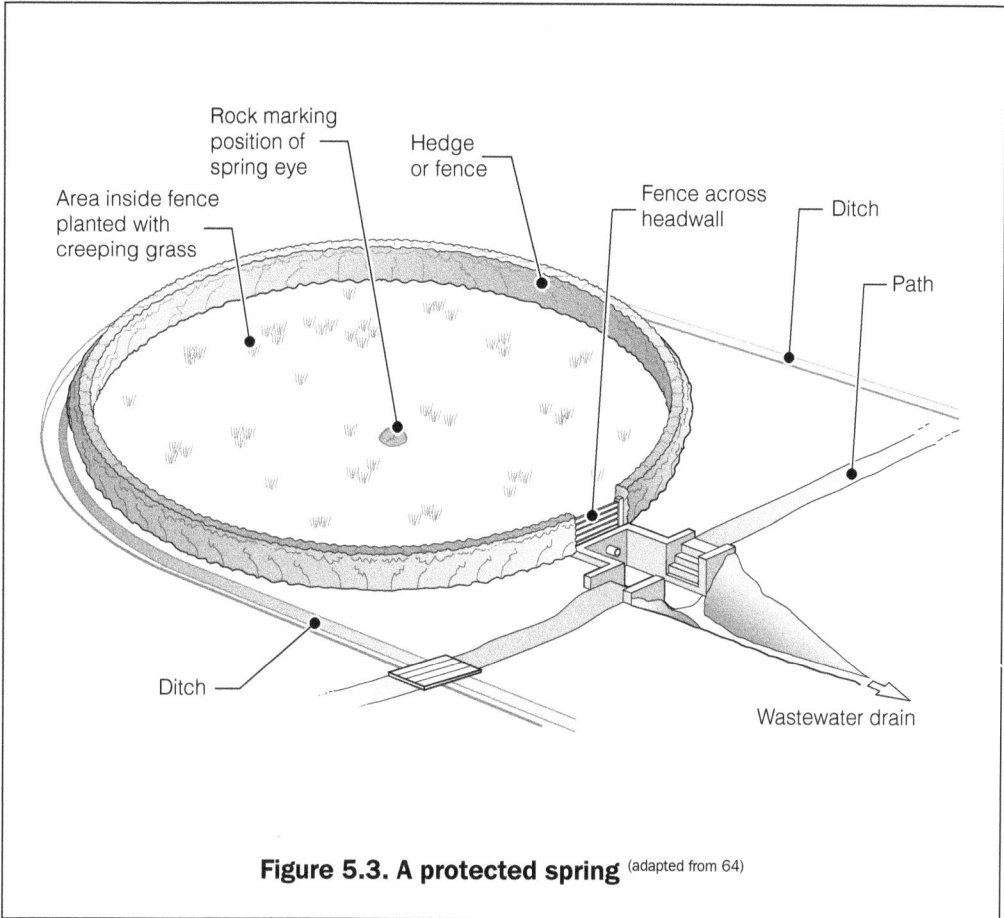

Figure 5.3. A protected spring (adapted from 64)

Rainwater harvesting: If rainwater is properly collected and stored it will usually be of good quality. The catchment area (e.g. roof, rock) and guttering or channels should be kept as clean as possible. The first minutes of rainfall are best discarded to avoid collecting unwanted material like dust, debris, or bird droppings. Alternatively, a silt trap can be installed. The storage tank must be built to prevent contamination by animals, insects, or polluted material [56]. The water should be withdrawn from the storage tank by a tap or pump to avoid contamination during collection. Rainwater is seasonal and large storage capacity is needed to bridge dry periods, so rainwater harvesting is not usually appropriate as the only source of water.

Borehole or tube-well: A properly constructed borehole with handpump usually produces good quality water. The tube-well should be sited a safe distance from sanitary structures. To avoid the seepage of contaminated surface water or shallow

63

groundwater into the tube-well, install a good grout seal. A watertight apron sloping away from the pump must extend for at least 1 metre around the tube-well. The borehole casing must be intact or else polluted water could enter. If water must be added to prime a suction pump, be careful to use clean water to avoid contaminating the water in the tube-well [43]. The apron must drain into a drainage channel that leads spilt water at least 4 metres away from the tube-well before disposing of it in a garden or soakaway. If possible, a fence or hedge should be installed around the borehole to keep animals at distance [82].

It is very difficult to assess whether the underground structures of existing tube-wells are adequate, and it is therefore best to assume that they are not. The apron and drainage channel should be intact and not have any cracks. There should be no ponding of water within 2 metres of the borehole, and no excreta (human or animal), refuse, or surface water should be within 10 metres of the tube-well [82]. A sanitary survey would identify any of these as risk factors that might contaminate the water in the tube-well.

Hand-dug wells: Water abstracted from a hand-dug well is usually of intermediate quality. Sanitary structures should be sited at sufficient distance from the well. The top three metres of the well lining must be watertight to prevent polluted surface water or shallow groundwater from seeping into the well. A space is often created during construction between the original soil and the lining. This must be properly sealed to prevent surface water from entering the well. There should be a watertight apron at least one metre wide around the well [82], and a drainage channel at least four metres long must lead spilt water away before discharging it properly [64].

If possible, water should be withdrawn using a system that prevents the vessel and rope from being contaminated (e.g. by being left on the ground). A headwall must be installed to prevent surface water or other contamination from entering the well. The headwall should discourage people from standing on it, as this could result in soil or spilt water contaminating the well. Children must be prevented from throwing material in the well [15]. Where possible, a fence or hedge should be installed to keep animals at distance. Figure 5.4 shows an appropriate hand-dug well.

If a hand-dug well is covered with a lid and a handpump is installed, several risk factors are eliminated or reduced. A raised manhole should be installed to ease maintenance, and to allow people to get to the water without demolishing the structure if the pump breaks down.

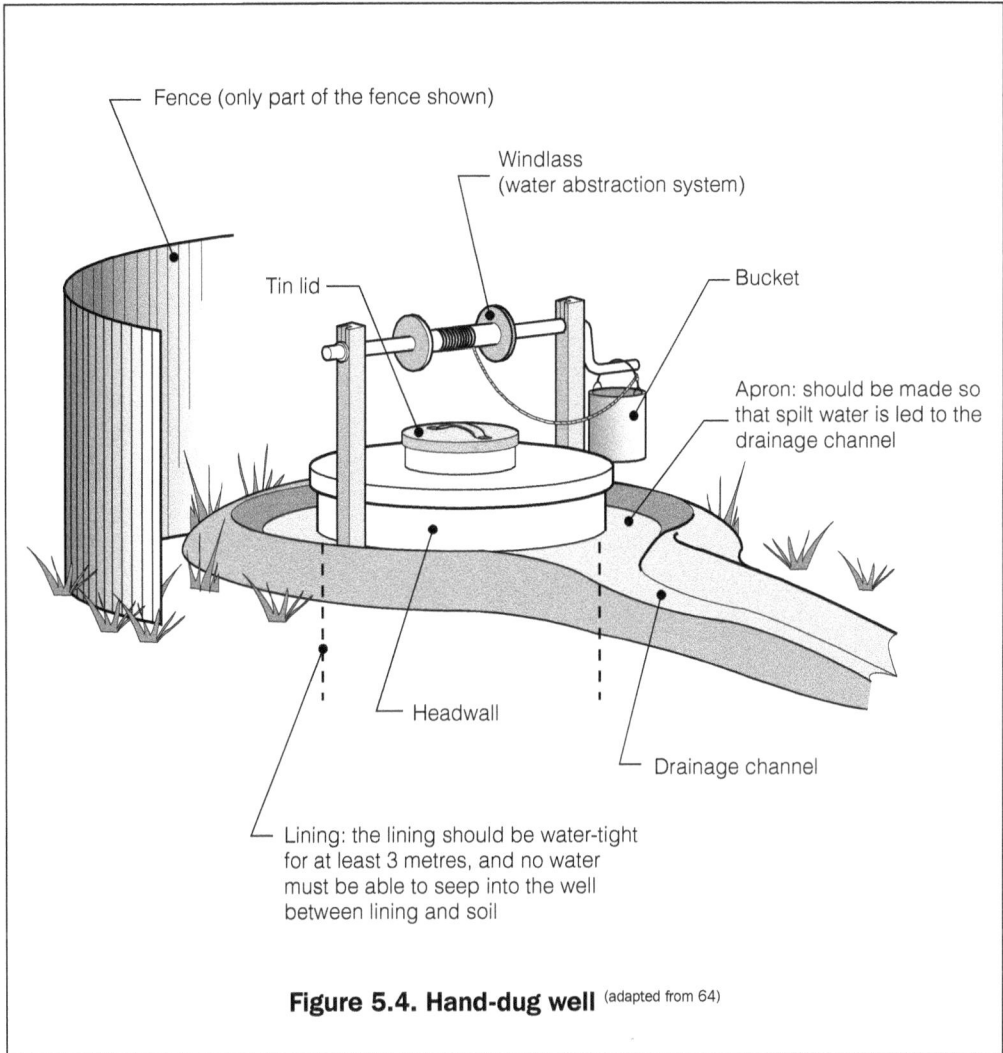

Fence (only part of the fence shown)

Windlass
(water abstraction system)

Tin lid

Bucket

Apron: should be made so
that spilt water is led to the
drainage channel

Headwall

Drainage channel

Lining: the lining should be water-tight
for at least 3 metres, and no water
must be able to seep into the well
between lining and soil

Figure 5.4. Hand-dug well (adapted from 64)

If existing wells are assessed in a sanitary survey, it is best to assume that the underground structures are not adequate. Risk factors to look for include broken or cracked apron and drainage channel, ponding of water within two metres of the well, and the presence of human or animal excreta, refuse, or surface water within 10 metres of the well [82].

Surface water: Any type of surface water must be assumed to be polluted or at risk of pollution. If surface water has to be used for drinking-water, the water should be abstracted as far upstream as possible. The river water will be less contaminated upstream of where people bathe, wash, or play in a stream, and animals come for watering. The quality of surface water can be improved by installing infiltration galleries in the riverbed or by digging riverside wells or infiltration wells [21].

When selecting a water source, seasonal fluctuations in water availability have to be considered. Surface water, water from shallow wells, and rainwater are all usually influenced by the seasons, and water may be in short supply at the end of the dry season.

Water quality beyond the source

Installing a water supply system that provides water of very good quality is of little use if the water is going to be contaminated at a later point. It is very common for water to be contaminated with faecal-oral pathogens during distribution, transport, collection, storage, or handling [48].

Distribution points, vessels, and reservoirs must be designed so that the risk of contamination during filling is minimal. Transport and storage vessels should have a small neck so that water cannot be dipped out. (Be practical, however, as the difficulty of filling a vessel with a small neck at a handpump must be considered.) The vessels should be properly covered to keep animals, insects, dust and other contaminants out. The water should be taken from the vessel either by pouring, or by using a tap. Vessels used for transporting and storing drinking-water should only be used for this purpose. If they have been used for something else, or have been empty for some time, they must be properly cleaned and possibly disinfected before being used for drinking-water. Vessels can be cleaned with boiling water or a chlorinated solution. Health and hygiene promotion will probably be needed to improve behaviour concerning water handling and storage.

A piped water system with intermittent supply is also at risk of pollution. Intermittent supply means that the pressure in the pipes will occasionally be lower than the pressure in the surrounding soil, which means that contaminated water can seep back into the pipes. Installing an electric pump to draw water from a piped water supply with a low water pressure, as often happens in cities in developing countries, can draw polluted water into the system.

Water treatment

The term water treatment is used here to mean manipulating the water to remove water-borne pathogens (e.g. those that cause diarrhoeal diseases). This will often be accomplished by chlorinating the water.

It is not always obvious whether water needs to be treated or not. It is more important to treat the water when many people are supplied by the same source, the water is contaminated, there is a risk of an outbreak of water-borne disease, and polluted water is playing a role in the occurrence of water-borne infections. In addition the local technical, financial, institutional, and logistical capabilities will have to be assessed to determine whether the capability exists to treat the water adequately. This assessment must look into both the current and future situation.

Water treatment at communal level requires funds and adequate support, while treatment at household level will rarely be reliable. The priority should therefore be to find a source that provides water of an adequate quality, and to maintain this quality by protecting the source.

Water from safe sources used by small communities does not usually need to be treated. The priority should be on health and hygiene promotion to both protect the source and handle and store the water properly.

A piped water supply to (peri-)urban areas should normally be chlorinated to reduce the risks of water-borne outbreaks of faecal-oral infections. In an emergency situation, water should be chlorinated if it is piped to more than 10,000 people. Water should also be chlorinated if an outbreak of faecal-oral infections is occurring, or if there is a risk of an outbreak [66]. Other than in emergencies or during a significant threat of an outbreak of faecal-oral disease, there is little use in introducing a water treatment system that could not be maintained when external support is withdrawn [15].

Although it is not possible to go into much detail on water treatment here, there are some important points concerning chlorination and boiling of water.

Chlorine added to water will work in three ways:

- Part of the chlorine will oxidise contamination, including pathogens. The more contamination there is, the more chlorine will be used up. This is 'consumed chlorine'.
- Part of the chlorine will combine with matter in the water, and form 'combined residual chlorine'. Combined residual chlorine functions as a disinfectant, but is less effective than 'free residual chlorine' [15].
- Part of the chlorine will form free residual chlorine. The free residual chlorine has a remaining or residual effect in water. If pathogens contaminate the water during distribution, handling, or storage, the free residual chlorine in the water will normally kill them.

Proper chlorination therefore has two effects: it kills pathogens present in the water at the time of treatment, and it will, to some degree, protect water from future contamination.

Normal chlorination of drinking-water is not effective against the cysts of faecal-oral protozoa (amoebiasis, giardiasis, cryptosporidiosis, and balantidiasis) [3].

In chlorinating drinking-water enough chlorine must be added to leave sufficient free residual chlorine without giving the water a bad taste or wasting the product. Normally a free residual chlorine content of 0.2-0.5mg/l at the point of distribution is adequate [22]. Annexe 4 shows how to determine the amount of chlorine that must be added to water.

After the chlorine is added, it needs time to react with the contamination and turn into combined residual chlorine. A contact time of at least 30 minutes should therefore be allowed before the water is safe to drink, or before the free residual chlorine can be measured. In a cold climate chlorine acts more slowly, and the contact time will have to be longer [15]. If the pH of the water is high, chlorine is less effective in killing pathogens. At a pH of over 8, the free residual chlorine content of the water should be between 0.4 and 1.0mg/l [22].

Sometimes the boiling of water is promoted to make it safe. To be certain that all pathogens are dead, water has to be boiled for 5-10 minutes, although bringing water above 75°C will normally kill the vast majority of the pathogens [28]. Unlike chlorination, boiling water is effective on water of high turbidity, and against protozoa. Boiling water has several disadvantages though, which often makes it less useful than chlorination. Around 1kg of firewood is needed to boil one litre of water, which will often make it environmentally and financially unsustainable. And unlike chlorinated water, boiled water has no residual effect against pathogens [21].

Assessing water quality

In the field there are two ways to assess water quality: conduct a sanitary survey in which all threats to the quality of water are evaluated, or test the water for specific bacteria (usually faecal coliforms and total coliforms) to check whether the water is contaminated. Testing for bacteria is relatively costly and complex, and some skill is needed to obtain reliable results. It also only indicates water quality at the time of the test. Although a sanitary survey does not give a measurable level of pollution, it is often more appropriate than bacterial testing as it does not need specialised material, is instant, and gives a more holistic view of the water quality and its threats.

Treated water should be free of any coliforms when it enters the distribution system. At the distribution point treated water should contain no faecal coliforms. The presence of (faecal) coliforms in treated drinking-water is an indication that treatment is not working properly, or that the water is being contaminated during distribution. Instead of determining which coliforms are present, it is often enough to verify that the water has a sufficient level of free residual chlorine, and that there has been enough contact time between the chlorine and water.

Unlike treated water, any source of untreated water can be expected to contain faecal coliforms, and it will be virtually impossible to obtain water free of faecal coliforms without treatment [15]. In rural areas it will often be difficult to reach WHO or national guidelines even with appropriate structures.

5.3 Additional health issues concerning water supply

A water supply can be a health threat because of its structure or because of poor design or maintenance. The main health risks will be a result of creating an environment in which vectors or intermediate hosts can breed or live.

5.3.1 Large water reservoirs

Artificial reservoirs used for water storage can create two major health problems. The reservoirs are potential breeding sites for *Anopheles* mosquitoes that transmit malaria and filariasis [36], and if people come in direct contact with contaminated water schistosomiasis can also be transmitted. An additional health risk could be created if the spillway of the reservoir creates shallow, turbulent, 'white water' in which the blackfly, the vector of river blindness, can breed [232,240].

5.3.2 Water distribution and storage

All water reservoirs used in the distribution or storage of water (e.g. service reservoirs, overhead tanks, small domestic water containers) should be adequately covered and maintained to prevent them from becoming breeding sites for *Anopheles* mosquitoes and *Aedes* mosquitoes [80].

5.3.3 Sullage

Chapter 7 goes into more detail on drainage, so here we will only briefly point out the health risks associated with the disposal of sullage (or domestic waste water).

All water supply systems will produce waste water in the form of used water, water spilled at the distribution point, and water leaking from pipes or taps. Although sullage normally contains fewer pathogens than sewage, it will often contain faecal pathogens, and could potentially transmit excreta-related infections to either people or animals.

If the casings or linings of boreholes or hand-dug wells are not properly sealed, waste water could seep back in, contaminating the water.

Where waste water keeps soil moist, a favourable environment for soil-transmitted helminths (e.g. hookworm and roundworm) or sandflies could be created [80].

Accumulated polluted waste water can become a breeding site for domestic flies, which transmit several faecal-oral infections and diseases spread by direct contact. *Culex* mosquitoes, which transmit filariasis and several arboviral infections, breed in polluted waste water too [21]. *Anopheles* mosquitoes can breed in ponds or puddles formed by unpolluted waste water.

Chapter 6

Sanitation

Sanitation is everything associated with excreta* in relation to people. It includes the structures used to deal with excreta (e.g. latrines), the materials needed to use these correctly (e.g. water), and people's behaviours and attitudes in relation to both excreta and the sanitary structures (e.g. acceptance of open defecation, washing hands after defecation).

This chapter looks at how excreta and excreta-related infections are linked, and how these infections can be prevented by improved sanitation. Several sanitation-related issues are considered in some detail, and we look at issues which are important to the planning, design, and construction of sanitary structures.

In addition to health benefits, the installation of adequate sanitation may bring people increased convenience and privacy. Improving sanitation can eliminate the unpleasant or unsightly living or working conditions which often result from poor sanitation. Where excreta is reused, people acquire a potential resource. And although this will not be the development worker's motivation, nice sanitary structures often increase the prestige of the owner.

The uncontrolled discharge of excreta, sewage, or effluent into surface water may result in environmental problems. The organic matter in excreta-related waste will use oxygen to oxidise, and it will draw its oxygen from the water. The amount of oxygen used is called the Biochemical Oxygen Demand (BOD) of the excreta. If the waste is discharged into surface water without being adequately treated, the natural aquatic life in the water may die from lack of oxygen.

---

* Excreta can be faeces and urine, and can be human as well as animal

71

6.1 The transmission of excreta-related infections

Infections are related to excreta in two ways: the pathogens leave the original host's body through excreta, or one of the vectors of the disease benefits from the lack of adequate sanitary structures or from accessible excreta.
Several disease-groups leave the body through excreta.

Faecal-oral infections are transmitted directly through faecally contaminated hands, food, water, or soil. The pathogen must be ingested to cause infection (see Section 2.4.1.1, Figure 2.2).

Schistosomiasis needs to develop in a freshwater snail before it can infect people. The pathogen infects people by penetrating skin which is in contact with infected surface water (see Section 2.4.2.2, Figure 2.4).

Water-based helminths with two intermediate hosts (e.g. fasciolopsiasis, clonorchiasis) need to develop in two freshwater intermediate hosts before they become infectious to people. Transmission occurs when the second intermediate host is eaten without being properly cooked (see Section 2.4.2.2 Figure 2.4).

Soil-transmitted helminths (e.g. hookworm disease and roundworm infection) have to develop in soil before they can infect people. Some of these helminths infect people by penetrating their skin when they are in contact with contaminated soil, others infect people when ingested (see Section 2.4.2.1, Figure 2.3).

Beef tapeworm and pork tapeworm have to be ingested by cattle or pigs and development in them. People are infected by eating poorly cooked beef or pork.

Cysticercosis, a complication of pork tapeworm, is transmitted like a faecal-oral infection from person to person (see Section 2.4.2.3).

Leptospirosis is mainly transmitted through direct skin contact with water or material contaminated with the urine of infected rats (see Section 2.4.1.2).

Vectors which benefit from inadequate sanitation include domestic flies, cockroaches, and *Culex* mosquitoes.

Domestic flies, which can transmit several faecal-oral infections including conjunctivitis, trachoma, and yaws, can breed in, and feed on, excreta [67].

Cockroaches, which have the potential to transmit several faecal-oral infections, can feed on excreta and hide in sanitary structures.

The mosquito *Culex quinquefasciatus*, a vector of filariasis and several arboviral infections, can breed in the polluted liquids in latrines and cesspits or septic tanks[61].

As there are many disease-groups related to excreta and sanitation, the following concept should help to assess when these infections could pose a risk.

If pathogen transmission is to succeed, the excreta has to come in contact with certain elements. For example, schistosomiasis can only be transmitted if the pathogen infects a freshwater snail, so transmission can only occur if the excreta is released into fresh surface water.

Table 6.1 shows the different elements that the pathogens have to come in direct contact with to be transmitted.

Table 6.1. Disease groups and the elements that play a role in disease transmission
(adapted from 60)

The element excreta must come in direct contact with:	Faecal-oral infections	Schistosomiasis	Water-based with two intermediate hosts	Soil-transmitted helminths	Beef and pork tapeworm	Leptospirosis	Guinea-worm infection	Spread by direct contact	Vector-borne infections
People	H/A				H(a)	A			
Animals	H/A				H	A			
Insects	H/A							(b)	(c)
Crops, food, vegetation	H/A				H	A			
Soil	H/A			H		A			
Surface water	H/A	H/A	H/A		H	A			(c)
Ground water	H/A								

H: Human excreta
A: Animal excreta
(a): Only cysticercosis, a complication of pork tapeworm
(b): Domestic flies can breed in excreta and can transmit conjunctivitis, trachoma, and yaws
(c): The mosquito *Culex quinquefasciatus*, vector of filariasis and several arboviral infections, can breed in sanitary structures or surface water polluted by excreta

Faecal and urinary transmission of infections

Most excreta-related infections are only transmitted by faeces. The exceptions are urinary schistosomiasis, which is common in Africa and which has no animal host; leptospirosis, which is transmitted mainly through animal urine; and (para-) typhoid fever, which is occasionally transmitted through urine [16].

The risk of children's excreta

As many excreta-related infections occur mainly in children, it is more likely that children's excreta will contain pathogens than adult's excreta, so special care must be taken in disposing their faeces. Health and hygiene promotion to mothers will usually be needed to improve the children's behaviour and reduce the risks of open defecation by children. Sanitary structures will have to be adapted and acceptable to children.

The risk of animal excreta

Many excreta-related pathogens can infect animals as well as people, and animals can be important reservoirs of disease. Cattle, pigs, dogs and rats are all potential hosts for several diarrhoeal infections, several water-based helminths, and leptospirosis. Chickens and wild birds can be the reservoir of pathogens that cause diarrhoea. More information on the potential animal reservoirs of specific diseases can be found in Annexe 1. Where animals are believed to be playing a role in the transmission of infections they will have to be controlled.

6.1.1   Risk-factors relating to excreta and sanitation

There are five major problems relating to excreta and sanitation which can result in a health risk:

- There is open defecation as people do not use sanitary structures.
- People do not wash their hands (properly) after defecation.
- Sanitary structures are not used correctly, are poorly designed, or are poorly maintained.
- Excreta is re-used as a fertiliser, fish food, building material, or for fuel.
- People come in contact with excreta of infected animals.

Several of these problems can be broken down further into specific risk-factors. These specific risk-factors with their associated disease-groups are presented in Table 6.2.

Several of these risk-factors will be looked at in more detail in Section 6.2.

Table 6.2. Specific sanitation-related risk-factors

Risk-factors relating to:
i   Open defecation
ii Poor personal hygiene
iii Poor functioning or design of structure
iv Excreta used as a resource
v   Animal contact

	Risk-factor	Faecal-oral infections	Schistosomiasis	Water-based with two intermediate hosts	Soil-transmitted helminths	Beef and pork tapeworm	Leptospirosis	Guinea-worm infection	Spread by direct contact	Vector-borne infections
i	Sanitary structures are not used (by all)					(a)		(b)		
ii	Poor handwashing after defecation				(c)					
iii	Poor hygiene of sanitary structure				(c)			(b)		
	Openings or cracks in sanitary structure							(b)	(d)	
	Collapse of sanitary structure or pit							(b)	(d)	
	Overflowing of sanitary structure							(b)		
	Excreta discharged in surface water							(b)	(d)	
	Sanitary structure pollutes groundwater									
	Excreta is handled in O&M							(b)		
iv	Excreta is re-used							(b)	(d)	
v	Access of animals to living quarters									
	Close contact between people and animals (work, play)									
	Animal faeces on domestic plot							(b)		
	Animals have access to well, spring, etc.									
	Animals have access to stored water or food									
	Animals have access to surface water									

Sanitary structure: latrine, sewage system
O&M: Operation and maintenance (of the sanitary structure)

(a): Leptospirosis, if transmitted by excreta, is usually transmitted by animal urine and therefore almost impossible to confine through improved sanitation
(b): A potential for breeding and feeding of domestic flies
(c): A risk of cysticercosis, a complication of pork tapeworm; all other 'positives' in this column can result in both cysticercosis and in infection of cattle or pork
(d): A potential for breeding of the mosquito Culex quinquefasciatus

Table 6.3. Reduction in occurrence of disease associated with improved sanitation		
Disease (group)	Reduction in occurrence	Remarks
Diarrhoea	36% [26]	improved sanitation
	42% [70]	sanitary facilities are well maintained (clean)
	44% [40]	hygiene improved in existing toilets in schools
	30% [70]	elimination of excreta from around the house
Infant diarrhoea	negligible [70]	improved neighbourhood sanitation but poor water quality
	25% [70]	improved neighbourhood sanitation with good water quality
Hookworm	4% [26]	improved sanitation only; reduction when improved sanitation and medical treatment were combined: 69%
Roundworm	29% [26]	improved sanitation and water supply; reduction when improved sanitation and medical treatment were combined: 80%
Tapeworms	important [73]	improved sanitation

6.1.2 The health impact of improving sanitation

Table 6.3 shows how different excreta-related infections can be reduced with improved sanitation.

6.1.3 The survival of excreta-related pathogens in the environment

Outside the host, excreta-related pathogens will usually die off over time. Most pathogens can remain viable in the environment for some time, however, and Table 6.4 shows the maximum time of survival of some. As a general rule, pathogens survive longer when they are in lower temperatures, in a moist environment, and protected from direct sunlight [28,31]. Again as a general rule, helminths and viruses will survive longer then bacteria and protozoa.

Except for roundworm, all the infections in Table 6.4 are faecal-oral. It is less useful to look at the survival times of pathogens which need intermediate hosts, as these usually remain viable for as long as the intermediate host survives.

Table 6.4. Maximum survival times (in days) of pathogens in different media (from 28)

Media in which pathogens survive (at 20 to 30°C)	Bacterial enteritis (by E.coli)	Salmonellosis	Shigellosis (bacillary dysentery)	Cholera	Amoebiasis	Faecal-oral viruses (e.g polio)	Roundworm
Fresh water and sewage	60	60	30	30	30	120	many months
Faeces, nightsoil, and sludge	90	60	30	30	30	100	many months
Soil	70	70	-	20	20	100	many months
On the surface of crops	30	30	10	5	10	60	60

The health risk of contaminated material (water, food, other objects) will usually decrease over time if no multiplication or recontamination occurs. As the number of pathogens discharged is often very large, the potential for transmission can remain high, even if most pathogens die off or if the excreta is diluted in surface water. A person with cholera can defecate up to 1×10^{12} bacteria per litre of diarrhoea, for example, a person with urinary schistosomiasis can discharge 50,000 eggs per litre of urine, and people infected with hookworm disease can shed 1×10^6 eggs per day [73].

Several bacteria and helminths can multiply outside the host. The bacteria *Salmonella* spp. (causing salmonellosis and (para-)typhoid), *Shigella* spp. (causing bacillary dysentery) [3] and *E.coli* (causing bacterial enteritis) [28] can all multiply in food. The food can be contaminated through faeces, hands, utensils, domestic flies, or cockroaches. Meat and dairy products pose the greatest risk. Thus food which is not initially harmful because it contains too little bacteria can become infectious over time because the bacteria have multiplied.

Several water-based helminths (schistosomiasis, fasciolopsiasis, fascioliasis, clonorchiasis, and opisthorchiasis) can multiply in freshwater snails, and strongyloidiasis can multiply in soil. Here again, a light contamination of water or soil can can become very infectious because the pathogen has multiplied outside the host.

Excreta poses a large and prolonged health risk because of its potentially high load of pathogens, the persistence of pathogens in the environment, and the potential for multiplication outside the host, so excreta-related wastes must be dealt with carefully.

6.2   Practical issues on sanitation

This section looks at several of the risk factors mentioned in Table 6.2. It also presents several aspects important to the planning, design, and construction of sanitary structures.

6.2.1   Open defecation

Open defecation allows the transmission of all excreta-related infections and is therefore a serious health threat. Open defecation is not acceptable close to the household plot, or in urban communities or other areas with high or medium population densities.

Each infected person usually has great potential to spread pathogens, so sanitary structures will only be effective in preventing disease if they are used by everyone, all the time. Even if only some people in the population (e.g. children) defecate in the open, the health benefits of sanitary structures will be limited. Some examples to illustrate this problem [adapted from 2,3,16,73]:

- A person with bacillary dysentery excretes 1×10^9 bacteria in a small stream. Ingesting 10 to 100 bacteria can cause infection. The number of pathogens excreted in the water could in theory pollute $10,000m^3$ of water with 100 bacteria per litre.
- A person with a hookworm infection can easily release 1,000,000 eggs per day. If this person does not always use a latrine, and we assume that 1 per cent of the eggs end up in favourable soil, become infectious, and remain viable for six weeks, then this person will be responsible for over 400,000 infectious larvae in the soil at any time for as long as the infection lasts.

Even though open defecation is a serious health threat, it should not be condemned categorically in areas with low population densities. Open defecation might be preferable to using poorly maintained latrines [57] which can become foci for the transmission of diarrhoea [40] and hookworm [9].

6.2.2   Poor hygiene of sanitary structures

Sanitary structures can play an important role in disease transmission if they are not kept clean [28]. Faecal-oral infections can be spread through direct contact with faeces, contaminated material, or through flies or cockroaches. Latrines with floors contaminated with faeces can transmit hookworm.

Sanitary structures must be kept clean to reduce health risks and to make them acceptable to users. Installing a SanPlat, which is a smooth concrete latrine slab,

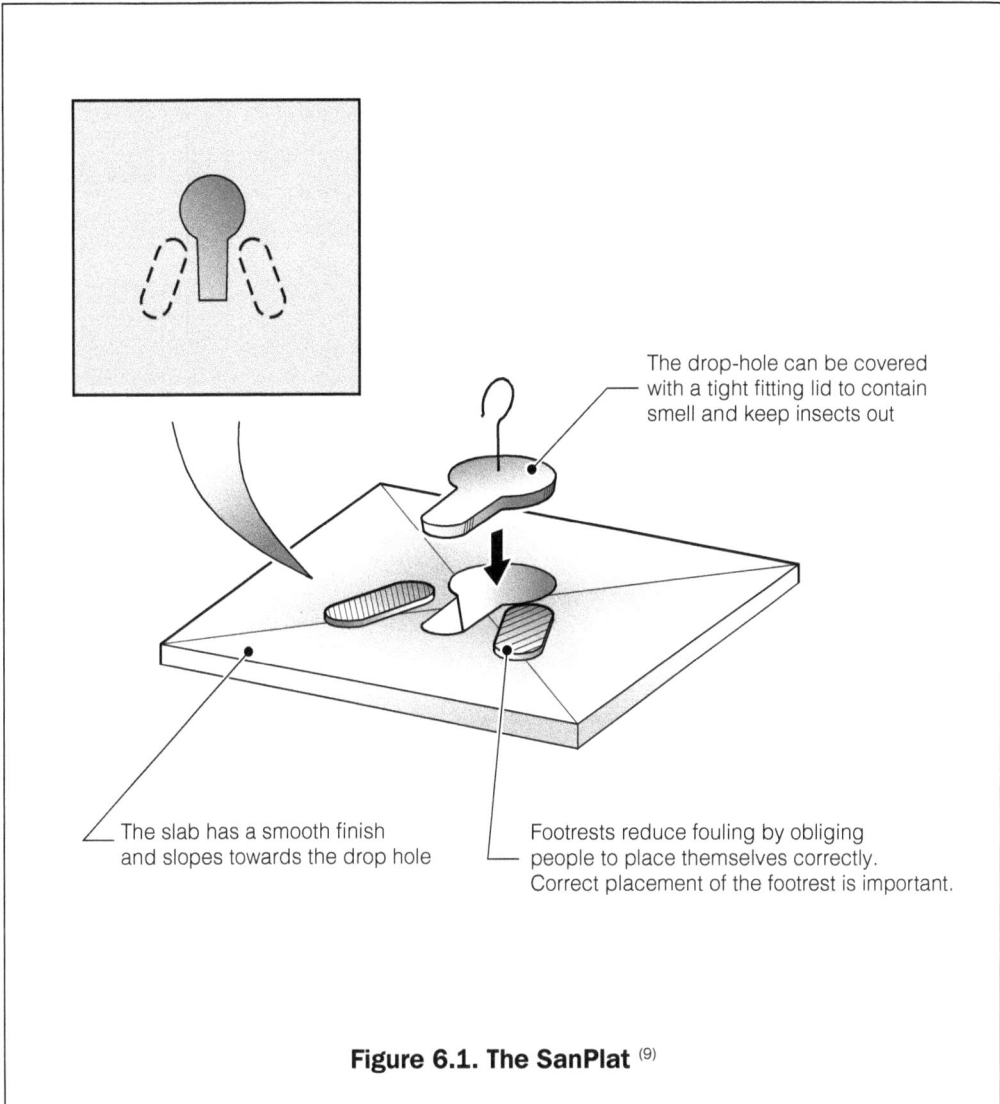

Figure 6.1. The SanPlat [9]

The drop-hole can be covered with a tight fitting lid to contain smell and keep insects out

The slab has a smooth finish and slopes towards the drop hole

Footrests reduce fouling by obliging people to place themselves correctly. Correct placement of the footrest is important.

makes it easier to clean the latrine. A SanPlat can be built into a new latrine or an existing latrine can be upgraded [9]. The slab should slope towards the drop-hole so that spilled water, or water used for cleaning, flows into the hole. Figure 6.1 shows an example of a SanPlat.

6.2.3   Water supply and the sanitary structure

There should be a reliable source of water near the sanitary structure. Water is used for handwashing and cleaning the structure, and possibly for flushing or anal cleansing. The water does not have to be high quality as it is not used for drinking.

Table 6.5. Water demands of a sanitary structure [66]	
Water use	Quantity needed
Handwashing	1-2 litres per person per day
Cleaning structure	2-8 litres per cubicle per day
Flushing (pour-flush)	3-5 litres per person per day
Flushing (sewerage)	20-40 litres per person per day
Anal cleansing	1-2 litres per person per day

Table 6.5 gives approximate quantities of water needed. A communal pour-flush latrine used by 20 people who use water for anal cleansing may need around 200 litres of water per day to work – and be used – correctly.

6.2.4 Discharge of excreta or effluent in surface water
Discharging excreta-related waste into freshwater causes different risks than discharging into seawater.

Discharging excreta in freshwater
Discharging excreta, nightsoil, or sewage into fresh surface water creates a serious health risk. Faecal-oral infections can be transmitted to people who drink the contaminated water, and water-based helminths (e.g. schistosomiasis, clonorchiasis) can infect their intermediate hosts. If cattle and pigs drink contaminated water, they can be infected with beef and pork tapeworm. Domestic flies, which transmit conjunctivitis and trachoma, and *Culex* mosquitoes, which transmit filariasis and several arboviral infections, can breed in surface water polluted with faeces.

The discharge of excreta, nightsoil, or raw sewage into fresh surface water should be limited as much as possible. The practise would only be acceptable where the waste was diluted in a large volume of moving water, where people are not in contact with the water (including people downstream), and where the risk from food taken from the river is very small. This combination is unlikely to occur in developing countries.

As conventional sewage treatment plants do not usually reduce the number of pathogens to a safe level (their main aim is generally to reduce the BOD to acceptable levels), their effluent is normally still very polluted. Exceptions to this are properly designed and functioning waste stabilisation ponds, plants with maturation ponds, and adequate filtration systems (see Section 6.2.6) [28].

Discharging excreta into seawater

Only faecal-oral infections pose a health risk if excreta, nightsoil or sewage are discharged into seawater. The cysts of protozoa and the eggs of helminths will settle out rapidly, so only viruses and bacteria will normally be a threat. It is unlikely that pathogens will travel more than a few kilometres from a sewage outfall.

As seawater is not used for drinking, the main health risk comes from handling or eating contaminated fish and shellfish. Fish can harbour pathogens in their body for weeks and can therefore be a risk if they are caught close to a sewage outfall. As shellfish can accumulate pathogens in their bodies, they are a larger health risk than fish. Fish and shellfish should always be properly cooked before eating.

The additional health risks from contaminated seawater will normally be limited if people already live in an environment with poor sanitation [28].

6.2.5   Groundwater pollution by sanitary structures

Polluted liquid seeping out of sanitary structures can sometimes percolate through the soil into the groundwater. The groundwater can thus be polluted with pathogens and chemicals from the excreta. Both types of pollution will be covered here, with the emphasis on pollution by pathogens.

Only faecal-oral pathogens will be transmitted by polluted groundwater, and unless the soil consists of fissured rock or coarse sands, only viruses and bacteria will pose a risk. Because of their large size, the cysts of protozoa and eggs of helminths will easily be blocked by the soil and will not seep down [42].

Groundwater pollution will only be a problem if the groundwater is used for drinking, or if water mains with intermittent supply are piped through polluted soil (see Section 5.2.3).

It is important to remember that the health risks from open defecation or from using inadequate sanitary structures are usually greater than the health risk of polluting the groundwater by sanitation.

If groundwater pollution is a serious risk, it is usually more appropriate to change to a piped water supply than to install off-site sanitation (e.g. a sewerage system).

Although groundwater pollution is often used as an argument against on-site sanitation (e.g. pit latrines), poorly constructed or maintained sewerage systems are just as likely to pollute the groundwater [62].

Pollution in the unsaturated zone

In the zone above the water table, polluted liquid from the sanitary structure will percolate downwards under the influence of gravity. The removal of pathogens in the unsaturated zone is very effective [31], and where groundwater pollution could be a problem, this distance should be maximised (e.g. by raising the latrine, using a shallow pit) [42]. If there is at least 2m of fine sand or loam between the source of pollution (e.g. the base of the pit of the latrine) and the groundwater table, most pathogens will be removed from the liquid [57]. Within months of a latrine being used an organic mat will form naturally in the soil. This mat is very effective in removing pathogens [42].

Pollution in the saturated zone

To understand the principles of pollution below the water table, the movement of groundwater in the saturated zone must be understood.

Shallow groundwater tables usually follow roughly the form of the terrain [34]. As water flows from high to low areas, groundwater will normally move in the same direction that water on the surface would flow. As a rough rule, the steeper the terrain and the coarser the soil particles (if there are no small particles like silt and clay), the faster the groundwater will flow [24].

When the polluted liquid meets the groundwater, the liquid will be carried with the groundwater flow. The liquid forms a 'tongue' which follows the flow of the groundwater, but the liquid and the groundwater do not really mix [30]. This is shown in Figure 6.2.

Bacteria will not normally travel further than the distance the groundwater flows in 10 days [42]. Predicting the exact distance that pathogens will travel from a sanitary structure is difficult, as this will depend strongly on the local situation. In terrain with a low gradient and medium to fine sands, bacteria will probably not travel further than 10 metres. Viruses can travel further, as can bacteria in coarse sands or fissured rocks [42]. In fine soils a safety distance of 15 metres will usually be adequate [57].

These values can be used for sanitary structures which have to deal with up to 50 litres of liquid per horizontal m^2 per day [30], and family structures will usually not exceed this.

Even though pathogens are removed from the flow, they are not necessarily killed, and if large volumes of liquid are suddenly discharged, viable pathogens which were 'stuck' may be flushed out. Pathogens will not travel as far if the same amount of liquid is discharged continuously than if it is discharged in gushes.

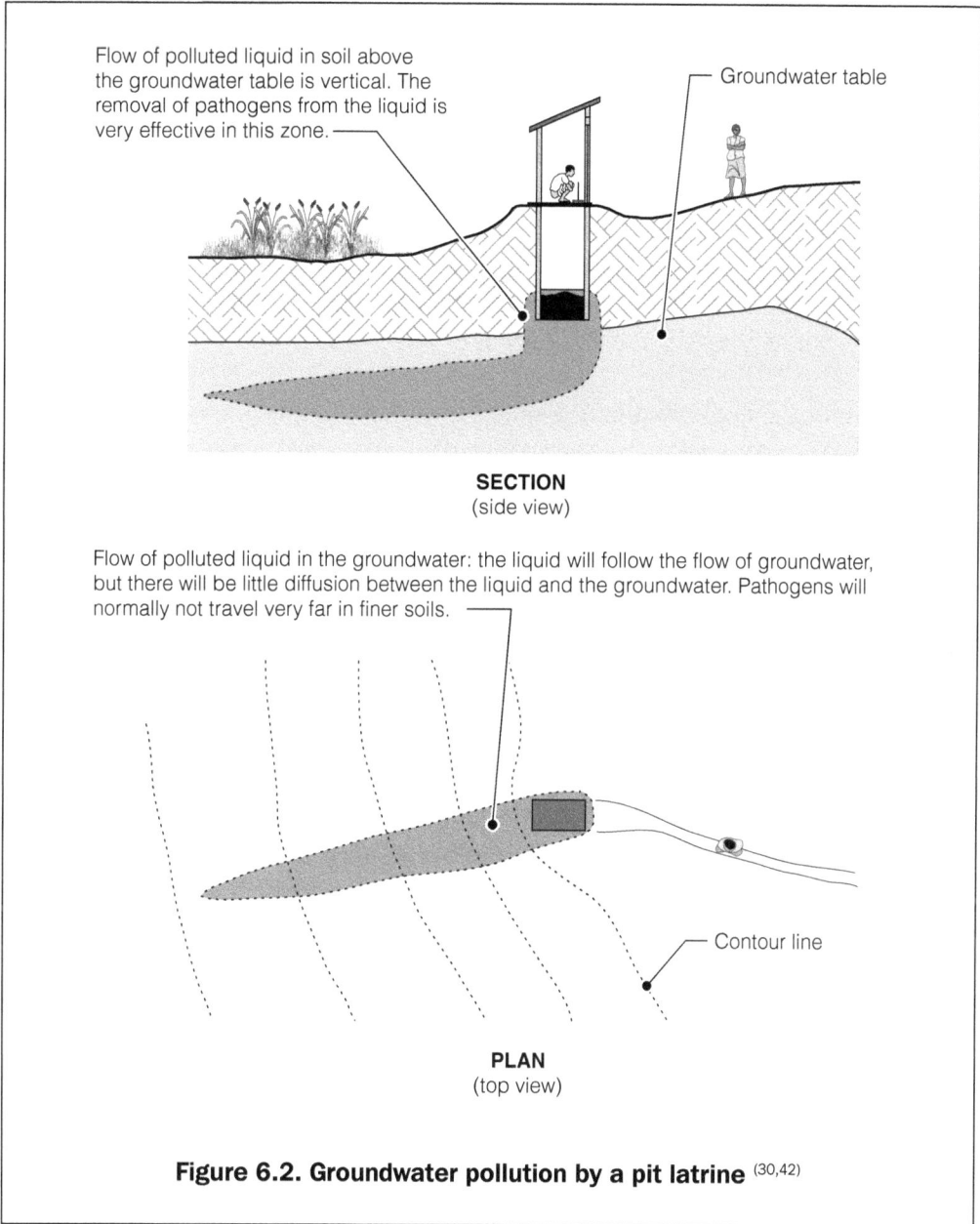

Flow of polluted liquid in soil above the groundwater table is vertical. The removal of pathogens from the liquid is very effective in this zone.

Groundwater table

SECTION
(side view)

Flow of polluted liquid in the groundwater: the liquid will follow the flow of groundwater, but there will be little diffusion between the liquid and the groundwater. Pathogens will normally not travel very far in finer soils.

Contour line

PLAN
(top view)

Figure 6.2. Groundwater pollution by a pit latrine [30,42]

If groundwater is abstracted through a properly sealed borehole well below the polluted layer, the water from the pump will be safe. This only works if water is abstracted in low volumes (e.g. with a handpump). Mechanised pumping can draw down the water table to such an extent that the pollution of deeper groundwater is possible [24,57]. A properly sealed borehole that pierces an impermeable layer would be even safer. It might sometimes be possible to install latrines and properly constructed tube-wells close together, but it is always better to have a minimum safe distance between the two.

Chemical pollution of groundwater through sanitation

The chemical pollution of groundwater is caused mainly by nitrogen (nitrate) and chloride [43]. The health risk of chloride in groundwater is limited [46] (chloride is a component of kitchen salt), but a high chloride content could make the water taste unacceptably salty. Nitrate can cause blue-baby syndrome in infants, but this risk seems to be limited [62,68]. Nitrate is possibly linked to gastric cancer and congenital deformities, but here again, the risks seem to be limited [62].

Unless there is a high population density, or some other cause of chemical pollution (e.g. using sanitary structures to discharge chemically polluted waste water), the health risk of chemical polluting groundwater by sanitary structures will usually be small.

6.2.6   Re-use of excreta

Excreta can be a valuable resource. Excreta-related wastes can be used for:

- fertilising or irrigating crops: nightsoil, sludge, sewage or composted wastes can be used to fertilise plants, and sewage or effluent can be used for irrigation (and fertilisation).
- Aquaculture: nightsoil, sludge or sewage can be used to feed fish in ponds.
- Gas production: nightsoil is used to produce biogas, a useful source of energy.

Fresh excreta, nightsoil, sludge, sewage, or effluent can all contain large quantities of pathogens, and thus pose a serious health risk to the people who handle the waste and those around them. People who work directly with waste or who live or work close to where excreta-related wastes can all be at risk from excreta-related infections. But excreta, effluents, and sludge can be treated to make them relatively safe to handle and re-use.

Treatment of excreta-related wastes

There are several ways to make excreta-related wastes safer. The waste may not be totally free of pathogens, but if one of the following techniques are used correctly, the risk of handling the treated waste will normally be negligible.

- Pass the waste through properly designed and working waste stabilisation ponds [15].
- Let the effluent from a sewage treatment plant sit for enough time in maturation ponds.

- Filter sewage treatment plant's effluent through a sand bed.
- Compost excreta, nightsoil or sludge under aerobic conditions, at temperatures of at least 62°C for over one hour, 50°C for over one day, or 46°C for over one week.
- Treat nightsoil or sludge with heat; temperatures and duration should be at least equivalent to those mentioned above [28]. The high financial and environmental costs of fuel will usually make this method inappropriate.
- Bury excreta, nightsoil, or sludge for two years [30] (e.g. use twin-pit latrines, bury nightsoil or sludge in trenches, or top with earth full latrines). In tropical climates most pathogens, except for roundworm, will not survive longer than one year when buried.
- Dry nightsoil or excreta for at least one year [28].

Fresh excreta, nightsoil, and any type of excreta-related sludge or effluent that has not been treated adequately can contain pathogens and should therefore be isolated as much as possible from people, animals, insects, food, crops, vegetables, soil, and water. Conventional sewage treatment plants usually do not reduce the number of pathogens to safe levels, and their effluent can still contain high levels of pathogens.

Use of excreta-related waste for fertilisation and irrigation
The main health risks of workers (and often of their families) who use excreta-related waste for fertilisation or irrigation are faecal-oral infections and soil-transmitted helminths (e.g. roundworm and hookworm). Where workers come in contact with contaminated surface water schistosomiasis could also be a problem.

Consumers of the crops are at risk of faecal-oral infections and ingested soil-transmitted helminths (e.g. roundworm and whipworm).

The health risks of using excreta-related waste for fertiliser should be reduced by minimising the contact between crops and pollution as much as possible (e.g. through subsurface irrigation). Excreta-related wastes should only be applied before the crops are planted or up to one month before the crops are harvested. This will reduce, though not eliminate, the risks of faecal-oral pathogens. The health risks of soil-transmitted helminths will not be reduced significantly.

The health threat to people can be reduced by feeding these crops to animals, though several infections (e.g. salmonellosis and beef and pig tapeworm) will remain a health threat to people through infections in the animals [28].

Use of excreta-related waste for aquaculture

Using excreta-related waste to feed fish ponds creates several health risks. People who handle, prepare, or eat undercooked fish from these ponds are at risk from the faecal-oral pathogens that are on the fish's body or in its intestines [28].

In addition to faecal-oral infections, consumers are at risk from water-based helminths which use fish as an intermediate host (e.g. clonorchiasis and opisthorchiasis). These pathogens can be transmitted to people or animals if the fish is not properly cooked. Other pathogens which have to reach surface water to develop (e.g. schistosomiasis) could also potentially be transmitted.

Keeping the live fish in unpolluted water for two to three weeks before eating them will reduce the health risks.

As the eggs of water-based helminths with two intermediate hosts settle out easily in water, the risk of these pathogens can be reduced by putting ponds in series, and only harvesting fish from ponds which have not been fed with excreta-related wastes [6].

Production of biogas

Handling excreta and the sludge that has to be removed regularly from a biogas plant could be a health risk. The sludge could be heavily contaminated with pathogens and should be handled and disposed of with the same care as fresh excreta.

6.2.7　Some practical issues on the planning and construction of sanitation

While not all practical sanitation issues can be considered here, some important issues need to be highlighted.

Assessment

To maximise the impact of improved sanitation, everyone must have access to adequate structures, and these structures must be used correctly.

The structures have to be adapted to local behaviour, traditional beliefs, and the population's needs. In addition, sanitation has to be affordable to the users, and appropriate for local institutional capabilities and restrictions. The structures also have to be adapted to the physical situation in which they will have to operate. A thorough assessment will be needed, and it is likely that different groups will identify different issues, needs, and preferences, and these must be identified and considered. It is especially important to address the problems of marginalised people to ensure that everyone has access to sanitation.

Household versus communal latrines
Each household should normally have its own sanitary structure so that responsibility for maintenance and cleanliness lies with the family.

In a stable situation, communal latrines should only be considered if it is impossible to install structures at household level (e.g. because there is no space or installation is unaffordable), or in public structures like schools or hospitals.

Where communal structures have to be installed, the issues of management, cleaning, maintenance, and operation must be worked out before construction begins. Usually people have to be employed to keep communal structures clean [56]. The facilities for men and women should be separated, and issues of privacy and safety for women using the structures, or walking to the structures, have to be addressed in the planning phase.

Numbers and location of latrines
People will only use sanitary structures if they do not lose too much time at them. This is achieved by having enough latrines available and siting them close to the users.

There should be no more than six cubicles per communical latrine [21], with not more than 20 [66] or at most 25 users per cubicle [21]. Structures should be sited less than 50 metres [66] from people's houses, and at most 250 metres [21].

If groundwater is the community's drinking-water source, latrines must be located and constructed so that the risk of contaminating groundwater is minimal. As a general rule, if the latrine is constructed in fine soils, there should be at least 15 metres between the water source and the latrine. If possible, the water source should be installed on higher ground than the latrine. Where the soil is coarse, or waste water is discharged in the structure, the distances between water source and latrine may have to be more. (The problem of groundwater pollution has been addressed in more detail in Section 6.2.5.) Latrines should be located so that the risk of flooding by stormwater or floodwater is minimised. The top of the latrine slab should be raised a minimum of 0.15 metres above surface level to prevent surface water or rainwater from entering the structure [30]. Pits should be dug some metres away from the foundations of buildings as this could weaken the foundation or cause collapse; and pits must not be dug against a road carrying heavy traffic as this can also collapse the pit.

Sanitation in emergencies

In the early stages of an emergency it is not usually feasible to provide household latrines or even enough communal latrines. It may be necessary to construct structures with 50 to 100 users per cubicle or metre of trench (if trench latrines are used) to begin with. This must be upgraded as soon as possible to communal latrines with 20 users per cubicle, or household latrines [47]. As it is not normally possible to provide adequate structures from the beginning, and the aim should be to decrease the health risks and increase the convenience to the users as quickly as possible.

Start by discouraging people from defecating near any water source used by people and animals, or in fields where crops for consumption are grown. As soon as possible defecation should be confined to specific areas: open defecation fields or trench defecation fields. The next step could be to install trench latrines, or communal borehole or pit latrines. Following that latrines could be installed at household level if feasible [64]. Provision should progress through these steps as soon as possible, to use the best feasible structures at all times.

If communal latrines are installed people have to be employed to maintain and clean them. Anal cleansing material, water and soap for handwashing, and soil to cover the excreta may have to be provided [66].

If insects can access the contents of the latrines, the excreta should be covered with 0.1 metre of soil every two to three days [21].

Some issues concerning construction

Structures are designed to last a certain period (the 'design life'). In a stable situation the pit of a latrine may be expected to last for up to 30 years [30]. The expected number of users at the end of the design life should be used when designing structures. Annexe 5 has information on the accumulation rates of solids in pit latrines, and how to estimate the infiltration capacity of the soil.

Where soil stability, soil erosion, or rats could become a problem, the top 0.5 metres of a pit should be protected with a closed lining. If the soil cannot carry much weight the superstructure should be light. It may be necessary to make a foundation in the form of a concrete ring beam to make the latrine structurally sound [30]. The more complex a latrine becomes, the more expensive and demanding its construction will be.

Latrines should be built so that insects cannot enter the pit. This can be achieved by installing a tight-fitting lid (this is difficult in a communal structure), a water seal (this will only be adequate if water or soft paper is used for anal cleansing), or a VIP-latrine (this type of latrine is probably less adapted to use at household level as they are expensive and rather complex; in addition, VIP latrines usually do not stop mosquito breeding). If the latrine is 'wet', polystyrene beads can be used to create a floating layer which will prevent mosquitoes from breeding in the pit [61]. All other openings which give access to the pit containing excreta should either be sealed or closed with flyproof netting.

Vandalism and theft must be prevented by sealing the lids of access-holes with mortar or locking them and by making structures as solid as possible; this is especially important in communal structures.

This example of a pit latrine (Figure 6.3) shows some of most important points for proper use.

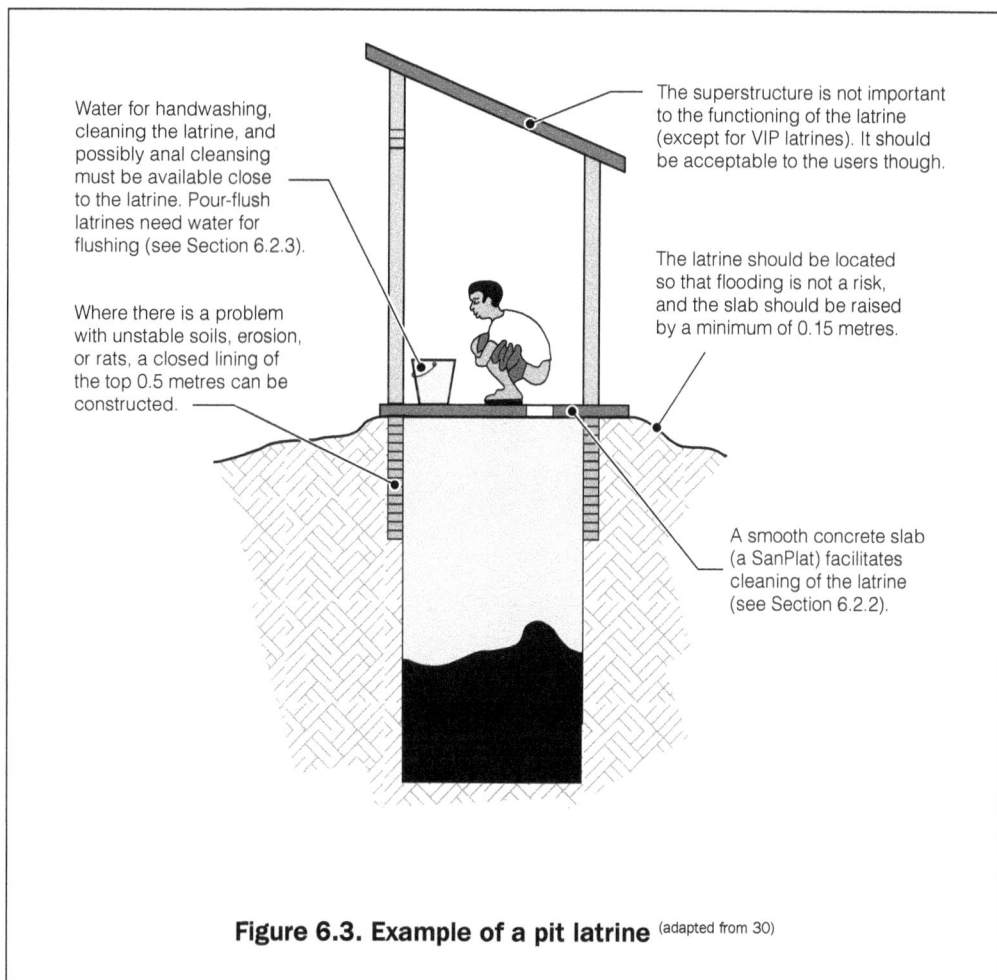

Water for handwashing, cleaning the latrine, and possibly anal cleansing must be available close to the latrine. Pour-flush latrines need water for flushing (see Section 6.2.3).

Where there is a problem with unstable soils, erosion, or rats, a closed lining of the top 0.5 metres can be constructed.

The superstructure is not important to the functioning of the latrine (except for VIP latrines). It should be acceptable to the users though.

The latrine should be located so that flooding is not a risk, and the slab should be raised by a minimum of 0.15 metres.

A smooth concrete slab (a SanPlat) facilitates cleaning of the latrine (see Section 6.2.2).

Figure 6.3. Example of a pit latrine (adapted from 30)

Chapter 7

Drainage

This chapter looks at the health risks caused by the presence of water[1] in the human environment and how this water can be drained. The purpose of drainage is to remove unwanted water from the human environment [17]. It is often difficult to make a clear separation between 'unwanted' and 'wanted' water, as people will usually use surface water, for example for irrigation or watering animals. What is unwanted, however, are the health risks associated with surface water.

From a health point of view, the properties of the surface water are usually more important than its origin. The WES specialist needs to separate the different sources, as different types of structure will be needed to deal with them properly. In the section on surface water and the transmission of disease we will look generally at surface water, while in the section on the practical aspects of drainage we focus on the sources of water and how to cope with them.

Drainage must handle water of different origins: domestic waste water (or sullage), rainwater (or stormwater, runoff), floodwater, and water from natural sources (e.g. springs).

Sullage includes used water (e.g. washing water), water spilled at the distribution point, water from leaks in the system, or from taps. Sullage is usually produced in low volumes, and without seasonal fluctuations.

Stormwater is that rainwater that has not infiltrated into the soil, was not intercepted by the vegetation, and did not evaporate. This surplus water will either collect in depressions in the surface, or flow over the surface until it reaches channels, streams, or rivers, through which it will be evacuated. Stormwater often occurs in large volumes, and is a seasonal problem.

Floodwater is generally water from overflowing rivers or channels. Flooding is a seasonal problem which usually involves large volumes of water [15].

---

[1] The health risks associated with water in the human environment are normally caused by fresh surface water

Natural water sources can result in unwanted water if the water is able to collect in large puddles or ponds.

In addition, industry, agriculture, mining, and other activities (e.g. medical facilities, abattoirs) may produce waste water. Most of the health risks related to these will be similar to the other types of surface water, but there may be specific health risks related to these types of waste water. These specific health risks are not covered by this manual.

Surface water can exist in many types of reservoirs. Naturally occurring surface water is found in lakes, marshes, natural ponds, streams, rivers, puddles – even leaf axils collecting rainwater can form 'reservoirs'. Artificial reservoirs of surface water include irrigation systems, channels, artificial water reservoirs (e.g. for hydroelectric power generation), overhead tanks, swimming pools, and pits resulting from construction work, agriculture, mining, brickmaking or other activities. Even small 'vessels' like old tyres, drums, blocked roof gutters, empty plant pots, or old cans that accumulate (rain)water may serve as a reservoir for 'surface water'.

Issues concerning drainage other than health

Stormwater, or floodwater, can kill people or animals, and can destroy buildings, roads or crops. Floods can make it impossible for people to move around. Poor drainage can cause landslides and mudflows, which may be a risk to people and their property. Stormwater can erode fertile soil, reducing production.

On the other hand improved drainage may degrade the environment if natural wetlands or ponds dry out or are filled in, if the local water-balance is disturbed, or if organically polluted drainage water is discharged into surface water, using up all its oxygen.

Artificial reservoirs are built to benefit people, for example by providing electricity or water for irrigation. In addition dams may benefit people downstream, as the flow of rivers or streams can be regulated, reducing the risks of floods or draughts. On the down side, people are often displaced and land and property lost when large artificial reservoirs are created. A dam may become a problem if people – or nature – are deprived of the water they depend on. If a dam bursts, a dangerous situation is likely to result.

7.1 Surface water and the transmission of disease

Drainage channels are frequently used for defecating, and the first rains after a dry period will often wash human and animal excreta from the surface into the drainage system. Water used for washing (people or clothes) will often contain faecal pathogens. Sullage or stormwater can therefore transmit faecal-oral infections directly to people and animals. If cattle and pigs can get to the water, they may become infected with beef and pork tapeworm. The chance of direct contact is increased if water stagnates in the drainage system because of blockages caused by soil, refuse, vegetation, or poor design or construction of the system.

If sullage or stormwater is discharged into fresh surface water (e.g. streams, rivers, lakes), the surface water will be polluted with excreta. This will result in a risk of faecal-oral infections and beef and pork tapeworm if people and animals use this water as drinking-water.

Any type of fresh surface water which is contaminated with urine or faeces can become a transmission risk for schistosomiasis. As the pathogen multiply in snails, even a light contamination of the water can create a large potential for transmission. Only fast-flowing rivers and streams, and deep water at a good distance from the shores, will be relatively safe [15]. Schistosomiasis is often associated with irrigation schemes and artificial reservoirs [36].

In addition to schistosomiasis, water-based helminths with two intermediate hosts can benefit from the discharge of faecally polluted drainage water into surface water.

Temporary pools and small containers (e.g. cans, drums, blocked gutters) full of relatively clean water are potential breeding sites for the *Aedes* mosquitoes which transmit filariasis, yellow fever, dengue fever, and several other arboviruses. The eggs of *Aedes* mosquitoes can survive for months outside the water, but must be in the water to hatch.

Where organically polluted water can accumulate (e.g. stagnant water polluted with waste from sanitary structures, organic refuse, or rotting plants), *Culex* mosquitoes, which transmit filariasis and several arboviral infections, can breed. *Culex quinquefasciatus* is often a problem in urban areas.

Where ponds or puddles of relatively clean water form, preferably with some form of vegetation, *Anopheles* mosquitoes, vectors of malaria and filariasis, can breed. *Anopheles* mosquitoes also breed in lakes, rice fields, and calm areas in slow streams [61]. Malaria is a problem associated with the presence of artificial reservoirs [6].

Surface water does not need to be permanent to be a risk; mosquitoes and snails can breed and survive in temporary or seasonal puddles and ponds. Mosquitoes can develop from egg to adult in less than two weeks [80]. Snails transmitting schistosomiasis can survive in ponds that dry up seasonally [5], and one snail can grow out into an infectious colony within two months [73].

A number of other infections could be a risk where drainage is poor.

If drainage water comes in contact with soil, it can become contaminated with soil-transmitted helminths (e.g. hookworm disease, roundworm infection). The soil-transmitted helminths need moist soil in which to breed, an environment which can be created by inadequate drainage. Sandflies, the vector of leishmaniasis, Bartonellosis and several arboviruses, breed in humid, organic soils [61].

Polluted water (e.g. from stagnant water in drainage channels) is a potential breeding site for the domestic fly [21], which can transmit faecal-oral diseases and infections transmitted by direct contact.

Rats are attracted to surface water, and can be a host for a multitude of infections including plague [80].

Turbulent, shallow 'white water', which can be created in the spillways of reservoirs, can become a breeding site for blackflies, which can transmit river blindness [6,15].

Table 7.1 presents the infections related to poor drainage.

The health risks of seawater and brackish water
The health risks linked to surface water are mainly related to freshwater.

The health threat of seawater is limited. The chance of transmitting excreta-related pathogens by seawater is small (see Section 6.2.4), and vectors and intermediate hosts can not survive in seawater.

Depending on the water's salt content, the chances of excreta-related pathogens surviving or being transmitted will be higher in brackish water (water with a salt content between that of seawater and freshwater) than in seawater.

Table 7.1. Disease categories associated with poor or absent drainage

Risk-factors related to drainage i Water accumulates ii The drainage functions poorly, or is badly designed	Faecal-oral infections	Schistosomiasis	Water-based with two intermediate hosts	Soil-transmitted helminths	Beef and pork tapeworm	Leptospirosis	Guinea-worm infection	Spread by direct contact	Vector-borne infections
i Clean surface water		(a)				(b)			(c)
Organically polluted surface water	(d)					(b)		(d)	(e)
Resulting in moist soil									(f)
ii Stagnant water in drainage						(b)		(d)	(e)
Poor disposal of drainage water						(b)		(d)	(e)

(a): as long as some food (plants, organic matter) is present in the water
(b): through rats being attracted to, and contaminating, the surface water
(c): *Anopheles* and *Aedes* mosquitoes
(d): through domestic flies
(e): *Culex* mosquitoes
(f): sandflies

Although most mosquitoes do not like salt water, some can breed in slightly salty water. *Anopheles* mosquitoes are in general more sensitive to salt water than *Culex* and *Aedes* mosquitoes [77]. Some species of *Aedes* mosquitoes are able to breed in coastal salt marshes [61].

7.2 Practical issues concerning drainage

This section looks at some practical issues concerning the drainage of sullage and stormwater, and how other sources of surface water can be dealt with. Issues concerning flooding by external water bodies or large artificial reservoirs are not covered as they are complex, and will not normally be dealt with by a WES specialist at field level.

7.2.1 The disposal of sullage

Domestic waste water can often be disposed of where it is 'produced' (on-site disposal).

Where waste water is not polluted with pathogens (e.g. water spilt at a hand-dug well or handpump), it can be fed directly into a garden or vegetation. Care should be taken that no ponding can occur.

Soakaway pits and trenches can be used where waste water could be polluted, space is available, and the infiltration capacity of the soil is sufficient. A soakaway will have to be adapted to the physical situation and the characteristics of the sullage to prevent blockage or overloading.

The infiltration surface area ('surface of infiltration') must be adapted to the amount of waste water discharged and the infiltration capacity of the soil. Sand can be assumed to have an infiltration capacity of around 200 litres per m² per day. Silt and loam will normally be able to deal with up to 100 litres per m² per day. The infiltration capacity of clay will normally be less than 50 litres per m² per day. These values are for soil above the groundwater table [57]. It must be assumed that the pores in the bottom of the pit will clog with settled material, so only the vertical sides of the pit are used to calculate the surface of infiltration. If a lining is used, only the surface of the bare soil should be considered.

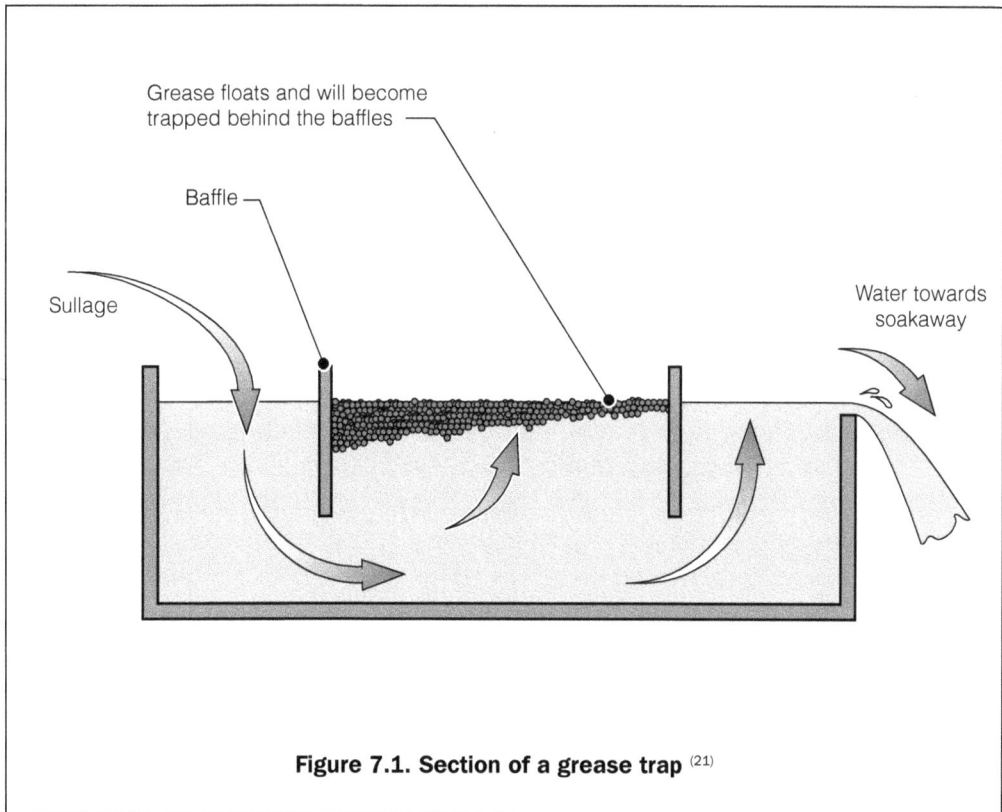

Figure 7.1. Section of a grease trap [21]

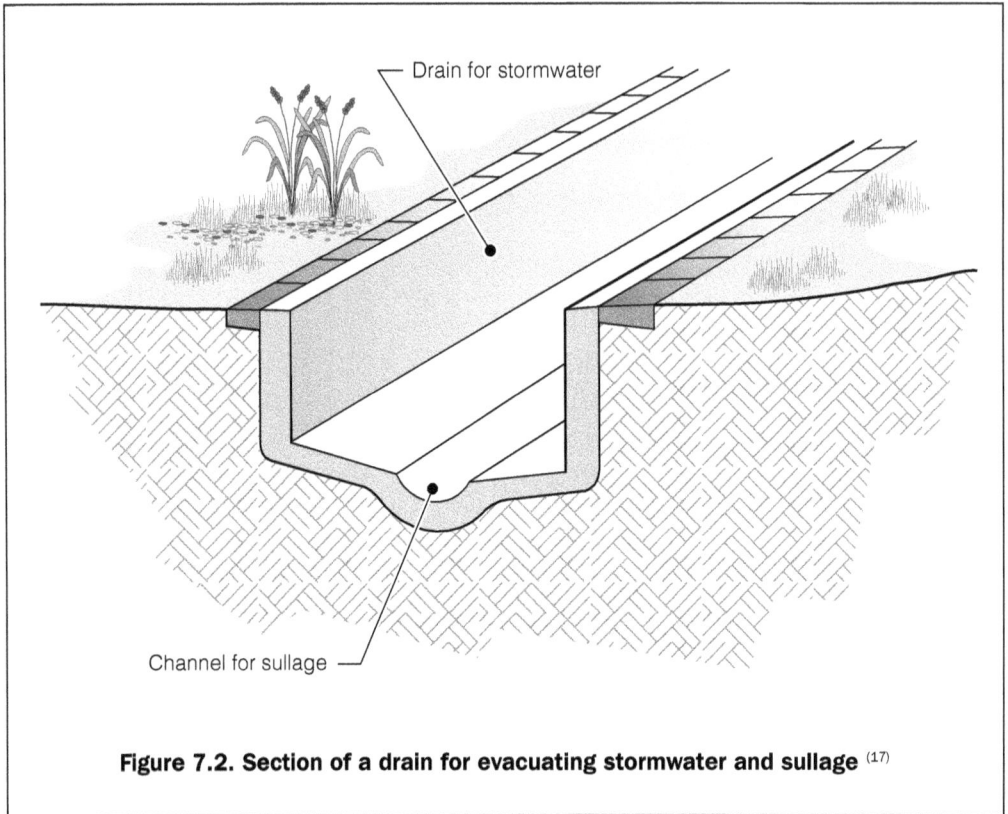

Figure 7.2. Section of a drain for evacuating stormwater and sullage [17]

Where sullage contains solids, they should be removed by straining the waste water or feeding it through a silt trap (i.e. a small reservoir which allows the solids to settle) . If the waste water contains grease or soap, a grease trap will have to be installed. Silt and grease traps should be impenetrable to insects and rats cannot enter. Figure 7.1 shows a model of a grease trap. Regular maintenance is necessary to ensure that these structure function properly.

Where enough surface is available and the climate is appropriate, evaporation pans or beds can be used. Eliminating waste water through evaporation is only possible where the climate is hot, dry, and receives very little rain throughout the year. Wind increases evaporation. Even in these ideal circumstances large surfaces are needed; open water will evaporate 5 to 10 litres per m^2 per day, an evaporation bed with vegetation can probably evaporate around 2 litres per m^2 per day [21].

Where the population density is high or the soil relatively impermeable, on-site disposal may not be possible. If there is a sewage system sullage can normally be discharged this way. If on-site disposal and sewerage are not present or possible, it may be necessary to dispose of the waste water in drains. Figure 7.2 shows a drain which can dispose of sullage as well as stormwater. The small channel in the drain is to discharge sullage, and its rounded form allows small amounts of water to flow at sufficient velocity to keep solids in suspension. This practise is not ideal as people, animals, and insects can come into direct contact with the waste water, but it is better than allowing waste water to pond. The health risks of discharging the waste water will have to be assessed, and if necessary, reduced.

Before considering using existing structures (e.g. pit latrines) for disposoing of waste water, investigate whether the existing structure can cope with the quantity of waste water that is to be discharged. Up to 80 per cent of the water supplied to users may become sullage [17].

Annexe 5 can be used to estimate the infiltration capacity of an existing pit already used for excreta. Discharging more liquid into the pit will also increase the distance that pathogens from the excreta in the soil will travel.

7.2.2 The drainage of stormwater

Where stormwater poses a risk to people, animals, or structures, or where it could pond and thus become a health risk, a drainage system will be needed to collect the stormwater and lead it away safely.

The size, type, and finish of the drainage system will depend on the availability of funds and the potential damage a flood could cause. The greater the risk, the greater the amount that should be invested in preventing flooding. Drainage systems need to be designed in combination with other structures (e.g. roads, buildings) to adapt the structures to one another.

In Annexe 6 a method is presented to calculate how much water would be discharged from a catchment area, and the size of the drain needed to discharge this amount of water. This method can be used to design a simple drainage system, or assess whether a proposed design is realistic. The design of a more complex system will be more demanding, and if the reader is not familiar with these procedures the design should be left to a specialist.

Refuse, soil, and the vegetation which accumulates in drainage channels will reduce the capacity of the system, and regular maintenance will be needed to keep it functional. Regular maintenance and inspection will also deal with collapse or other structural damage in the system.

The responsibilities of all actors in maintenance and structural repairs must be addressed early in the planning phase. Drainage systems are usually communal, but the basic maintenance of the system at neighbourhood level (e.g. removing blockages, cleaning the channels) is probably best done at household level [17]. The problem of solid waste management should be addressed in the planning phase of the drainage system as poor management of refuse (e.g. domestic waste or waste from construction) will result in inappropriate waste ending up in the drainage system.

Where the channels are not protected with a lining, erosion can be a problem if water flows at high speed or if the sides of the drains are too steep.

If tools or other materials are required for maintenance, these must be available to those who need them.

7.2.3   Other types of surface water
Temporary ponds or unwanted reservoirs can be filled to reduce the health risks. No new ponds should be created when sourcing the filling material. Where filling is not feasible, the vegetation along the sides of the water can be removed to make it less attractive to snails and mosquitoes, or the shoreline can be made steeper to control the vegetation.

The best way to deal with potential breeding sites for *Aedes* mosquitoes depends on the situation: solid waste must be removed, water tanks and drums must be covered with a lid or mosquito-proof netting, gutters should be maintained, hollow construction blocks or bricks should be filled, containers that are needed but not used should be turned upside down, and holes in trees must be filled [61]. It will only be possible to control *Aedes* by teaching people to be very vigilant and attentive to the problem.

Where springs result in ponding they can be protected (see Figure 5.3) to reduce the health risks.

Chapter 8

Solid waste management

Solid waste management is about dealing with refuse. This chapter looks at communicable disease in relation to solid waste, and presents some practical issues about managing refuse. Solid waste management up to neighbourhood level, including local health structures, is considered, but the management of wastes from industries, mining, or structures like large hospitals or abattoirs are more specialised, and will not be covered here.

Poor solid waste management will result in an unpleasant and often unsafe environment to live or work in. In addition, piles of refuse can be a fire hazard [15].

In urban areas refuse often ends up in drainage systems, creating drainage problems (see Chapter 7).

Pollution caused by poor management of waste can create serious environmental problems. For example, one litre of diesel can in theory make around 80,000m³ of water undrinkable according to European standards [46].

8.1 Solid waste management and infectious disease

Solid waste is often contaminated with human or animal excreta. Those who handle the waste, and those who live or work where the waste accumulates, will therefore often be at risk from excreta-related infections. The specific health risks they will be exposed to will depends on their contact with the excreta (see Table 6.1).

As drainage systems are frequently used for defecation, the solid waste that accumulates in the system is often contaminated, and is a health risk to those who have to handle it [39]. (For the health risks related to blocked drainage systems see Chapter 7.)

Organic waste from households, restaurants, and markets attracts rats, which are potential hosts for many infections (e.g. leptospirosis, plague). Organic waste also serves as food and a place to rest and hide for domestic flies, which can transmit faecal-oral infections and infections spread by direct contact, and cockroaches, which can transmit faecal-oral infections.

Other animals which use refuse dumps to rest and hide include mosquitoes; sandflies, vector of leishmaniasis, bartonellosis, and several arboviruses; and reduviid bugs, which can transmit American trypanosomiasis [61,80].

Refuse often includes materials which can collect rainwater, such as tin cans, jars, and old car tyres. *Aedes* mosquitoes, which transmit filariasis, urban yellow fever, dengue fever, and several other arboviral infections, can breed in these small water-filled vessels [67].

Poorly managed waste often ends up in ponds, reservoirs, or drainage systems. The refuse often blocks drainage channels, resulting in the ponding of water. As these surface waters are often polluted with organic waste, breeding sites for *Culex* mosquitoes and domestic flies are created [21,61].

Table 8.1 summarises the health risks relating to poor solid waste management.

8.2 Practical issues about solid waste management

A solid waste management scheme can be a large, complex, and expensive enterprise, with many people, materials, and funds required for good operation. Although it is not possible to go into much detail on solid waste management here, we will look at some important issues.

It is not always necessary to collect waste. In rural areas much of the refuse is re-used (e.g. feed for animals, containers, toys) and solid waste will often be less of a problem. In high-density (peri-) urban areas, however, waste may become a serious problem if poorly managed.

If on-site burial or burning are not possible, waste has to be collected. If affordable, household bins will usually be the most appropriate way of collecting and storing household wastes. Where this is not feasible, communal storage of the waste will be necessary. Collection points must be convenient if they are to be used, and their location must be chosen in collaboration with users. The structures should be designed and built so that insects, rats, and rainwater are kept out, and so that people are discouraged from using them for defecation. The emptying and maintenance of the structures by workers must be made as easy as possible.

Table 8.1. Disease groups where poor solid waste management playa a role in transmission (adapted from 60)

Risk factors of poor solid waste management: i Animals have access to organic waste ii No regular collection iii Other	Faecal-oral infections	Schistosomiasis	Water-based with two intermediate hosts	Soil-transmitted helminths	Beef and pork tapeworm	Leptospirosis	Guinea-worm infection	Spread by direct contact	Vector-borne infections
i Rats									(a)
Domestic flies/cockroaches									
ii Refuse accumulates	(b)							(b)	(c)
Containers in refuse									(d)
Refuse blocks drainage					(e)			(b)	(f)
III Organic waste in water	(b)							(b)	(f)
Excreta in refuse									

(a): Flea-borne infections (plague, murine typhus fever)
(b): The risk is caused by domestic flies
(c): Vectors use refuse as a hiding/resting place: mosquitoes, sandflies, reduviid bug
(d): *Aedes* mosquitoes
(e): For humans: cysticercosis; for cattle and pork: beef and pork tapeworm
(f): *Culex* mosquitoes

The collection points have to be managed correctly, otherwise they will become a health threat. Regular collection is essential. In hot climates flies and rats can be attracted to solid waste within two days, so the refuse probably needs to be collected daily or every other day [17,21].

Waste is often dumped in public areas or on wastelands. The uncontrolled discharge of waste must be discouraged, and the displaced wastes have to be collected. Part of solid waste management is making sure that refuse does not end up in drainage systems or surface water. The actual volume of wastes produced will depend on the situation. In low-income urban communities in developing countries one should count on a volume of 1 to 2.5 litres per person per day, with a weight of up to 1kg per person per day [15,17].

In developing countries burying the refuse will usually be the most practical way of disposal. To prevent animals from accessing the refuse, it should be covered daily with 0.15m of soil. The last layer of soil covering the waste should be at least 0.5m thick [253,350]. Incineration is usually not feasible because of the frequently high content of moist (organic) waste, which would use too much fuel to burn.

Disposal of medical wastes

In addition to 'normal' wastes, health centres, feeding centres, and specialised medical centres (e.g. cholera treatment centres) will produce medical waste.

There are different types of medical waste: sharp objects (e.g. needles, syringes, blades), material which has been in contact with blood, puss, or other body fluids (e.g. bandages or cotton wool), and organic waste (e.g. placentas).

There are many infections which could be transmitted through these wastes, and it is therefore important that they are disposed of so that the pathogens are isolated from people or animals.

Sharp objects should be collected in sturdy, closed containers with a small opening just large enough to pass the objects through. When these containers are full they should be discarded in a waste disposal pit. A disposal pit for medical wastes should be deep, with a superstructure with a small opening that can be locked securely. The superstructure must keep people, animals, insects, and surface water out. The pit is quite similar to a pit latrine.

Contaminated bandages and other materials should be wrapped in plastic bags reserved for and identified as medical waste. The bags should be burnt in an incinerator. It should be assumed that incinerated waste is still infective, and the ashes must be disposed of in the waste disposal pit [21].

It will be difficult to incinerate organic wastes, so these wastes should be wrapped in plastic bags and thrown into the waste disposal pit.

To make sure the medical waste is properly dealt with, and to ensure that scavengers (e.g. children, animals) do not have access to it, the waste should not leave the compound of the health structures. The incinerator and waste disposal pit should be near each other, and should be fenced off to keep people and animals away.

Although the medical waste disposal pit is similar to a pit latrine, latrines should not be used for medical wastes as there is a risk of contaminating the slab or superstructure.

Whether normal waste from the health structure can be disposed of without special precautions will depend on how well the medical and uncontaminated waste are separated. If there is any doubt, all normal waste should be treated as medical waste and incinerated.

People dealing with waste in a health centre must be aware of the health risks, and be provided with protective clothing and adequate tools.

Disposal of the dead

The health risk of a dead body is usually negligible, and the risk of an outbreak due to the presence of dead bodies after a disaster is extremely small [66]. Although rapid disposal of the dead is normally not necessary for health reasons, it may be demanded by the people, and this demand will have to be considered.

The exceptions are people who die during outbreaks of cholera, louse-borne typhus, or plague [21]. The dead bodies of people who die during these epidemics should be handled carefully. The bodies (and clothes) should be disinfected or treated rapidly; and the bodies should be manipulated as little as possible before burial or cremation.

Annexe 1

Listing of diseases related to water and environmental sanitation

Annexes

Bacterial enteritis, Campylobacter enteritis, Diarrhoea, Gastroenteritis

A diarrhoeal disease with fever. Often the diarrhoea contains blood (dysentery). Usually a disease of infants. The infection will often be transmitted by domestic animals.

Pathogen : *Campylobacter jejuni, C.coli* [3] (Bacterium)
Distribution : worldwide [15]
Symptoms : an infection with acute diarrhoea, often with blood and mucus [35], abdominal pain, malaise, vomiting [3]. Fever is intermittent or relapsing [4]. In developing countries most cases occur in children under 2 years of age [3]
Severity : the severity is variable [3], complications do occur but are rare [44]
Incubation period : 2 to 5 days [16]
Duration : often 2 to 5 days, usually no more than 10 days [3]. Up to 20% of the people who get sick have a relapse, or prolonged illness [44]
Communicability : cases who are not treated can be carriers of the pathogen for up to 7 weeks. Animals can be permanent carriers [3]

Transmission cycle [3]

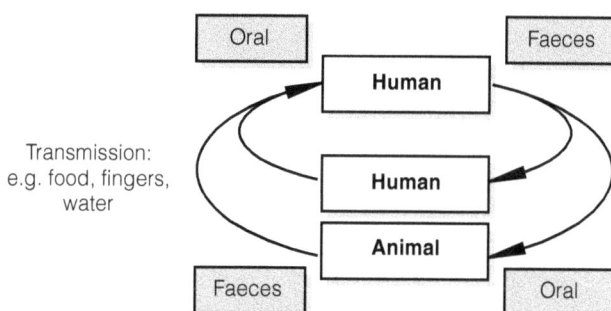

Oral — Human — Faeces

Transmission: e.g. food, fingers, water

Human

Animal

Faeces — Oral

Transmission : transmission takes place through contaminated food, water, or through contact with infected animals. The infective dose is around 500 bacteria [16]
Reservoir : humans, cattle, poultry, swine, sheep, cats, dogs, rodents, birds. Animals (especially poultry and cattle) [3] are the major reservoir for the pathogen. *C.jejuni* can survive for up to 5 weeks in milk or water at 4°C [16]
Vector/int. host : none
Water-related : water-washed and water-borne (in developing countries transmission often occurs through surface water contaminated by animals) [16]
Excreta-related : faecal-oral [15]
Environment : an environment with poor sanitation, poor personal hygiene [44], inadequate water availability, use of water of poor quality, close contact between food or people and reservoir animals (e.g. poultry, cattle, goats and dogs) [16]
Risk in disaster : the infection is a risk where poor sanitation is combined with mass feeding [3]
Remarks : an estimated 5-14% of all diarrhoea worldwide is caused by *C.jejuni* [3]

Preventative measures	Potential effect
Improving the quality of drinking water	(++) [29]
Improving water availability	(+++)
Improving handwashing practise [3]	(+++) [73]
Improvement of sanitation	(++) [73]
Improving food hygiene (especially dairy products and poultry)	(++) [73]
Care in contact with domestic animals (especially poultry or their faeces and puppies/kittens with diarrhoea) [3]	(++) [73]
Health and hygiene promotion	

People with symptoms should not handle food or come in close contact with institutionalised persons [1]

Epidemic measures : groups of patients should be reported to health authorities. If feasible the source of infection should be determined and eliminated [3]

Bacterial enteritis (caused by *Escherichia coli*), Diarrhoea, Gastroenteritis

A diarrhoeal infection with a wide range of symptoms. The infection can be severe, and one group of *E.coli* is able to cause dysentery outbreaks.

Pathogen : *Escherichia coli* [15] (Bacterium).
The bacteria *E.coli* is naturally present in human intestines. Most strains (groups) of *E.coli* are harmless, but some strains can cause intestinal infections [45]

Distribution : worldwide [15]

Symptoms : depends on the group of bacteria which cause the infection: from bloody diarrhoea, caused by *E.coli* 0157:H7, which has the potential of causing outbreaks, and which could be mistaken for shigellosis (dysentery outbreaks) [47]; to watery diarrhoea, abdominal cramps, vomiting, and fever [3]. Children under 5 are particularly affected [44]

Severity : depends on the strains of the bacteria. The infection can be fatal. Children are especially at risk [3]

Incubation period : 9 hours to 8 days, depending on the strain causing the infection [3]

Duration : 1 to 10 days, depending on the strain [44]

Communicability : *E.coli* 0157:H7 can be excreted by children for up to 3 weeks. For the other categories communicability may be prolonged [3]

Transmission cycle [3]

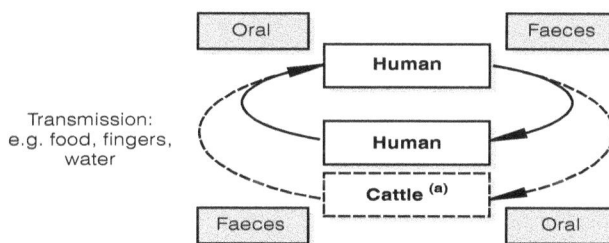

Transmission: e.g. food, fingers, water

(a) : cattle is a reservoir for *E.coli* 0157:H7

(a) : cattle is a reservoir for *E.coli* 0157:H7

Transmission : through the ingestion of contaminated food or water, or through contact with an infected person. For *E.coli* 0157:H7, contact with cattle. The infective dose of *E.coli* 0157:H7 is very low [3]

Reservoir : for most strains: only humans [3], though dogs are mentioned as a potential reservoir [73]. *E.coli* can multiply outside the host on food. Cattle is a reservoir for *E.coli* 0157:H7 [3]

Vector/int. host : none

Water-related : water-washed and water-borne [15]

Excreta-related : faecal-oral [15]

Environment : an environment with inadequate sanitation, poor personal hygiene, poor water availability, poor drinking water quality [44]

Risk in disaster : *E.coli* 0157:H7 can cause outbreaks [47]

Remarks : *E.coli* is one of the most common causes of diarrhoea in humans. In some surveys up to 30% of the cases of gastroenteritis are attributed to it [16]. *E.coli* is estimated to be the cause of 70% of travellers diarrhoea [4].
E.coli occurs naturally in the normal intestinal flora, and is often used as indicator for faecal contamination of drinking water

Preventative measures	Potential effect
Improving the quality of drinking water	(++) [29]
Improving water availability	(+++)
Improving handwashing practise [3]	(+++) [73]
Improvement of sanitation	(+) [73]
Improving food hygiene	(++) [73]
Health and hygiene promotion [3]	

People who are sick should not handle food, or work with institutionalised persons [3].

Epidemic measures : in outbreaks the source of infection should be searched for and eliminated [3]

Bacterial enteritis, Salmonellosis, Diarrhoea, Gastroenteritis

An acute diarrhoeal disease. Outbreaks of salmonellosis are often food-borne.

Pathogen	: *Salmonella* spp. [15] (Bacterium)
Distribution	: worldwide [3]
Symptoms	: diarrhoea, headache, nausea, abdominal pain, fever, vomiting [3]. The infection is rare in adults [16]
Severity	: the infection can be severe, but fatal infections are rare in a healthy adult population. Children and the weak are most at risk [3]. The number of bacteria which cause the initial infection influences the outcome of the disease [16]
Incubation period	: 6 hours to 3 days [3]
Duration	: symptoms usually last for several days [3]
Communicability	: usually several weeks. Chronic human carriers are rare, still, 5% of the infected children will pass bacteria for over one year. In animals chronic carriers are more common than in humans [3]

Transmission cycle [3]

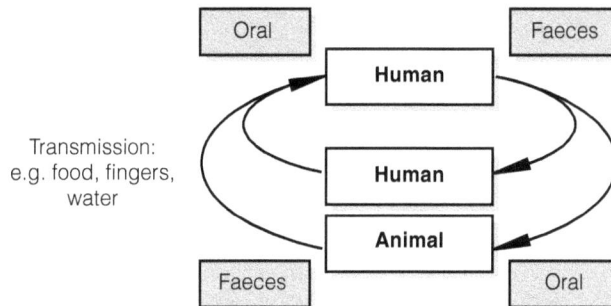

Transmission	: cattle, pigs, poultry, dogs, cats, birds, and turtles, are potential reservoirs of the pathogen. Sick people or carriers are also important sources of the pathogen. Usually transmission occurs through contaminated animal products (poultry, meat, egg). Other ways of transmission are contaminated water (though water-borne transmission is rare) [16], or contact with infected persons or animals. Transmission through contaminated hands can be important. The bacteria can multiply in infected food (especially milk) [3]. The infective dose is from very small to high [16]
Reservoir	: human, dogs, cats, cattle, pigs, poultry, rodents, turtles, tortoises [3]
Vector/int. host	: none
Water-related	: water-washed and water-borne [15]
Excreta-related	: faecal-oral
Environment	: an environment with inadequate sanitation, poor water availability, poor personal hygiene, and poor food hygiene
Risk in disaster	: the infection is a risk where poor sanitation is combined with mass feeding [3]
Remarks	: -

Preventative measures	Potential effect
Improving the quality of drinking water	(++) [29]
Improving water availability	(+++)
Improving handwashing practise	(+++) [73]
Improvement of sanitation	(++) [73]
Improving food hygiene (especially animal products) [3]	(++) [73]
Care in contact with domestic animals [3]	
Health and hygiene promotion	

Adequate food hygiene during the slaughtering of animals, and the preparation and distribution of food is important. Cooked food and raw meat should not be brought into contact with each other [16]. People who are sick should not handle food, or care for institutionalised persons. Individuals handling food should have clean fingernails [3]

Epidemic measures : the source of the infection should be identified, and dealt with [3]

Bacterial enteritis, Yersiniosis, Diarrhoea, Gastroenteritis

An acute diarrhoeal disease which sometimes produces bloodstained faeces.

Pathogen : *Yersina enterocolitica, Y.pseudotuberculosis* [3] (Bacterium)
Distribution : worldwide [15]. The infection is more common in temperate climates than in the tropics [16]
Symptoms : acute diarrhoea, in 25% of the cases bloodstains are found in the diarrhoea [16]. Adults frequently have pains in joints. The infection can display symptoms of acute appendicitis. Yersiniosis is most common in younger people [3]
Severity : -
Incubation period : 3 to 7 days [73]
Duration : usually 2 to 3 weeks [3]
Communicability : in untreated cases, up to 3 months. Prolonged asymptomatic carriers are reported [3]

Transmission cycle [3]

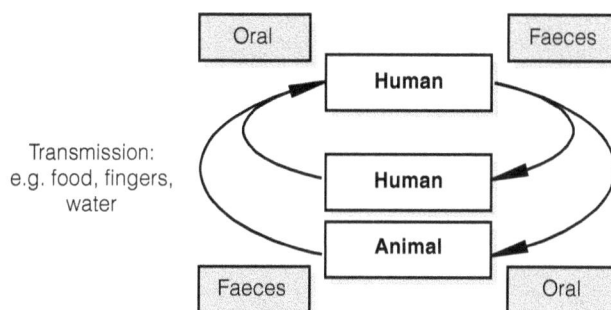

Transmission : occurs through consumption of contaminated food or water [73], or through contact with infected persons (this is rare [16]) or animals. As the pharynx of pigs can be heavily infected, pork can be contaminated during slaughtering[3]. The infective dose is medium to high [15]
Reservoir : the pig is the main reservoir of *Y.enterocolitica*. Other reservoirs are humans, dogs, cats, birds, rodents, and other mammals [3]
Vector/int. host : none
Water-related : water-washed and water-borne [15]
Excreta-related : faecal-oral
Environment : an environment where close contact between domestic animals and people, poor food hygiene [3], and/or poor personal hygiene exist
Risk in disaster : usually not a problem [3]
Remarks : Surveys have shown that less than 1% of the cases with acute diarrhoea are caused by yersiniosis [16]

Preventative measures	Potential effect
Improving the quality of drinking water	$(++)$ [73]
Improving water availability	$(+++)$
Improving handwashing practise [3]	$(+++)$ [73]
Improvement of sanitation (human and animal)	$(+)$ [73]
Improving food hygiene (especially food with pork)	$(++)$ [73]
Care in contact with domestic animals [3]	
Health and hygiene promotion [3]	

Infected people should not handle food or care for institutionalised persons [3]

Epidemic measures : groups of patients should be reported to health authorities. The source of infection should be determined and eliminated [3]

Bacillary dysentery, Shigellosis

The most important infection causing dysentery [83]. The infection is a disease of poor and crowded communities [16]. Shigellosis has the ability to cause large outbreaks, especially in displaced populations [47].

Pathogen	:	*Shigella* spp. [15] (Bacterium)
Distribution	:	worldwide [3]
Symptoms	:	typical symptoms are bloody diarrhoea with mucus, cramps, and fever. Still, shigellosis will often present itself as watery stools [3]. The number of stools can be up to 100 per day. Many infections in adults are asymptomatic. Where the disease is endemic, most infections occur in children under 10 years of age [16]
Severity	:	depends of the host and the pathogen. The case fatality rate of hospitalised people can vary from negligible to 20%. Most at risk of severe illness are children, the elderly, and the undernourished [3]
Incubation period	:	1 to 7 days [73]
Duration	:	the illness will usually last 4 to 7 days [3]
Communicability	:	if untreated, usually up to 1 month after the illness. The carrier state exists, but is rare. Medical treatment will usually reduce the duration of communicability to a few days [3]

Transmission cycle [3]

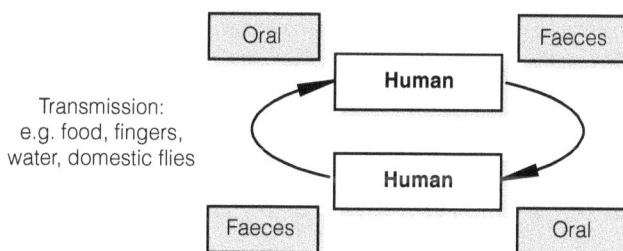

Transmission:
e.g. food, fingers,
water, domestic flies

Transmission	:	shigellosis is highly contagious. Transmission takes place through ingestion of contaminated material. Ingestion of 10 to 100 bacteria can be enough to cause infection [16]. Transmission through close contact between carriers or recovering patients and susceptible persons is common [4, 47]. Domestic flies can play a role in transmission of *Shigella* spp. [16]. Excreta of the sick contain 10^5 to 10^8 bacteria per gram [44]. The bacteria can multiply in food, which increases the chance of food-borne transmission [3]
Reservoir	:	human [16]
Vector/int. host	:	domestic flies can act as mechanical vector [3]
Water-related	:	water-washed and water-borne [15]
Excreta-related	:	faecal-oral [16]
Environment	:	where the population has a poor personal hygiene (poor availability of water), lives in crowded conditions, and where sanitation is inadequate [3]; another risk factor is the use of drinking water of poor quality [44]

Risk in disaster : a serious risk where overcrowding is combined with poor personal hygiene and poor sanitation [4]

Outbreaks : the signs for potential outbreaks are an unexpected increase of cases of dysentery in a population, or an increase in the number of death caused by bloody diarrhoea. In an outbreak, all age groups will be attacked (contrary to endemic shigellosis, which mainly occurs in children). Epidemic dysentery is caused by Sd1 (Shigella Dysenteriae type 1) which has a case fatality rate of 5 to 15% [83]. With appropriate treatment this can be reduced to 2 to 5% or lower [47].

In a stable population around 5% [47] to over 10% [16] of the total population can be expected to develop the disease. Of the sick around 10% will need hospitalisation [47].

In a refugee setting however, over 30% of the population may fall ill, with weekly attack rates of 2 to 10% of the total population. The total attack rate seems to be related to population density [47]

Remarks : In many places *Shigella* spp. is responsible for 5 to 10% of normally occurring diarrhoeal diseases [4]. *Shigella* is estimated to be responsible for around 600,000 deaths per year worldwide, most of which are children.

It must be assumed that only a small proportion of the total number of cases will be reported [3].

The pathogen can develop resistance to antibiotics during an epidemic [83]

Preventative measures	Potential effect
Improving the quality of drinking water	(++) [29]
Improving water availability	(+++)
Availability of soap	(++) [47]
Improving handwashing practise	(+++) [73]
Improvement of sanitation	(++) [73]
Improving food hygiene (especially dairy products)	(++) [73]
Control of domestic flies [73] (see Annexe 3)	
Health and hygiene promotion [3]	

People who are infected should not handle food, or care for institutionalised persons or children. Fingernails should be kept clean and short [3]

Epidemic measures : groups of patients should be reported to the health authorities, the source of infection should be determined and reacted upon [3]. During large outbreaks the places where dysentery cases are treated should be isolated from other health services [47]. Management of the outbreak should be similar to that of cholera [73]. If malnutrition is a problem, sufficient food should be made available. If people have no easy access to soap, it must be made available if appropriate [47].

Cholera

A diarrhoeal disease with a potential of causing large outbreaks. The disease is a serious health threat where poor sanitation, crowding and poor hygiene exist.

Pathogen	:	*Vibrio cholerae* [15] (Bacterium)
		There are two biotypes (categories) of *V.cholerae*: the classical biotype, and the El Tor biotype which has now largely replaced the classical biotype.
		The El Tor biotype tends to become endemic if it has reached a location with poor personal hygiene and poor sanitation, while the classical biotype tends to strike and disappear [2]
Distribution	:	all developing countries [3]
Symptoms	:	severe cases will develop acute diarrhoea with rice-watery stools, often combined with vomiting [3]. Most infections will not show any symptoms though. Infections with the classical biotype will have around 5 carriers for every symptomatic case. Infections with the El Tor biotype will have 30 to 50 carriers for every symptomatic case [16].
		Of those who develop the disease, 90% will have a mild or moderately severe illness [83] with diarrhoea [3]. Of the people who develop typical cholera normally less than 10% will suffer from moderate to severe dehydration. Where the infection is highly endemic, it is mainly a disease of young children [83]
Severity	:	severe cases can die within hours. If not treated, 50% of those developing the severe form can die. With proper treatment this can be reduced to below 1% [3]
Incubation period	:	1 to 5 days [73]
Duration	:	the disease lasts for up to one week [2]
Communicability	:	infected persons without symptoms will discharge bacteria for up to 2 weeks [83]. The sick will often discharge pathogens for up to some days after recovery. Some persons will become carriers for several months. Chronic carriers do exist but are very rare. If antibiotics are effective against the type of *V.cholerae* causing infection, treating people with these will reduce the period of communicability [3]

Transmission cycle [2]

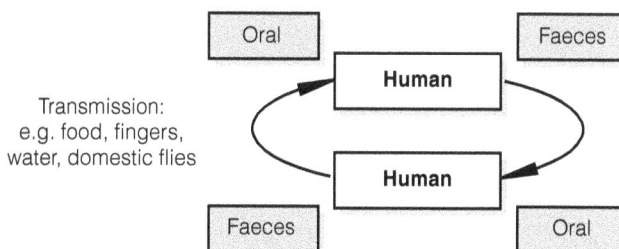

Transmission:
e.g. food, fingers,
water, domestic flies

Transmission	:	the main mode of transmission is through contaminated food or drinking water. As well faeces as vomit are infectious [2]. Cholera is rarely transmitted directly from person to person [83]. Transmission of the disease through drinking water seems to be less common with the El Tor biotype than with the classical biotype [2]. Persons with asymptomatic infections play an important role in the transmission of the infection [83].

The usual infective dose is 10^6 to 10^8 bacteria, though with some persons 10^3 may suffice. A severe case can excrete 10^7 to 10^9 *Vibrio*/ml of diarrhoea while an asymptomatic case may shed 10^2 to 10^5 *Vibrio*/mg of faeces [73].

Reservoir : humans are the only host [16], marine shellfish and plankton can be reservoirs [83], and *V.cholerae* can survive in association with these reservoirs for several months. Some information on the viability of the bacteria in food [16]:

	Time of survival (in days)	
	At 30 to 31°C	At 5 to 10°C
Fruits	1-3	3-5
Cereal	1-3	3-5
Cooked foods	2-5	3-5
Fresh vegetables	1-7	7-10
Fish and seafood	2-5	7-14
Milk and dairy products	7-14	more than 14

Vector/int. host : domestic flies are a possible mechanical vector [47]

Water-related : water-washed and water-borne [3]

Excreta-related : faecal-oral [3]

Environment : an environment with poor personal hygiene (poor availability of water), inadequate sanitation [2], and a population living in crowded conditions [3]. Where people use drinking water of poor quality [73]. Where cholera is endemic, it tends to be a disease of the poor [3].

Risk in disaster : a serious risk where the disease is endemic, overcrowded conditions, and where sanitation is poor [3]

Outbreaks : where an outbreak is likely, the preparation must start well before an outbreak occurs. In a refugee setting a number of precautions must be taken: an early detection system must be operational and units where cholera cases can be treated must be planned. When the risk of an outbreak increases, material to deal with the outbreak should be present and cemeteries must be planned. Medical personnel should be trained in detecting cases and dealing with them. The population should receive health and hygiene promotion [47].

The attack rates in a population will depend on the level of overcrowding, the situation concerning sanitation, and the level of immunity in the population. In a refugee setting, around 5% of the population can be assumed to develop a severe form, though higher attack rates are possible. In Goma (1994) 8% of the total population was struck. In a refugee camp an epidemic will generally last 3 weeks to 3 months.

In an open setting, 1-2% of the total population can be expected to develop a severe form of the disease [47].

Some information on logistics: in a refugee setting around ¾ of the severe cases will need 8 litres of Ringer Lactate (intravenous rehydration fluids) [47]. The needs of a patient in fluids can sometimes be over 20 litres per day [73]. Large quantities or ORS (Oral Rehydration Salts) should be available. In an open setting the requirements will be lower than those in a refugee setting [47].

To calculate the number of beds needed in a displaced population (assuming the outbreak will last around 1 month and 5% of the population is severely ill) [adapted from 47]:

$$\text{Number of beds needed} = \frac{\text{Population at risk}}{200}$$

In an open setting the number of beds needed would probably be around 20% of what would be needed in a refugee setting

Remarks : the disease must be notified to the WHO in Geneva [73].
Although this is often practised, a strict isolation of patients is not necessary for health reasons [3] (as long as the wastes are disposed of hygienically)

Preventative measures	Potential effect
Improving the quality of drinking water	(+++) [29]
Improving water availability	(+++)
Improving handwashing practise	(+++) [73]
Improvement of sanitation	(++) [73]
Improvement of food hygiene (especially marine animals and salad)	(++) [73]
Control of domestic flies where contaminated waste is present [47] (see Annexe 3)	
Prompt and hygienic burial of the dead [73]	
Health and hygiene promotion [3]	

Corpses of people who died of cholera should be disinfected. Travel restrictions are not effective in preventing the disease [47], neither are the restrictions of food movements [3].

Epidemic measures : if feasible, the source of the outbreak should be determined and eliminated. Treatment facilities separated from other health services should be arranged to be able to deal adequately with the potentially large numbers of cases. Drinking water should be chlorinated. Where possible, sanitation should be improved [3].
If soap is not easily available to the population, it should be supplied [47] if feasible and adequate.

Viral enteritis, Acute viral gastroenteritis, Viral diarrhoea, Diarrhoea

An acute diarrhoeal disease. Relatively little is known on the transmission of the disease and its prevention.

Pathogen : rotavirus [15] (virus)
Distribution : the infection occurs worldwide [15]
Symptoms : often asymptomatic. Symptoms are watery diarrhoea, vomiting and fever [3]. The infection affects mainly 4 month to 3 year olds [16]
Severity : the infection is often severe and can be life-threatening [3]
Incubation period : 2 to 3 days [44]
Duration : usually 4 to 6 days [3] but illness of up to 3 weeks does occur [16]
Communicability : literature does not agree on the period of communicability; possibly longer periods [3,16]

Transmission cycle [3]

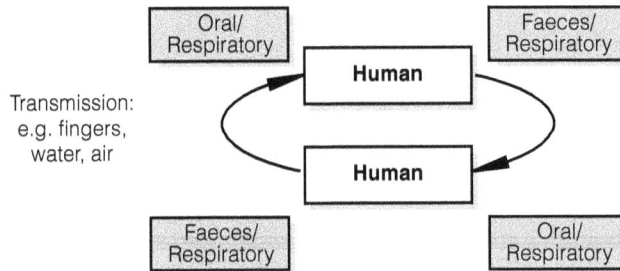

Transmission: e.g. fingers, water, air

Transmission : transmission from person to person is probably the main way the pathogen is spread [3]. Water-borne transmission does occur [16]. Rotavirus can be present in lung secretions and respiratory transmission is possible [3,73]. In tropical zones the disease occurs throughout the year with a slight increase in the cool period. In temperate zones the infection occurs in the colder seasons[3]. The infective dose is 10^2 to 10^4 viruses. An infected person can excrete 10^{11} pathogens per ml of faeces [16]
Reservoir : humans are the only known reservoir [3]
Vector/int. host : none
Water-related : water-borne [16]
Excreta-related : faecal-oral [73]
Environment : unknown. The infection often occurs in institutions like school or hospitals [44]

Risk in disaster : the infection could be a potential risk [3]
Remarks : rotavirus is responsible for about 1/3 of the cases of diarrhoea in children under 5 years admitted in hospital. It is estimated that rotavirus causes 870,000 deaths each year [3].
Even though the infection affects mostly children, outbreaks involving adults can occur if new strains of rotavirus are introduced in a susceptible population[3].

Prevent. measures : effective preventative measures are not obvious [3]. The infection is as frequent in developing countries as in developed countries, and it is therefore unlikely that improved personal and environmental hygiene could prevent the infection [16]

Epidemic measures : if possible, the source of infection should be identified [3]

Viral enteritis (epidemic), Viral gasteroenteropathy, Acute viral gastroenteritis, Viral diarrhoea, Diarrhoea

A diarrhoeal disease. Usually the disease is mild to moderately severe.

Pathogen	: several viruses (e.g. Norwalk agent) [3]
Distribution	: the distribution is worldwide [3]
Symptoms	: diarrhoea, abdominal pain, malaise, headache, vomiting [3]
Severity	: the infection is usually of mild to moderate severity [3]
Incubation period	: usually 1 to 2 days [3]
Duration	: intestinal problems normally last for up to 2 days [3]
Communicability	: communicability is up to 2 days after the diarrhoea ends [3]

Transmission cycle [3]

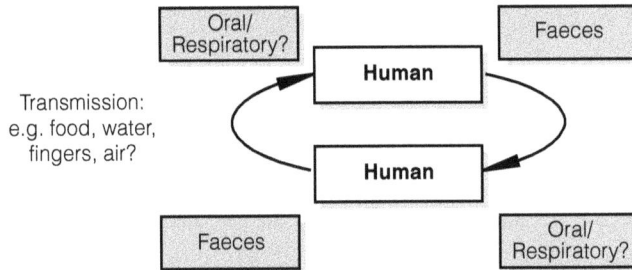

Transmission	: probably faecal-oral transmission. Food and water have been linked to outbreaks. Airborne spread is suggested [3]
Reservoir	: only humans have been identified as reservoir [3]
Vector/int. host	: none
Water-related	: the infection is probably water-borne and water-washed [3]
Excreta-related	: most likely faecal-oral [3]
Environment	: -
Risk in disaster	: the infection can a potential problem [3]
Remarks	: it is believed that 40% of non-bacterial diarrhoea is caused by Norwalk agent [4]

Preventative measures	Potential effect
Improving the quality of drinking water	
Improving water availability	(+) [29]
Improving handwashing practise	(+)
Improvement of sanitation	(+) [73]
Improving food hygiene	(+) [73]
Health and hygiene promotion [3]	

Epidemic measures : if possible, the source of infection should be identified and eliminated [3]

Dysentery (amoebic), Amoebiasis

A very common diarrhoeal infection. A typical symptom is gradually developing bloody diarrhoea. Where sanitation is poor, over 50% of the population may be carrier of the pathogen.

Pathogen : *Entamoeba histolytica* [15] (Protozoon).
Amoeba can be found in two forms: a parasitic (fragile) form and an infective (resistant) cyst [4]

Distribution : the infection occurs worldwide [15]

Symptoms : most infections are asymptomatic. In tests only 1 out of 5 persons who ingested amoebic cysts developed amoebic dysentery. 3 out of the 5 persons developed an asymptomatic infection.
Typical symptoms are gradually developing diarrhoea [2] with blood/mucus, abdominal discomfort, fever, and chills. Sometimes diarrhoea and constipation alternate [3]. A small percentage of the asymptomatic carriers will develop amoebiasis in a later stage [44]. Amoebiasis is rare in children under 5 years of age [3]

Severity : usually the infection is not very serious. Dangerous complications can sometimes occur though [74]

Incubation period : 2 to 4 weeks [73]

Duration : if the patient is not treated, the infection can last for up to 5 years (if the person is not re-infected). Symptomatic attacks usually last up to 6 weeks, and symptoms can reappear for years. In some infections the person with amoebiasis will have bloody diarrhoea for years [2]

Communicability : the period of communicability can be years [3]

Transmission cycle [3]

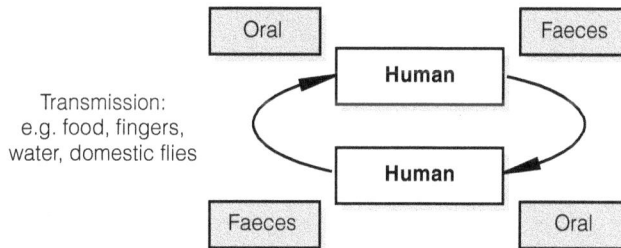

Transmission : transmission is faecal-oral, mainly through ingestion of contaminated food. Water-borne transmission is less common [2]. Asymptomatic carriers are the main source of transmission [3]. Where sanitation is poor, over half the population can be carrier of the pathogen [4]. Where amoebiasis is endemic, outbreaks are uncommon [2].
The infective dose of the pathogen is low [15]

Reservoir : human carriers without symptoms are the main reservoir [16]. Humans are the only known reservoirs [3].
In faeces cysts can remain infective for at least 8 days at 34-38°C, and for up to one month at 10°C [16]. In water they can survive for weeks [4]. Cysts are also relatively resistant in seawater, sewage and wet soil. On the surface of hands, cysts will survive for one minute, while under fingernails they can remain viable for up to 45 minutes [16]

Vector/int. host	:	domestic flies can function as mechanical vectors, and can carry the cysts for up to 5 hours [73]
Water-related	:	water-washed and water-borne [15]
Excreta-related	:	faecal-oral
Environment	:	common in an environment with poor personal hygiene, inadequate sanitation [2], poor food hygiene, and use of drinking water of poor quality [16]. The infection can be a problem in mental institutions [3]
Risk in disaster	:	the disease could be a potential problem [3]
Remarks	:	It is estimated that around 480,000,000 people are infected worldwide, and that the infection causes around 100,000 deaths per year [44].

Preventative measures	Potential effect
Improving the quality of drinking water	
Improving water availability	(++) [29]
Improving handwashing practise	(++) [73]
Improvement of sanitation	(++) [73]
Improving food hygiene	(+) [73]
Control of domestic flies [73] (see Annexe 3)	
Health and hygiene promotion [3]	

Cysts are killed at temperatures over 50°C [3]. Chlorination of drinking water at normal concentrations is not very effective against cysts [3]. A chlorine concentration of over 3.5 mg/l is needed to kill the cysts (recommended chlorine concentration for drinking water: 0.2-0.5 mg/l at distribution point). Iodine is more effective against the pathogen than chlorine [73].

Epidemic measures : the source of infection should be identified, and dealt with [3]

Giardia enteritis, Giardiasis

A common diarrhoeal infection.

Pathogen : *Giardia lamblia* [15] (Protozoon)
Giardia exists in the form of infective, resistant cysts (the form which transmits the infection), and parasitic trophozoites (the form which causes the disease) [4]

Distribution : the infection occurs worldwide [3]

Symptoms : 25 to 50% of the persons infected with *Giardia* will develop a symptomatic infection [44]. Symptoms are chronic diarrhoea, flatulence, and abdominal cramps [3]. Where giardiasis is endemic, the disease will be most common in infants and young children [16], and adults will rarely have symptomatic infections [2]

Severity : the infection can be severe, though this is uncommon [2]

Incubation period : 5 to 20 days [73]

Duration : normally symptoms will last for up to some months; then the infected person will become an asymptomatic carrier [2]

Communicability : as long as the infection lasts transmission can occur, this will usually be for months [3]

Transmission cycle [3]

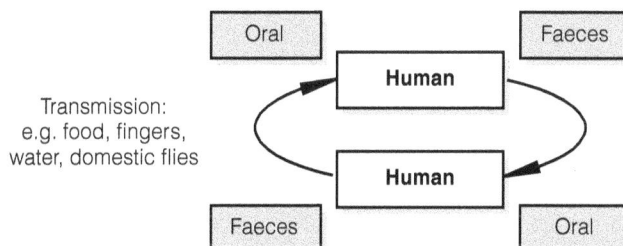

Transmission:
e.g. food, fingers,
water, domestic flies

Transmission : faecal-oral. Transmission seems to occur mainly through hand to mouth contact [3]. Water-borne and food-borne transmission do take place, but are probably less common than transmission through contaminated hands [16]. Still, water-borne outbreaks have occurred where people have used contaminated water supplies [2]; and small food-borne outbreaks have happened [3].
The infective dose is 10 to 100 cysts [16]

Reservoir : the main reservoirs are humans and contaminated surface water [16]. An animal reservoir seems to exist [3], but its role in human infections is not clear [16]. The cysts of *Giardia* are resistant, and in cold water they can remain viable for months [44]

Vector/int. host : none

Water-related : water-washed and water-borne [15]

Excreta-related : faecal-oral [44]

Environment : a common infection where sanitation is poor [2], personal hygiene is inadequate, and the quality of drinking water is poor [16]

Risk in disaster : the infection will normally not be a risk [3]

Remarks : Where *Giardia* is highly endemic most infections are asymptomatic. In developing countries 20 to 30% of the population may be infected [3]

Preventative measures	Potential effect
Improving the quality of drinking water	(++) [2]
Improve water availability	(++) [29]
Improving handwashing practise	
Improvement of sanitation	(+) [73]
Improving food hygiene	(+) [73]
Health and hygiene promotion [3]	

Normal chlorination of drinking water is not effective against giardia cysts [73].

Epidemic measures : if clustered cases occur, the source of infection should be determined and dealt with [3]

Cryptosporidiosis

A diarrhoeal disease which is common in developing countries.

Pathogen : *Cryptosporidium parvum* [3] (protozoon).
The two forms of *Cryptosporidium* are infective cysts which are passed in stools, and the parasitic sporozoites [4]

Distribution : the infection occurs worldwide [15]

Symptoms : asymptomatic infections are common. Symptoms are (often watery) diarrhoea, abdominal pain with cramps, and sometimes fever and vomiting. The disease is most common in children under 2 years of age [3]

Severity : usually not severe, though the disease can lead to death in imunodeficient persons [3]

Incubation period : 1 to 12 days, usually one week [73]

Duration : repeating attacks over a maximum of one month in otherwise healthy persons [54]

Communicability : the period of communicability can be up to 6 months [73]

Transmission cycle [3]

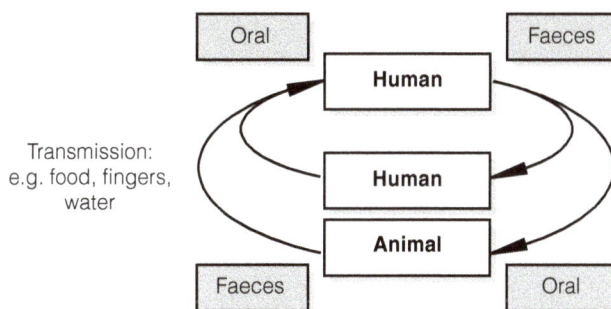

Transmission : the transmission is faecal-oral: person to person, animal to person, water-borne, or food-borne. Asymptomatic persons are a source of transmission of the pathogen [3]. Outbreaks have occurred where the supply of drinking water has been contaminated [16].
The infective dose is very low [73]

Reservoir : reservoirs are humans, cattle, sheep, dogs, cats, poultry, fish and reptiles [73].
The cysts of *Cryptosporidium* are very resistant. In a moist environment they can remain infective for up to 6 months [3]

Vector/int. host : none

Water-related : the infection is water-washed and water-borne [3]

Excreta-related : faecal-oral [73]

Environment : the infection can mainly be found in conditions of poor personal hygiene and poor quality of drinking water [73]. Persons working closely with animals are especially at risk. The infection is common where people are institutionalised [3]

Risk in disaster : normally not a problem [3]

Remarks : In developing countries the infection can be responsible for 4 to 17% of the cases of childhood diarrhoea [16], and the pathogen may be found in the stools of in 3 to 20% of the population [3]

Preventative measures	Potential effect
Improving the quality of drinking water [73]	
Improving water availability	
Improving handwashing practise [3]	
Improvement of sanitation (human and animal) [3]	
Improving food hygiene	
Care in contact with domestic animals [73]	
Health and hygiene promotion [3]	

Persons with an infection should not handle food, or work with institutionalised people. Chlorination of drinking water will not kill the pathogen [3].

Epidemic measures : if cases occur in clusters, the source of infection should be determined, and eliminated [3]

Dysentery (Balantidial), Balantidiasis

A relatively rare diarrhoeal disease. The source of human infection is usually pigs.

Pathogen : *Balantidium coli* [15] (Protozoon)
Distribution : the distribution is worldwide [15]
Symptoms : up to 80% of the infections are believed to be asymptomatic [16]. Typical symptoms are diarrhoea (with or without blood), nausea, and vomiting [3]
Severity : the infection can be life-threatening in a weak person [3] if not treated [16]
Incubation period : days [73]
Duration : -
Communicability : the period of communicability lasts the entire period of infection [3]

Transmission cycle [3]

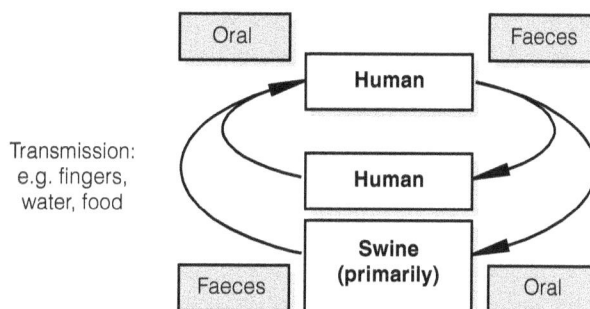

Transmission : transmission is faecal-oral. Pigs seem to be the main source of infection [2]. Single cases occur through hand to mouth contact, or through ingestion of contaminated water or food. Outbreaks are often water-borne [3]. The infective dose is low [15]
Reservoir : the main reservoir transmitting the disease to people are pigs. Other reservoirs are humans, rodents [2] and primates [3]. Cysts of *B.coli* are rapidly destroyed in hot and dry conditions but can survive for several weeks in a moist environment [16]
Vector/int. host : none
Water-related : water-washed and water-borne [15]
Excreta-related : faecal-oral [15]
Environment : an environment with close contact between pigs and humans [16]. Use of poor quality drinking water; where personal hygiene is poor and sanitation inadequate [3]
Risk in disaster : the infection does not pose a large risk [3]
Remarks : the disease is relatively rare in humans [3]. In some places 40 to 90% of the pigs are though to be carriers of the pathogen [16]

Annexes

A1

Preventative measures	Potential effect
Improving the quality of drinking water [3]	
Improving water availability	
Improving handwashing practise [3]	
Improvement of sanitation (human and swine faeces) [2]	
Improving food hygiene [3]	
Care in contact with pigs [16]	
health and hygiene promotion [3]	

Chlorination of drinking water is not effective in killing the cysts of *B.coli* [3]

Epidemic measures : if a group of infections appears, the source of infection should be looked for and eliminated [3]

Typhoid, Enteric fever, Typhoid fever/Paratyphoid, Paratyphoid fever

Faecal-oral diseases that cause sustained fever. Typhoid is more severe and more easily transmitted than paratyphoid. (Small) outbreaks can occur. Permanent carriers do exist and play an important role in transmission.

Pathogen : typhoid: *Salmonella typhi*
paratyphoid: *Salmonella paratyphi* [3] (Bacteria)

Distribution : typhoid and paratyphoid have a worldwide distribution [15]

Symptoms : mild infections are frequent. Typical symptoms are: sustained fever, headache, enlarged spleen, malaise, sometimes a rash, disorientation, and loss of appetite. In adults constipation is more common than diarrhoea [3]. Typhoid can produce stools with blood [4]. In endemic areas typhoid is most common in the age-group 5-19 years [3]

Severity : before antibiotics, the mortality rate of typhoid was over 10%. If the infection is treated adequately, mortality rates should be under 1% [4]. Paratyphoid is milder than typhoid, and has a much lower fatality rate [3]

Incubation period : for typhoid: 1 to 3 weeks, though it can be up to 3 months. The time depends on the number of pathogens that cause infection [3].
For paratyphoid: 1 to 10 days [73]

Duration : typhoid: usually around 3 weeks. Relapses occur in 5 to 10% of the untreated cases, and may be up to 20% in treated cases [3].
Paratyphoid: up to 3 weeks or longer [2] relapses do occur in around 3 to 4% of the cases [3]

Communicability : Typhoid: 2 to 5 % of the untreated cases will turn into chronic carriers [3] (who do not necessarily have a history of being sick [4]).
Permanent carriers in paratyphoid exist, but are less common than in typhoid fever [3].
Urinary carriers excreting pathogens after the third month of infection are rare, except in persons with urinary schistosomiasis [16]

Transmission cycle [3]

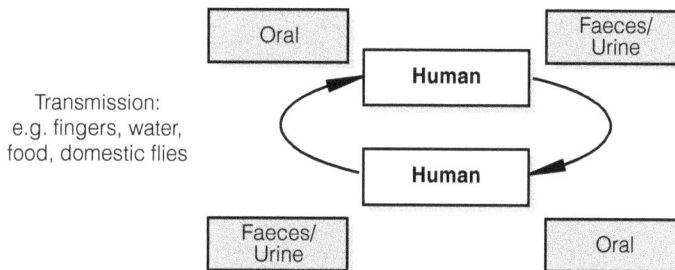

Transmission:
e.g. fingers, water,
food, domestic flies

Oral — Human — Faeces/Urine

Faeces/Urine — Human — Oral

Transmission : transmission occurs through ingestion of food or water contaminated with faeces or urine of a patient or carrier [16]. Carriers play an important role in the transmission of the infections [73]. If *S.typhi* or *S.paratyphi* contaminate food, for example through domestic flies, or dirty hands, they can multiply [73]. Where human excreta is used as fertiliser, raw fruit and vegetables are important vehicles of transmission. Shellfish from coastal waters polluted by sewage can be a danger [16]. Typhoid has a much lower infective dose than paratyphoid [3] (the infective dose of typhoid is 10^3 to 10^9 bacteria [73]). The higher the ingested dose of bacteria is, the higher the attack rate will be [2]. While typhoid is more frequently transmitted by water than by food [4], paratyphoid is less often water-borne as it has a high infective dose [16].

In an outbreak of typhoid fever the number of cases can be expected to double every 2 weeks [47]

Reservoir : humans are the only reservoir for typhoid, and the normal reservoir for paratyphoid. Domestic animals can be a sporadic reservoir for paratyphoid [3].

In fresh water *S.typhi* can survive for up to 4 weeks, in raw sewage possibly for over 5 weeks [73]. *S.typhi* can survive in sea water, which makes seafood dangerous [4]

Vector/int. host : domestic flies can be mechanical vectors [3]

Water-related : both infections are water-washed and water-borne [15]

Excreta-related : faecal/urinary-oral [73]

Environment : an environment with poor personal hygiene, inadequate sanitation [2], poor quality of drinking water, and inadequate food hygiene [45]

Risk in disaster : large outbreaks are unusual, but smaller outbreaks or single cases can appear over longer periods [47]. The infections can be a problem where sanitation is inadequate, and the quality of water poor [3]. Typhoid is often a problem after disasters involving flooding [74]

Remarks : every year roughly 17,000,000 cases of typhoid occur worldwide, of whom around 600,000 will die [3]

Preventative measures	Potential effect
Improving the quality of drinking water	(+++) [29]
Improving water availability	(+++)
Improving handwashing practise	(+++) [73]
Improvement of sanitation	(++) [73]
Improving food hygiene (especially dairy products and shellfish)	(++) [73]
Control of food, and persons who handle food [73]	
Control of domestic flies [73] (see Annexe 3)	
Health and hygiene promotion [73]	

Carriers should not handle food or work with institutionalised persons [3]. Fingernails should be kept short and clean [73]. Pasteurisation of milk at 60°C is effective in killing typhoid bacteria [73].

Epidemic measures : the ultimate source of infection is always a person [16]. If possible this source of infection should be identified and dealt with. Food believed to play a role in transmission should be avoided. Water used for drinking should be chlorinated [3]

Hepatitis A, Infectious hepatitis or Jaundice/Hepatitis E, Non-A non-B hepatitis

Faecal-oral diseases with fever and jaundice. Hepatitis E occurs mainly in outbreaks, and is very dangerous to pregnant woman.

Pathogen	: Hepatitis A virus Hepatitis E virus (viruses)
Distribution	: both diseases have a worldwide distribution [15,3]
Symptoms	: many asymptomatic infections occur [73]. Typical symptoms are fever, loss of appetite, jaundice [3] (yellowing of skin or whites of the eyes [45]) , and depression [3]
Severity	: the severity of the illness can range from mild to severely disabling for months. The average case fatality rate in both diseases is normally less than 1 per 1,000 cases. The diseases become more dangerous with age: persons over 50 have a case fatality rate of 27 per 1000. A particularity of hepatitis E is that it is very dangerous to pregnant women, in whom a case fatality rate of up to 20% may occur [3]
Incubation period	: the incubation period for hepatitis A is 15 to 50 days [73]; for hepatitis E the incubation period is 15 to 64 days [3]
Duration	: the duration of the diseases range from one week to several months [3]
Communicability	: the period of communicability for hepatitis A is usually up to the first week of onset of jaundice. The period of communicability for hepatitis E is not known [3]

Transmission cycle [3]

Transmission:
e.g. water, food,
fingers
(Hepatitis A: blood
and secretions?)

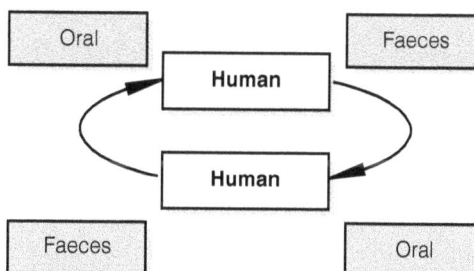

Transmission	: transmission occurs through the ingestion of contaminated water or food [73]. Transmission from person to person is possible [4]. Faeces of people in the incubation period of hepatitis A contain very large numbers of viruses [16]. Outbreaks of hepatitis A are uncommon as people are normally infected at an early age and develop immunity [73]. The risk of an outbreak increases though if part of the population is not immune because of improved sanitation and personal hygiene [3]. The carrier state in hepatitis A is not important. Salads, cold meat and raw seafood are often implied in the transmission of hepatitis A [73]. Hepatitis A can possibly be transmitted through blood and secretions [4]. Hepatitis E occurs mainly in outbreaks [73], with the highest attack rates in young adults. Outbreaks of hepatitis E are often caused by water-borne transmission [3]. The infective doses for the infections are high [73]
Reservoir	: humans are the main reservoir for the hepatitis A virus. In exceptional cases

primates can be a reservoir. The reservoirs for the hepatitis E virus are not known, and animal reservoirs

are possible. The virus can be transmitted to certain primates and pigs [3]

Vector/int. host	:	none
Water-related	:	the infections are water-washed and water-borne [15]
Excreta-related	:	faecal-oral
Environment	:	the diseases occur where people have poor personal hygiene, inadequate sanitation, live under crowded conditions, and have drinking water of poor quality [3]
Risk in disaster	:	a potential problem where crowding, poor sanitation and poor water supply occur [3]. Hepatitis E will probably pose the largest risk.
Remarks	:	people who have been infected with hepatitis A are probably immune for life [3], though there are indications that people can be re-infected if they ingest a large quantity of pathogens [73].

Preventative measures	Potential effect
Improving the quality of drinking water [73]	
Improving water availability	(+) [29]
Improving handwashing practise [73]	
Improvement of sanitation	(+) [73]
Improving food hygiene	(+) [73]
Health and hygiene promotion [3]	

Epidemic measures : the source of infection should be determined and dealt with. Personal hygiene, sanitation and the quality of the drinking water should be brought up to standard [3]

Polio, Acute poliomyelitis

A highly contagious faecal-oral disease. The infection has disappeared from most parts of the world. A typical symptom which appears in a small number of infected persons is lasting paralysis.

Pathogen : Poliovirus [15] (virus)

Distribution : until recently the infection was endemic worldwide [16]. It has disappeared from most areas as a result of immunisation campaigns. The infection is still a problem in certain African and Asian countries [3]

Symptoms : the majority of the infections are asymptomatic or just a mild illness. Symptoms are fever, general malaise, and headache. Paralysis only occurs in some of the cases [73]

Severity : if infection takes place at a young age, about 1% of the cases will develop some form of paralysis. The risk of paralysis becomes larger with an increasing age of the infected person [73]

Incubation period : 5 to 30 days [73]

Duration : the illness lasts from some days to months. The paralysis is permanent [44]

Communicability : probably up to 6 weeks, though longer is possible [3]

Transmission cycle [3]

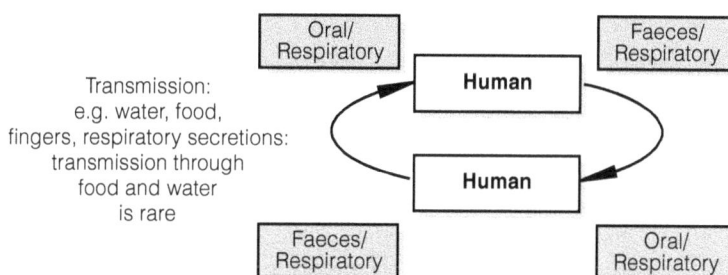

Transmission: e.g. water, food, fingers, respiratory secretions: transmission through food and water is rare

Transmission : poliomyelitis is a very contagious infection [4], and is mainly spread by direct person to person contact. Respiratory transmission is possible, and can be important if sanitation is adequate [3] or during outbreaks [47]. It is rare that food or water are associated with transmission [3]. Transmission of poliomyelitis will stop in a population when 80 to 85% of the people have been immunised successfully [50].
The infective dose of the infection is low [15]

Reservoir : human [3]

Vector/int. host : none

Water-related : water-washed and sporadically water-borne [15]

Excreta-related : faecal-oral

Environment : the disease is linked to poor personal hygiene [73]. In the tropics a small seasonal increase in cases can be expected in the hot and rainy season. Outbreaks can occur in regions where people have a low immunity to the infection (either because they have not been immunised, or because the infection is not endemic) [3].

Risk in disaster : a potential problem where crowding, poor sanitation, and poor personal hygiene are found in a non-immune population [3, 73]

Remarks : to prevent epidemic poliomyelitis, improved sanitation should be accompanied by good immunisation coverage; otherwise there is a risk of creating a non-immune population in which an epidemic could develop [73]

Preventative measures	Potential effect
Improving water availability	(+) [29]
Improving handwashing practise	
Improvement of sanitation (after immunisation of the population) [73]	
Improved food hygiene	(+) [73]
Mass immunisation (vaccination)	(+++) [3]
Health and hygiene promotion [3]	

Epidemic measures : mass immunisation (vaccination) [3]

Tapeworm (dwarf), Hymenolepiasis

A usually asymptomatic faecal-oral disease.

Pathogen : *Hymenolepis nana* [15] (Helminth).
Hymenolepis is a tapeworm. The adult worm is roughly 40 mm long and lives in the human intestine [44]
Distribution : the infection occurs worldwide [15]
Symptoms : the infection is usually asymptomatic. Heavy infections can cause abdominal pains, occasionally with diarrhoea [3]
Severity : the infection is mild [3]
Incubation period : the incubation period is variable [3]
Duration : the infection can last for several years [3]
Communicability : communicability can be years [3]

Transmission cycle [3]

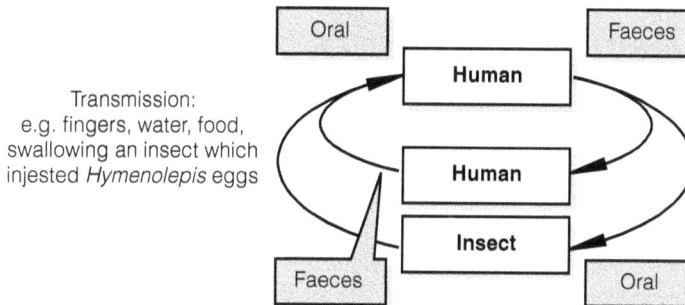

Transmission:
e.g. fingers, water, food,
swallowing an insect which
injested *Hymenolepis* eggs

Transmission : faecal-oral. The eggs are often directly infective when excreted. Transmission is water-borne, food-borne, or hand to mouth [3]. Insects (e.g. fleas [45]) which ingested eggs of *Hymenolepis* can transmit the pathogen when swallowed [3]
Reservoir : humans, mice could play a role as a reservoir, insects [3]
Vector/int. host : contaminated insects could transmit the pathogen if ingested [3]
Water-related : water-washed and water-borne [15]
Excreta-related : faecal-oral [15]
Environment : more common in warm and dry climates [3]
Risk in disaster : the infection is not a risk in a disaster [3]
Remarks : -

Preventative measures	Potential effect
Improving the quality of drinking water [3]	
Improving water availability	(+) [29]
Improving handwashing practise [3]	
Improvement of sanitation	(+) [73]
Improving of food hygiene	(+) [73]
Control of rodents [3]	
Health and hygiene promotion [3]	

Epidemic measures : -

Pinworm infection, Enterobiasis, Oxyuriasis

An 'anal-oral' infection with mild symptoms.

Pathogen : *Enterobius vermicularis* [15] (Helminth)

Gen. description : enterobiasis is caused by a thin, white worm with a length of about 10 mm [74] . The infection is common and occurs worldwide. It is often asymptomatic. Symptoms are anal itching and irritability. The infection is mild [3]. Infection occurs mainly in children [4] and under crowded conditions [16]

Transmission : the eggs are not excreted through faeces. The female worm leaves the body through the anus to deposit her eggs outside the body [73]. The eggs become infective within a few hours [3]. The activity of the female worm causes an itch. When the infected person scratches, the eggs are picked up by the fingers [73]. Transmission is hand to mouth. Anything that becomes contaminated (clothing, bedding, food) can transmit the pathogen. Airborne transmission is possible [3]

Reservoir : humans are the only host. Eggs can survive for up to 2 weeks outside the host [3]

Water-related : the infection is water-washed [73]

Preventative measures	Potential effect
Improving water availability	(+) [29]
Improving handwashing practise [73]	
Washing of clothing and bedding [73]	
Improvement of cleanliness of sanitation [3]	
Health and hygiene promotion [3]	

Long fingernails can more easily gather eggs and should therefore be kept short [3]

Epidemic measures : systematic treatment of cases, their family, and other contacts [3]

Hydatid (cystic) disease, Unilocular echinococcosis

The source of this potentially severe infection is dog faeces (or faeces of other canines). Transmission of the disease is faecal dog – human oral.

Pathogen   : *Echinococcus granulosus* [3] (Helminth) [73].
The 3 to 6 mm long tapeworms live in the small intestine of the dog [2]. People are infected by the infective embryos of the worm which can form cysts in the human body [3].

Distribution   : the infection occurs worldwide [3]

Symptoms   : cysts form in the body. The cysts are usually 1 to 7cm in diameter [3], but larger cysts are possible. The symptoms will vary with the organs affected [44], and the size and numbers of cysts. Symptoms are similar to those of a slow growing tumour [3]. 66% Of the cysts are formed in the liver, 10% in the lungs, 7% in the brain, other organs may be affected [73]

Severity   : the infection is severe and can be fatal [2]

Incubation period : from 12 months [3] up to 20 years [44]

Duration   : prolonged

Communicability   : the infection in a dog lasts for around 6 months, but tapeworms may survive for up to 3 years [3]

Transmission cycle [3]

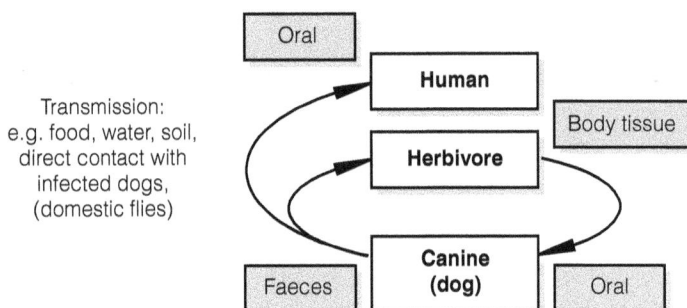

Transmission   : dogs or wild canines excrete infective eggs. The normal transmission cycle involves herbivores (e.g. sheep, cattle) who ingest the eggs, and develop cysts in their body. When the herbivores are eaten by dogs, the tapeworms will develop in the intestines of the dog, completing the transmission cycle [2].

The eggs excreted by dogs and canines can cause an infection in humans which is similar to the infection in herbivores. People can be infected by the eggs through food, drinking water [73], soil, or any other object contaminated by dog faeces [3]. Transmission is possible through direct close contact with dogs (through touching their fur, or being licked) [73]. Occasionally domestic flies have transmitted the pathogen [3]

Reservoir   : the reservoirs of the adult worm are canines: dogs, jackals, and wolves [73]. The infective eggs can survive for several months in the environment [3]

Vector/int. host	: the normal intermediate hosts are sheep, pigs, goats, cattle, camels, horses and other herbivorous animals [73]. Humans function as an intermediate host, but are a dead end in the transmission cycle
Water-related	: water-washed [3] and water-borne [73]
Excreta-related	: the pathogen leaves canines (dogs) through their faeces [73]. The infection is canine faecal - human oral
Environment	: the infection occurs mainly where sheep and cattle are reared [2] and people and dogs live in close association [73]
Risk in disaster	: the infection is not a priority in disasters [3]
Remarks	: the pathogen is common in the Turkana region in Kenya [73]

Preventative measures	Potential effect
Improving water availability	(++) [29]
Improving handwashing practise [3]	
Dogs should be controlled (wild and stray dogs should be eliminated, domestic dogs at risk should regularly be treated against worms, dogs should not be fed potentially infective body parts of herbivores) [3]	
Dogs should be kept away from potentially infective carcasses [3]	
Dogs should be kept away from water sources and food gardens [73]	
Health and hygiene promotion [3]	

Epidemic measures : control of dogs (elimination of wild and stray dogs and treatment of domestic dogs), slaughtering of reservoir animals should be controlled so that dogs have no access to any parts of the carcass [3].

Schistosomiasis, Bilharziasis

A very common infection affecting around 200,000,000 people worldwide. The infection is associated with engineering schemes like irrigation systems and artificial lakes.

Pathogen : *Schistosoma* spp. (Helminth)
The blood flukes causing this infection are 10 to 20 mm long. Male and female fluke live in association, 'coupled together' [2].
Several species infect humans:
Schistosoma haematobium (which causes urinary schistosomiasis), the adult flukes live in veins surrounding the bladder.
Schistosoma mansoni, *S.japonicum* and other *Schistosoma*, whose adult flukes live in veins in the intestines [3]

Distribution : *S.haematobium*: is found in Africa and the Middle-east
S.mansoni: occurs in Africa, the Middle East and the north-eastern part of South America
S.japonicum: is limited to China, Taiwan, the Philippines, Indonesia and Celebes
Other *Schistosoma*: are found in South-east Asia and Africa [3]

Symptoms : many infections are asymptomatic, and symptoms are often ignored by people [16]. The main health problems from schistosomiasis are caused by the eggs produced by the flukes. If these eggs become trapped (over 50% are) [73], they can cause small scars in tissue [2]. The symptoms of the infection are linked to the number and the location of the trapped eggs. The main symptoms are:
S.haematobium: urinary problems including blood in urine, painful urination [3], and reduced bladder capacity [2].
Other *Schistosoma*: intestinal problems including diarrhoea, enlarged liver and spleen, and intestinal pain [3].
Occurrence in age-groups: *S.haematobium* is most common in 10 to 14 year olds; *S.mansoni* has a peak prevalence at 10 to 24 years; and *S.japonicum* does not seem to have a typical age-distribution [16]

Severity : the severity of the infection is usually related to the number of flukes causing the infection [16]. *S.japonicum* is in general more severe than the other *Schistosoma* [73]. In the majority of cases the infection is not severe, but (fatal) complications do occur [2]

Incubation period : the incubation period is variable [73]

Duration : the flukes normally live for 3 to 5 years, but some survive for up to 30 years [2]. Reinfection will often occur though

Communicability : people with infections can release eggs (infective to snails) for over 10 years, or the time the infection lasts. Snails remain infected for life and can release infective cercariae for up to 3 months [3]

Transmission cycle [73]

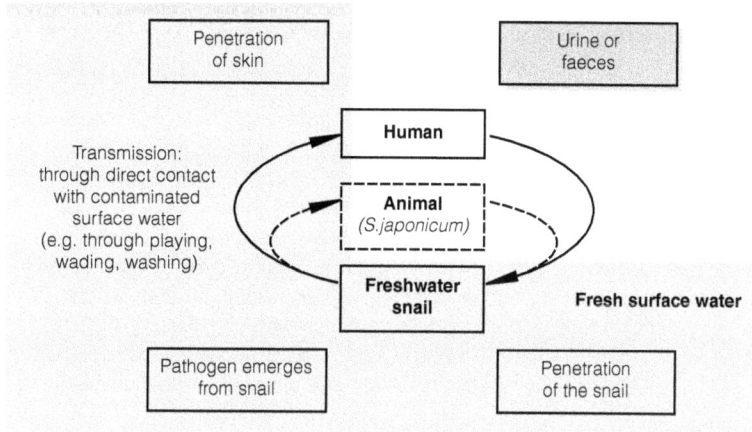

| Transmission | : | The eggs of persons infected with *S.haematobium* leave the body through urine. The eggs of the other *Schistosoma* leave the body through faeces [73]. In fresh water, the eggs can turn into miracidia, which can infect specific freshwater snails that serve as intermediate hosts. In the snails the miracidia will multiply, and turn into cercariae (this process takes a few weeks) [2]. One single miracidium can multiply into many thousands of cercariae [16]. The cercariae emerge from the infected snails; *S.heamatobium* and *S.mansoni* at mid-day to late afternoon, and *S.japonicum* late in the evening. The longer the period between emergence from the snail and infection of a person, the smaller the chance of successfully infecting a person [73]. Cercariae are able to survive for up to 48 hours in water [16]. The pathogen needs water temperatures between 10°C and 30°C [73]. People are infected when a cercarium penetrates the skin which is in direct contact with infective fresh water [2] |

Reservoir : *S.haematobium*: humans are the only reservoir.
S.mansoni: humans are the main reservoir, though animal hosts are possible.
S.japonicum: humans are an important reservoir, but in addition animals can serve as a reservoir to the pathogen. Some important reservoirs are dogs, cattle, pigs, rats, and water buffaloes.
Children are particularly important as reservoirs as the infection is most common in this age-group and because of their behaviour [16]

Vector/int. host : freshwater aquatic snails are the intermediate hosts for schistosomiasis. The genera that act as intermediate host:
S.haematobium: the genus *Bulinus* (preferring still, or very slow moving water).
S.mansoni: most commonly the genus *Biomphalaria* (which can live in slow flowing water, generally occurring in streams and irrigation systems).
S.japonicum: usually the genera *Oncomelania* (an amphibious snail) and *Tricula* [15].
Usually only 1 to 2% of the snails are infected. As these snails discharge high numbers of cercariae (up to 3,000 per day), the potential to infect people remains high [73]. The snails which transmit *Schistosoma* can survive for up to months outside water, which takes the infection from one wet season to another [16,73]. The snails can reproduce themselves very rapidly; one snail can grow out into an infective colony within 60 days [73]

Water-related	: the infection is water-based. The pathogen penetrates the skin in contact with contaminated fresh surface water [15]
Excreta-related	: *S.haematobium* is excreted by urine. The other *Schistosoma* are excreted through faeces [73]
Environment	: the infection is most common in rural areas of developing countries, but is not limited to this environment [16]. As the snails adapt themselves easily, they can be found in a wide variety of water bodies. From lakes and seasonal or temporary ponds, to rice-fields or slow-flowing streams [73]. The infection has become a large problem around many man-made structures like artificial lakes and irrigation schemes [15]
Risk in disaster	: the infection will not be an urgent problem in an emergency [47]
Remarks	: the dynamics of transmission can change rapidly in an endemic area where a water resource development scheme is taking place [16]. The distribution of the pathogens in a mass of water is not necessarily regular; while the pathogen may be present in one zone, it may be absent in another. The distribution depending on the presence of snails [73]. It is estimated that 200,000,000 persons are infected worldwide [16], and that the infection could cause up to 1,000,000 deaths per year [59]. In many regions the occurrence of the infection is on the rise [15]

Preventative measures	Potential effect
Reducing water contact (through health and hygiene promotion and water supply)	(+++) [29]
Improvement of sanitation	(+) [73]
Control of freshwater snails (through engineering, biological and chemical measures) [73]	
Mass treatment of infections [73]	
Health and hygiene promotion [73]	

The effect of improving sanitation is often limited as only a few infected persons need to contaminate the surface water to maintain an infected snail population [73].
As the snails can reproduce very quickly, the use of chemical control of snails as only measure will usually not be very effective. It can be effective however where the environment can be controlled, and in combination with treatment of infected persons [2]

Epidemic measures : mass treatment [73], reducing the contact of the population with contaminated water [3]

Fasciolopsiasis, Giant intestinal fluke infection

An infection which has to go through two water-based intermediate hosts: a freshwater snail and a freshwater plant. Reservoirs of the pathogen are pigs and people, who are infected when ingesting the cysts which are found on uncooked freshwater plants.

Pathogen : *Fasciolopsis buski* [15] (Helminth)
The fluke causing the infection is up to 7.5 cm long and lives in the upper parts of the small intestine [2]

Distribution : the infection occurs in the south of China, India, Bangladesh, Thailand, Malaysia, Borneo, Myanmar and Sumatra [16]

Symptoms : usually the infection is asymptomatic [16]. Symptoms are diarrhoea alternated with constipation, and swelling of face or legs. Sometimes flukes are passed in stool or vomit [3]. If the infection is heavy (hundreds - thousands of worms), symptoms may be more severe. Children over 5 years of age are most affected [16]

Severity : in heavy infections the flukes can cause severe health problems [16], and in weakened children the infection may be fatal [73]

Incubation period : 3 months [73]

Duration : around 1 year [3]

Communicability : if untreated, eggs are probably shed for around 1 year [3]

Transmission cycle [3]

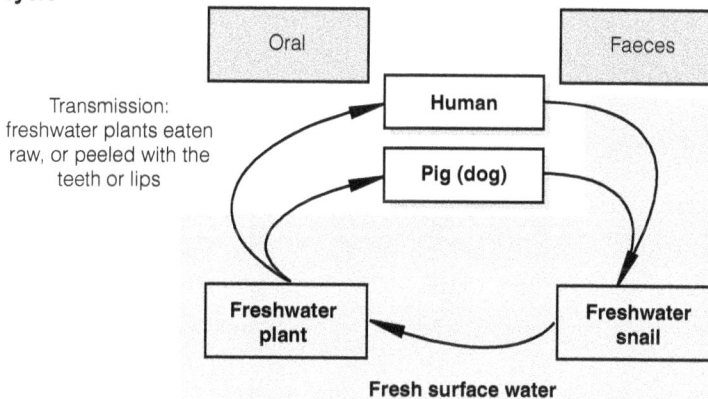

Transmission : the eggs of the fluke leave the body through faeces. The eggs will produce miracidia after a development of 3 to 7 weeks in fresh water [3]. These miracidia can infect freshwater snails. The pathogens multiply in the snail, and are released as cercaria. The cercaria form cysts on water plants (e.g. water caltrop, water chestnut, water bamboo) [73]. If these plants are eaten raw, or peeled with teeth or lips while still raw, the cysts can be ingested, and infection can follow [3]

Reservoir : reservoirs of the pathogen are pigs, humans, and occasionally dogs [3]

Vector/int. host : the pathogen has to go through developmental stages in two intermediate hosts. The first is a freshwater snail of the genus *Segmentina*. After a development in the snail the pathogen has to form a cyst on freshwater plants [73]

Water-related	:	the intermediate hosts of the pathogen are water-based [15]
Excreta-related	:	the pathogen leaves the host through faeces [15]
Environment	:	the infection is most common where human and animal excreta are used to grow freshwater plants [2], and where these plants are eaten raw [16] or the raw plants are peeled with the teeth [73]. The infection is more common where pigs are kept [3]
Risk in disaster	:	the infection will not be a problem in case of a disaster [3]
Remarks	:	where the infection is endemic, it can be expected that around 20% of the population is infected [16]

Preventative measures	Potential effect
Improving sanitation	(+) [73]
Not using human and pig excreta to enrich ponds from which freshwater plants are harvested [16]	
Improve the hygiene in the preparation of freshwater plants (drying or submerging the plants in boiling water will kill the cysts) [3]	(+++) [73]
Control of pigs. Pigs should be kept away from cultivation ponds [73] and should not be fed freshwater plants [3]	
Health and hygiene promotion [3]	

Epidemic measures : improve sanitation, identification of plants that play a role in transmission, and health and hygiene promotion [3]

Annexes

A1

Fascioliasis, Sheep liver fluke infection

An infection with two water-based intermediate hosts: a freshwater snail and freshwater plant. Infection follows the ingestion of uncooked water plants.

Pathogen : *Fasciola hepatica* and *Fasciola gigantica* (helminths)
F.gigantica is less common than *F.hepatica.* The infection is caused by 3 cm long flukes living in the bile ducts [3]

Distribution : *F.hepatica* occurs in South America, the Caribbean, the Middle East, Asia, Australia and Europe.
F.gigantica is found in Africa, the western parts of the Pacific, and Hawaii [3]

Symptoms : pain in the liver region, enlargement of the liver, jaundice [3]

Severity : the infection can cause considerable liver damage [73] and serious anaemia [2]

Incubation period : the incubation period is variable [3]

Duration : the infection persists [3]

Communicability : prolonged [3]

Transmission cycle [3]

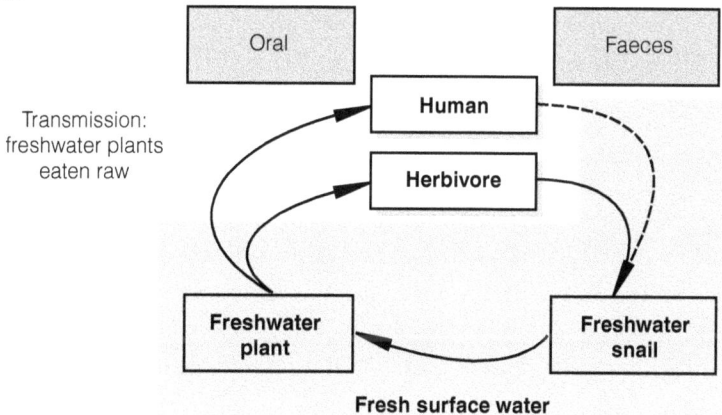

Transmission:
freshwater plants
eaten raw

Oral — Human — Faeces

Herbivore

Freshwater plant — Freshwater snail

Fresh surface water

Transmission : the pathogen leaves the body through faeces in the form of eggs. These eggs release miracidia after a development of 2 weeks in fresh water [3]. The miracidia infect freshwater snails [73], in which they go through a development, multiply, and form cercariae. These cercariae will attach to freshwater plants and become cysts. Infection follows the ingestion of freshwater plants containing these cysts [3]

Reservoir : the reservoirs of *F.hepatica* are usually sheep, cattle and goats [73]. The reservoirs of *F.gigantica* are cattle, water buffalo, and other large herbivores. People are infected accidentally and do not play an important role as reservoir [3]

Vector/int. host : the intermediate hosts of the pathogen are freshwater snails (*Lymnaea* spp.) and water-plants living in fresh water [73] (e.g. watercress) [2]

Water-related : the intermediate hosts are water-based [73]

Excreta-related : the pathogen leaves the host through faeces [73]

Environment : the infection is more common where sheep or other reservoir animals live in close association with humans [73]

Risk in disaster : the infection is not a problem in disasters [3]
Remarks : -

Preventative measures	Potential effect
Care in disposal of faeces of reservoir animals (faeces should not be used to fertilise water plants) [3]	
If appropriate, control of freshwater snails [3]	
Care in consumption of water plants (e.g. watercress) [3]	
Health and hygiene promotion [3]	

Epidemic measures : the source of infection should be determined and dealt with [3]

Clonorchiasis, Chinese liver fluke disease, Oriental liver fluke disease/ Opisthorchiasis, Cat liver fluke infection

Two similar infections with two water-based intermediate hosts: freshwater snails and freshwater fish. People are infected by eating poorly cooked fish.

Pathogen	:	Clonorchiasis is caused by *Clonorchis sinensis* (*Opistorchis sinensis*) [73]. The fluke causing infection is 10 to 25 mm long [2]. Opistorchiasis is caused by *Opisthorchis felineus* and *Opisthorchis viverrini* [3]. These flukes are around 10 mm long. The pathogens are helminths which live in the bile passages [2]
Distribution	:	*C.sinensis*: can be found in South-east Asia, China, Japan, Taiwan and Korea [3]. *O.felineus*: occurs in Eastern Europe; mainly Poland and Russia [2]. *O.viverrini*: is found in South-east Asia, especially in Thailand [3]
Symptoms	:	most infections show no specific symptoms [16]. Symptoms are diarrhoea, abdominal discomfort, and loss of appetite. In a later stage, liver problems can occur. Where *C.sinensis* is endemic, it is most common in adults over 30 years of age [3]
Severity	:	the infection is usually mild, but complications are possible [3]
Incubation period	:	months [73]
Duration	:	the duration of infection of clonorchiasis can be up to 30 years or longer [3]
Communicability	:	*Clonorchis* can survive for 20 to 50 years in an infected person. During this time eggs are passed in stools [4]

Transmission cycle [73]

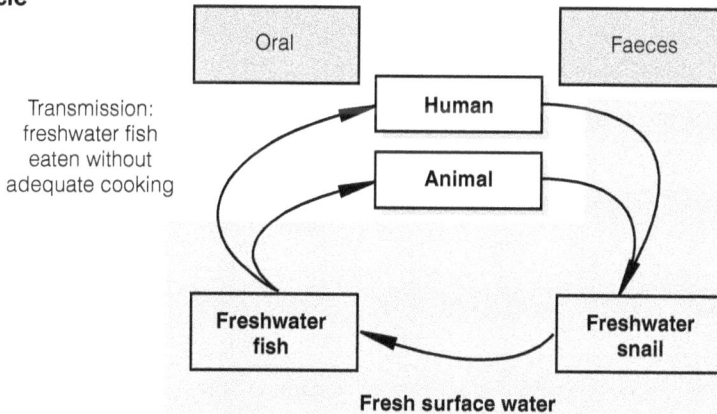

Transmission: freshwater fish eaten without adequate cooking

Oral — Human — Animal — Faeces — Freshwater snail — Freshwater fish

Fresh surface water

Transmission	:	the infected host sheds the eggs from the pathogen through faeces. When these eggs are ingested by a freshwater snail, the pathogen will multiply in the snail, and cercariae will be released in the water [3]. The cercariae will actively seek freshwater fish, and encyst in its flesh or under its scales [73]. When people ingest the infective fish raw or undercooked, infection occurs [16]. Smoking or pickling the fish will not necessarily kill the pathogen [73]
Reservoir	:	the reservoirs of the pathogen are humans, dogs, cats, pigs, rats, and other animals which eat fish [3]

Vector/int. host	:	the intermediate hosts are freshwater snails (*Bulimus* spp., *Bithynia* spp. and *Parafossarulus* spp.) [73] and freshwater fish (many species are potential intermediate hosts) [3]
Water-related	:	the intermediate hosts are water-based [15]
Excreta-related	:	the pathogen leaves the host through faeces [73]
Environment	:	where fish is eaten without adequate preparation
Risk in disaster	:	the infections are not a problem in disasters [3]
Remarks	:	an estimated 30,000,000 are infected with *C.sinensis* [73] and over 20,000,000 people are believed to be infected with *Opisthorchis* [16]. In parts of Northern Thailand, over 50% of the population is infected with *O. viverrini*. Pla ra, fermented fish eaten in Northern Thailand, will not transmit the pathogen [2]

Preventative measures	Potential effect
Improving sanitation (if possible human and animal sanitation) [3]	(+) [73]
Where possible the practise of raising fish in ponds receiving excreta as fertiliser should be prohibited [3]	
Improve preparation practices of freshwater fish	(+++) [73]
Control of domestic animals (reservoir animals should be kept away from fishponds)	
Health and hygiene promotion [3]	

Epidemic measures : search for the source of the outbreak, and eliminate it [3]

Annexes

A1

Tapeworm (fish) Diphyllobothriasis

A usually mild infection transmitted to humans through poorly prepared freshwater fish.

Pathogen   : several species of *Diphyllobothrium* [15] (Helminth)
The pathogen is a tapeworm of up to 10 metres long [44] living in the intestines [73]

Gen. description : the infection occurs in sub-arctic, temperate and tropical regions. In general infections are asymptomatic. Persons frequently carry several worms, and occasionally infections of over 100 worms do occur [16]. Even though these worms take an important amount of nutrients, the main problem is the absorption of vitamin B_{12} by the pathogen [73]. In 1 to 2% of the infections this develops into a deficiency of vitamin B_{12} [44] which can lead to anaemia. The tapeworms can survive for several years [3]

Transmission cycle [73]

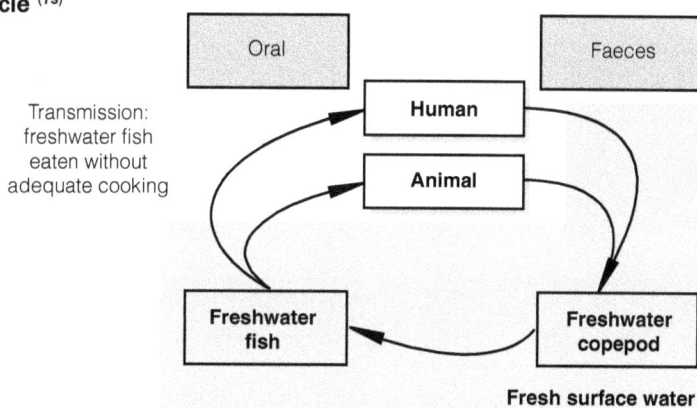

Transmission: freshwater fish eaten without adequate cooking

Oral

Faeces

Human

Animal

Freshwater fish

Freshwater copepod

Fresh surface water

Transmission   : the pathogen leaves the body through faeces. When the eggs come in contact with water, a coracidium emerges, which is ingested by a copepod. When the copepod is eaten by a fish, the pathogen works its way into the muscles of the fish. Infection of people follows when this fish is eaten without proper cooking [73]

Reservoir   : the most important reservoir of the pathogen are humans [16]. Other reservoirs are dogs, cats [73], pigs, other fish-eating mammals [3], and birds [16]

Vector/int. host : the intermediate hosts are freshwater copepods (species of *Cyclops* and *Diaptomus*) and freshwater fish (e.g. pike, salmon, perch, turbots) [3]

Water-related   : the intermediate hosts are water-related [16]

Excreta-related : the pathogen leaves the host through faeces [73]

Environment   : the infection is generally found in cooler regions, close to lakes [73]

Remarks   : it is believed that 13,000,000 are infected worldwide [73]

Preventative measures	Potential effect
Improving sanitation	(+) [73]
Correct preparation of freshwater fish (the pathogen is killed at 56° for 5 minutes or –18° for 24 hours) [73]	(+++) [73]
Mass detection and treatment of infections [16]	
health and hygiene promotion [16]	

Paragonimiasis, Lung fluke disease

A pathogen which has to go through two water-based intermediate hosts: a freshwater snail and a freshwater crustacean (freshwater crab, crayfish, or shrimp). Infection occurs through eating inadequately prepared infective crustaceans.

Pathogen : *Paragonimus* spp. [3] (Helminth)
the pathogen is a fluke with a length of about 10 mm living in the lungs [2]

Distribution : the infection occurs in the far East, South-east Asia, Oceania, West Africa [2], and South, Central and North America. The infection is most common in Asia [3]

Symptoms : the symptoms are coughing, chest pain, and sputum (lung secretions) with orange-brown flecks [3]. The infection can be mistaken for tuberculosis [2]

Severity : the infection can be severe if the flukes develop in other organs than the lungs [2], and deaths are reported [16]. In the lungs, only heavy and repeated infections will cause problems in the lung function [2]

Incubation period : variable, but normally long [3]

Duration : the flukes may live for up to 20 years [16]

Communicability : eggs may be discharged by a person for up to 20 years [3]

Transmission cycle [3]

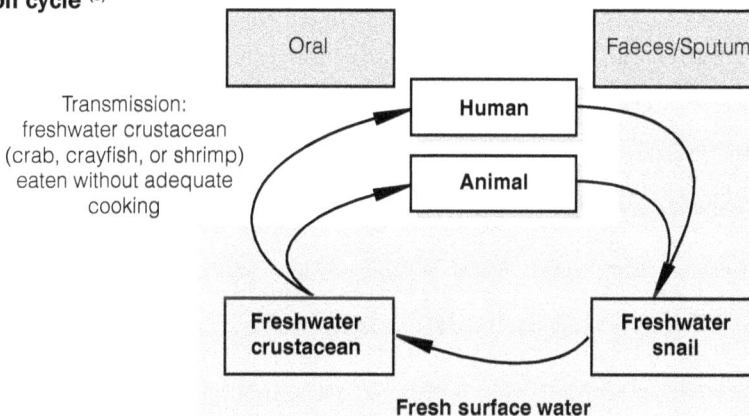

Oral		Faeces/Sputum

Transmission:
freshwater crustacean
(crab, crayfish, or shrimp)
eaten without adequate
cooking

Human

Animal

Freshwater crustacean

Freshwater snail

Fresh surface water

Transmission : eggs leave the body through sputum or faeces. Miracidia are released from the eggs after 2 to 4 weeks. These miracidia infect freshwater snails. In the snail a development of around 2 months will take place before cercariae emerge. The cercariae penetrate the body of crabs, crayfish [3], or shrimps [16] and form cysts. When infected crustaceans are eaten without proper cooking, infection can follow [3]. Ingestion of the cysts during preparation of the crustaceans is possible [16]

Reservoir : the main reservoirs of the infection are wild and domestic cats [16]. Dogs can play an important role as reservoir too [73]. Other reservoirs are humans, pigs and wild carnivores [3]

Vector/int. host : freshwater snails (*Semisulcospira*, *Thiara*, *Aroapyrgus* and other genera) [3], and freshwater crabs, crayfish [73] and shrimps are the intermediate hosts of the pathogen [16]

Water-related : the intermediate hosts are water-based [2]

Excreta-related : the pathogens leaves the body through faeces if sputum is swallowed [73]

Annexes

A1

Environment : the infection is likely to occur in endemic regions where freshwater crabs, crayfish or shrimps are eaten without adequate cooking

Risk in disaster : the infection is not a priority in disasters [3]

Remarks : in China around 10,000,000 people are believed to be infected. In Ecuador the number of infections is estimated at 500,000 [3]

Preventative measures	Potential effect
Improvement of sanitation	(+) [73]
Safe disposal of sputum [3]	
Improve preparation of freshwater crustaceans (crabs, crayfish and shrimps) [16]	(+++) [73]
Control of reservoir animals [3]	
Control of freshwater snails where appropriate [3]	
Health and hygiene promotion [3]	

As carnivores play an important role as reservoir, the effect of improved sanitation as only measure is limited. The most effective preventive measure is correct preparation of Crustaceans. Pickling processes are often not effective in killing the pathogen [2].

Epidemic measures : the source of the infection should be determined and dealt with [3]

Hookworm disease, Ancylostomiasis, Necatoriasis

A very common infection; ¼ of the world's population is estimated to be infected with this pathogen. People become infected when larvae which developed in soil penetrate bare skin.

Pathogen
: *Ancylostoma duodenale, Necator americanus,* and *Ancylostoma ceylanicum* [3] (Helminths).
  Hookworms are 5 to 13 mm long worms which live in the small intestine. Every worm taps 0.03 to 0.3 ml of blood per day [44]

Distribution
: *A.duodenale* and *N.americanus* cover jointly more or less the entire world, but are most common in tropical and subtropical zones. *A.ceylanicum* is found in South-east Asia [3]

Symptoms
: light infections are usually asymptomatic [3]. Symptoms are tiredness, breathlessness, pain in muscles, and pale skin [2] caused by anaemia (low levels of haemoglobin in the blood) [3]

Severity
: the severity of the infection depends on the number of worms; the more there are, the higher the blood loss they cause [16]. Light infections are usually no problem. Heavy infections can lead to severe disability, death is uncommon however [3]. The infection poses the biggest health threat to growing children and pregnant women [73]

Incubation period
: weeks to months [73]

Duration
: the worms can survive in the human body for 5 to 6 years [16], reinfection will be common

Communicability
: eggs can be passed for several years [3]

Transmission cycle [73]

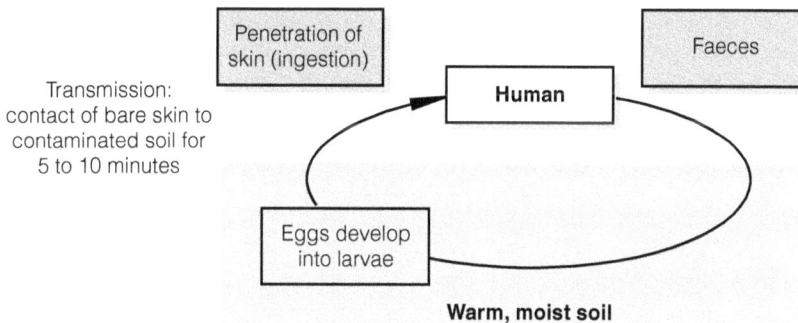

Penetration of skin (ingestion) — Faeces — Human

Transmission: contact of bare skin to contaminated soil for 5 to 10 minutes

Eggs develop into larvae

Warm, moist soil

Transmission
: the eggs excreted by an infected person will develop into larvae in the soil. These larvae cause infection in humans by penetrating (intact) skin. A contact time of 5 to 10 minutes of the skin with the infected soil is necessary for successful penetration [44]. In addition to penetrating the skin, *Ancylostoma* can be transmitted by ingestion of the developed larvae [3]

Reservoir
: man is the only reservoir for *A.duodenale* and *N.americanus* [16]. Dogs and cats are reservoirs for *A.ceylanicum* [3]. In warm and damp soil the infective form can live for several months [73] though up to 2 years is mentioned [16]

Vector/int. host
: none

Water-related
: no

Excreta-related
: the pathogen leaves the body through faeces [2]

155

Environment	:	the infection is common where inadequate sanitation occurs in a warm and wet climate [3]. The ideal environment for the pathogen outside the host is moist, shaded, humus-rich soil at a temperature of 25°C to 30°C [73]. In cooler or drier climates transmission may be seasonal in the hot or wet season [16]. Where the climate is unfavourable, the infection can occur where conditions are warm and humid, for example in mines [3]. If human faeces are used as fertiliser, the risk of infection is high [16]. Latrines must be kept clean; if excreta can soil the floor of latrines, these can become foci for transmission of hookworm [9,57]
Risk in disaster	:	the infection will not be an urgent problem in a disaster [3]
Remarks	:	it is believed that around 25% of the world's population is infected with hookworm [4]

Preventative measures	Potential effect
Improvement of sanitation (sanitation should be clean)	(+++) [73]
Care should be taken in use of excreta as fertiliser [16]	
Wearing closed shoes [2]	
Mass treatment (effective in reducing the number of cases quickly, not in preventing reinfection) [73]	(+++) [26]
Health and hygiene promotion [3]	

The number of eggs released by a single female worm can be up to 35,000. Persons with heavy infections can be host to 1,000 worms [16]. This means that the potential of contamination of the environment is huge. As it is unlikely that everybody will use the sanitary structures correctly, improved sanitation as only preventive measure is usually not very effective if many people remain infected. Improved sanitation as preventative measure is very important to reduce the reinfection of people though, and a combination of mass treatment and improved sanitation is very effective in reducing the infection in a population (a reduction of 80% is mentioned) [26].

Epidemic measures : a combination of mass treatment, health and hygiene promotion and improvement of sanitation [3]

Threadworm infection, Strongyloidiasis,

A pathogen which leaves the body through faeces, and develops in warm and moist soil. The pathogen can either go through its reproductive adult form in the human body, or in soil.

Pathogen : *Strongyloides stercoralis, S. fülleborni* [3] (Helminth)
The adult worms are 2 mm long and live in the small intestine of people, or in soil [2]

Distribution : (roughly) worldwide [3]

Symptoms : most infections are asymptomatic [16]. Symptoms are upper abdominal pain, diarrhoea [2], nausea [3], and loss of weight [2]

Severity : most infections are mild [2]. Hyper-infection does occur in rare cases, and can be fatal [44]. Most at risk are people who are undernourished or suffer from other illnesses [16]

Incubation period : variable [73]

Duration : the infection can last decades if autoinfection occurs (40 years is mentioned) [2]

Communicability : as long as the infection lasts [3]

Transmission cycle [73]

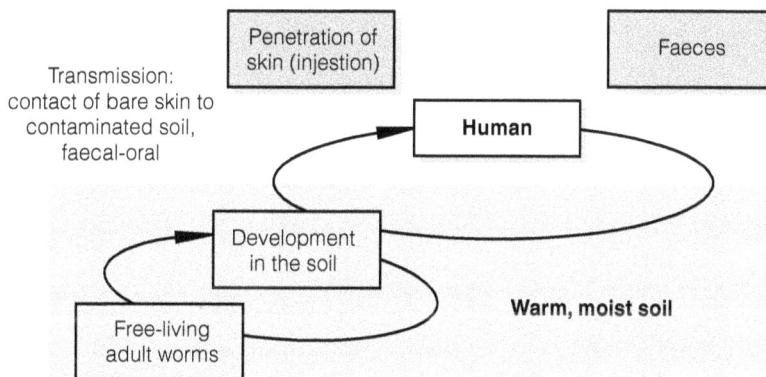

Transmission : the eggs hatch in the intestine of the person [4], to form rhabditiform larvae which leave the body through faeces. Either the rhabditiform larvae develop directly into infective filariform larvae, or they start a free-living cycle. The free-living cycle occurs when the larvae are in warm and moist soil [2]. The larvae will become adults which can reproduce [73]. This cycle outside the human body can be repeated many times [2].
People are usually infected by filariform larvae in soil which penetrate the skin [44]. Autoinfection can occur: rhabditiform larvae penetrate the intestinal mucous membrane without leaving the body. Faecal-oral transmission is also possible [73]

Reservoir : humans and soil are the most important reservoirs. On rare occasions dogs and cats do transmit a similar infection to humans. In Africa, primates can be a reservoir for *S. fülleborni* [3].
Infective larvae can remain viable in suitable soil for many weeks. Larvae will not survive in dry conditions, or temperatures under 8°, or over 40° [16]

Vector/int. host	: none
Water-related	: no, though the risk of faecal-oral transmission is probably slightly reduced by improving handwashing practise
Excreta-related	: larvae leave the body through faeces. Faecal-oral transmission is possible, but this is not the usual way of spreading [44]
Environment	: The infection flourishes in warm and wet regions [3] with overcrowding [16]. Although the pathogen can be found in an environment similar to hookworm [4], *Strongyloides* prefers wetter conditions [2]
Risk in disaster	: the infection is not a risk in disasters [3]
Remarks	: the disease is common in parts of tropical Brazil, Colombia and South-east Asia [16]

Preventative measures	Potential effect
Improvement of sanitation (sanitation should be clean)	$(+++)$ [73]
Wearing closed shoes [3]	
Health and hygiene promotion [73]	

Epidemic measures : the infection is not epidemic [3]

Roundworm infection, Ascariasis

A very common disease; one billion people are estimated to be infected. The pathogen leaves the body through faeces. Infection occurs through ingestion of contaminated soil. The eggs are very resistant and can survive for years in suitable soil.

Pathogen : *Ascaris lumbricoides* [15] (Helminth)
The cream-coloured worms are 15 to 40 cm long, and live in the small intestine. The worms feed on the contents of the intestines [2]

Distribution : the infection occurs worldwide [15]

Symptoms : most infections are asymptomatic. Sometimes worms are excreted. Children between 3 and 8 years old are usually most affected [3]

Severity : the infection is normally mild. The severity will depend on the number of worms causing the infection [2]. The worms take up nutrients which should have benefited the infected person [73]; and heavy infections will worsen nutritional insufficiencies [3].
In 0.05 to 0.2% of the infections more severe (potentially fatal) complications occur [44]

Incubation period : 10 to 20 days [73]

Duration : adult worms usually live around 1 year, but up to 2 years is possible [3]. Reinfection is likely to occur

Communicability : people shed eggs as long as infection lasts [3]

Transmission cycle [3]

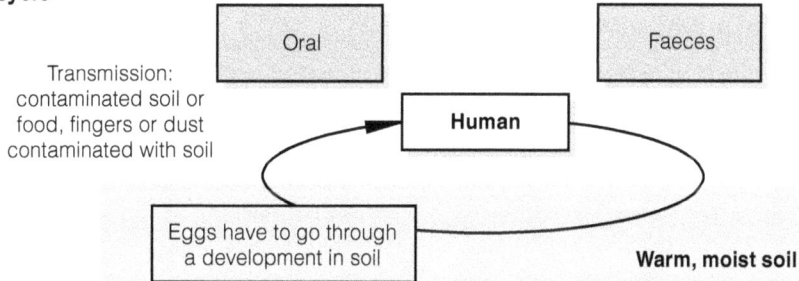

Transmission: contaminated soil or food, fingers or dust contaminated with soil

Oral

Faeces

Human

Eggs have to go through a development in soil

Warm, moist soil

Transmission : female worms discharge around 200,000 eggs per day [2]. These eggs leave the body through faeces. Eggs become infective after a development of 2 to 3 weeks [3] in warm [44], shady, and damp soil [16]. A person is infected after ingestion of eggs from contaminated soil. Infection can occur when children play around the house [16] or when food gets contaminated by soil. Hands contaminated with soil play an important role in transmission too [16]. Feet can take contaminated soil into the house. Contaminated dust can also play a role in transmission [3]. Outbreaks have occurred where raw sewage or waste-water were used for irrigation, and where contaminated vegetables were imported [16]

Reservoir : humans. The infective eggs are very resistant to drying or cold [73] and can remain infective for years in soil [3]. Temperatures over 45°C or direct sunlight will kill the eggs [16].
A similar infection of pigs (*A.suum*) can infect humans [2], but this is rare [3]

Vector/int. host : cockroaches and other animals can serve as mechanical vectors by ingesting, and excreting viable eggs [16]

Water-related : the infection is water-washed [73]

Excreta-related : eggs leave the body through faeces [2]

Environment : the infection is most common in moist, tropical zones [3] in a population with poor personal hygiene, inadequate sanitation, and poor food hygiene [73]. Where the climate is drier, the period of transmission is limited to the rainy season [16]

Risk in disaster : roundworm infection will not be a priority in a disaster [3]

Remarks : the infection is very common, and it is estimated that one billion people are infected worldwide [73]. In parts of Africa 95% of the population are infected [16]

Preventative measures	Potential effect
Improving water availability	(++) [29]
Improve handwashing practise	(++) [73]
Improvement of sanitation	(+++) [73]
Care should be taken in use of excreta as fertiliser [16] or contact with composted excreta [57]	
Improving food hygiene	(+) [73]
Mass treatment (especially of children) [2]	(+++) [26]
Health and hygiene promotion [3]	

Increased water availability has been associated with a reduction of 12 to 37% in hookworm infection; improved water availability combined with improved sanitation with a reduction of around 29%; and improved water availability and sanitation in combination with mass treatment has been associated with a reduction of 80% in roundworm infection [26]. Mass treatment alone will result in a short term reduction in the number of infections, but will not be effective on the long run, as the cause of infection has not been removed.

Epidemic measures : mass treatment, health and hygiene promotion, and improved sanitation [2, 3]

Whipworm infection, Trichuriasis

A very common, usually mild, infection. The pathogen leaves the body through faeces, develops in soil into an infective form, and infects people through the oral route.

Pathogen : *Trichuris trichiura* [15] (Helminth)
The greyish-white [16] worm is 2 to 5 cm long and lives in the large intestine, where it feeds on tissue juices [2]

Distribution : the infection occurs worldwide [15]

Symptoms : most infections are asymptomatic [2]. Symptoms are abdominal pain and diarrhoea [4].
Because of their behaviour children are most at risk of infection [16]

Severity : the infection is usually mild. In heavy infections dysentery (bloody stools with mucus), rectal prolapse (the rectum comes out of the anus), and retarded growth can occur [3]

Incubation period : no incubation period can be given [73]. It takes the worms 3 months to mature after being ingested [2]

Duration : the duration of the infection can be several years [3]

Communicability : several years [3]

Transmission cycle [73]

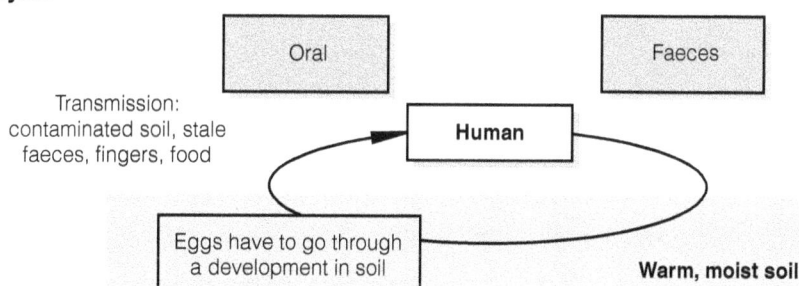

Transmission : the pathogen leaves the human body through faeces. In warm, moist soil the eggs will become infective after a development of 2 weeks [2]. Infection occurs when the infective eggs from stale faeces or contaminated soil are ingested by a person. Transmission is often through hand to mouth contact [16], or through contaminated food [73]

Reservoir : primarily humans and soil. The eggs in the soil are resistant to low temperatures, but need moisture to survive [16]. Pigs can be infected with a similar worm (*T.suis*) which is able to infect humans [2,16]

Vector/int. host : none

Water-related : the infection is water-washed [73]

Excreta-related : the eggs leave the body through faeces [73]

Environment : the infection is common where poor sanitation is combined with high rainfall and humidity, and dense shade [16]. In urban slums the infection can become a public health problem [2]. Persons who handle pigs have a higher incidence of the infection [16]

Risk in disaster : the infection is not a problem in disasters [3]

Remarks : the infection is very common, and over 500,000,000 people are estimated to be infected [73]

Preventative measures	Potential effect
Improving water availability	(+) [29]
Improve handwashing practise [3]	
Improvement of sanitation	(+) [73]
Improving food hygiene	(+) [73]
Mass treatment [16] (if the infection is a severe problem)	
Health and hygiene promotion [3]	

Epidemic measures : the infection is not epidemic [3]

Tapeworm (beef), Taeniasis

A mild infection which is transmitted through eating poorly cooked beef.

Pathogen	:	*Taenia saginata* [15] (Helminth)
		The infection is caused by a tapeworm which lives in the small intestine, and which can become up to 10 m long [2]
Distribution	:	the infection occurs worldwide [3]
Symptoms	:	the infections are usually asymptomatic [16]. Symptoms are insomnia, loss of weight, abdominal pain, and finding segments of worms in faeces [3]. People who are infected will often carry several worms [16]
Severity	:	the infection is usually mild [73]
Incubation period	:	10 to 14 weeks [73]
Duration	:	worms may survive for 30 years or longer [3]
Communicability	:	the period of communicability is as long as the tapeworm persists, which can be over 30 years [3]

Transmission cycle [3]

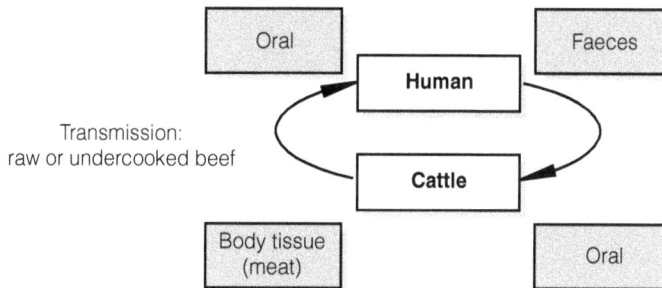

Transmission	:	the eggs leave the host through faeces, either individually, or in complete segments of the worm [2]. Cattle is infected by ingesting the eggs. After ingestion, the pathogen will implant itself in the flesh of the cow as cysticerci [3]. Cattle can become infected when its pastures are polluted with human faeces, or by drinking water contaminated with sewage [73]. Birds can play a role in taking the pathogen from sewage outflows to pastures [2]. Possibly domestic flies can play a role in the transmission of the eggs to cattle [73]. People are infected through ingesting raw or undercooked beef containing the pathogen [3]
Reservoir	:	humans are the only definitive host of the pathogen [16]. The eggs can survive for months in the environment [3]
Vector/int. host	:	cattle is the intermediate host of the pathogen [2]
Water-related	:	no
Excreta-related	:	the pathogen leaves the human body through faeces [2]
Environment	:	the pathogen is often found in areas of cattle breeding [44]. The infection is common in poorer areas where beef is eaten raw, or without proper cooking [16]
Risk in disaster	:	the infection is not a priority in disasters [3]
Remarks	:	it is estimated that over 60,000,000 people are infected worldwide [73]. The infection is very common in the highlands of Ethiopia [16]

Preventative measures	Potential effect
Improving sanitation (assuring cattle can not come in contact with human excreta, care in disposal of sewage)	(+++) [73]
Correct preparation of beef (beef will be safe after a minimum of 5 minutes at over 56°C [4] or 7 to 10 days at -20°C [44])	(+++) [73]
Inspection of meat	(+) [3]
Health and hygiene promotion [3]	

Epidemic measures :   -

Tapeworm (pig) , Taeniasis, Cysticercosis

This pathogen causes two different infections. The first infection is by the adult tapeworm which is transmitted through eating improperly cooked pork. Although this infection is mild, the hosts and their contacts are at serious risk of cysticercosis. Cysticercosis is the second infection caused by the pathogen. It is caused by the larvae of the worm, is transmitted through the faecal-oral route, and is potentially a severe disease.

Pathogen : *Taenia solium* [15] (Helminth)
The adult tapeworm can become up to 7m long [45] and lives in the small intestine [2]. Humans can be infected by the larvae of the tapeworm which can form cysts anywhere in the body [3]

Distribution : the infection occurs worldwide [3]; but is common in Africa, India, Indonesia, Mexico, Chile and Russia [73]

Symptoms : people can have two forms of infection: infection by the adult worm, or by the larval stage of the pathogen which causes cysticercosis (cysts in body tissues).
Infections by the adult worm are usually asymptomatic [16]. Symptoms are insomnia, loss of weight, abdominal pain, and finding segments of worms in faeces [3].
Cysticercosis can be asymptomatic. When the brain is affected, epilepsy [2] and psychiatric problems can result [3]

Severity : the infection with the adult worm is mild [2], but the hosts and people close to them are at risk of cysticercosis [16].
Cysticercosis is potentially a severe and dangerous infection [2]

Incubation period : infections with adult worms: 8 to 12 weeks [73]. Cysticercosis has an incubation period which ranges from days, to over 10 years [3]

Duration : worms may survive for 30 years or longer [3]

Communicability : as long as the tapeworm persists, which can be over 30 years [3]

Transmission cycle [3]

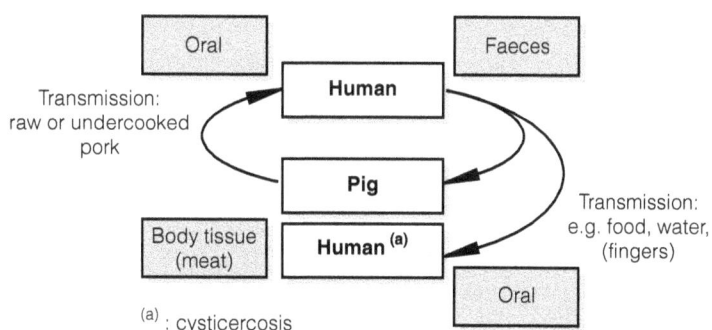

Oral — Human — Faeces
Transmission: raw or undercooked pork
Pig
Body tissue (meat) — Human [a]
Transmission: e.g. food, water, (fingers)
Oral

[a] : cysticercosis

Transmission : the eggs leave the human body through faeces [2]. Pigs are infected by ingesting these eggs through eating human faeces, or ingesting water or food contaminated with human faeces or sewage. The ingested eggs will implant themselves in the flesh of the pig as cysticerci. People are infected with the adult tapeworm when raw or undercooked pork containing the pathogen is eaten [3].

The eggs excreted by a person are directly infective through the faecal-oral route. This results in cysticercosis. The eggs can either infect the host carrying the adult worm, or persons around the host [73]

Reservoir : humans are the only definitive host of the pathogen [16]. The eggs can survive in the environment for months [3]

Vector/int. host : the intermediate host of the pathogen is the pig. In cysticercosis people function as intermediate host (though they are a dead end in the transmission cycle) [2]

Water-related : cysticercosis is water-washed [3] and water-borne [73]

Excreta-related : the pathogen leaves the human body through faeces [2]. Cysticercosis is spread through the faecal-oral route [73]

Environment : the infection can occur where pigs have access to human faeces, or to food or water contaminated by human faeces or sewage, and where pork is eaten without adequate preparation

Risk in disaster : the infection is not a priority in disasters [3]

Remarks : pork tapeworm is less common than beef tapeworm [2]

Preventative measures	Potential effect
Cysticercosis: improving water availability	
Cysticercosis: improve handwashing practise [3]	
Improving sanitation (pigs and humans must not have access to human faeces (either direct, or through sewage))	(+++) [73]
Correct preparation of pork (pork will be safe after a minimum of 5 minutes at over 56°C [4] or 7 to 10 days at -20°C [44])	(+++) [73]
Inspection of meat	(+) [3]
People with the infection should be treated [3]	
Health and hygiene promotion [3]	

Epidemic measures : -

Weil's disease, Leptospirosis

A usually mild infection which is mainly transmitted through skin contact with water or other material contaminated with urine of infected animals.

Pathogen	:	*Leptospira* spp. [15] (Bacterium)
Distribution	:	the infection occurs worldwide [15]
Symptoms	:	the majority of the infections are asymptomatic, or too mild to diagnose [3]. Symptoms will often be similar to influenza [16]: fever, headache, chills, malaise, muscular pain in legs, and vomiting [3]. Severe cases can result in jaundice and kidney failure [16]
Severity	:	severe infections are rare [16], but can be fatal [3]
Incubation period	:	4 to 18 days [73]
Duration	:	the duration of the illness ranges from some days to 3 weeks, though longer is possible [3]
Communicability	:	communicability is usually up to 1 month after illness, but can possibly be up to 11 months. Animals which are carriers can be infective for life [3]

Transmission cycle [3]

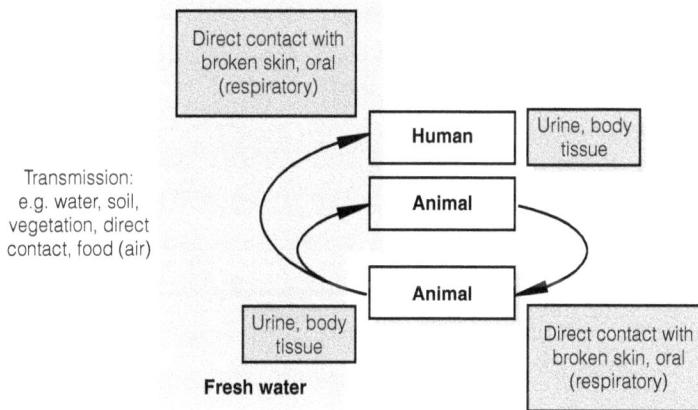

Transmission	:	transmission occurs mainly when abraded or broken skin, or mucous membranes, come in contact with water, moist soil, or vegetation contaminated with the urine of infected animals. Direct contact with urine or body tissue of infected animals can transmit the pathogen too. Sporadically transmission occurs through food contaminated with urine of rats carrying the infection, inhaling droplets of contaminated fluids [3] or the bite of an infected rat [16]. Transmission from person to person is uncommon [3]
Reservoir	:	rats and rodents are the main reservoir [73] and pose the largest risk for transmission to humans. However, most mammals can become carriers and spread the infection [16]. Some other important reservoirs are pigs, cattle, dogs, and many wild mammals. Humans are not important as reservoir [3].

The pathogen can survive for longer periods in a moist, non-acidic environment. In fresh water with a pH of about 7, survival of *Leptospira* can be up to 4 weeks. In a pH of 5, the pathogen will survive for up to 2 days. *Leptospira* will not survive in saline water [16] and is sensitive to chlorine [73]

Vector/int. host : the disease is spread through animals (the main risk comes from rats); these are final hosts and not vectors or intermediate hosts

Water-related : water contaminated with infected urine plays an important role in the transmission of the disease [3]

Excreta-related : the pathogen is mainly spread through contact with urine from infected animals [16]

Environment : the infection is common where rats are numerous and the environment is favourable [73]. The infection is a hazard to people in direct contact with fresh water, urine, or body tissues of animals [3], and is linked to specific occupations like workers in sugar-cane plantations or rice-paddies, mine workers, farmers, people working with fish, in canals, or in sewerage systems [73]

Risk in disaster : the infection could be a potential problem in regions with a high water table, or where flooding has occurred [3]

Remarks : -

Preventative measures	Potential effect
Improving the quality of water people come in contact with; workers who come in contact with fresh surface water must be properly protected	(+++) [29]
Improving food hygiene (protection of food from rats)	(++) [73]
Control of rats and rodents, especially where transmission is likely (where food is stored, animals butchered, where domestic animals are kept) [73]	
Control of domestic animals [73]	
Health and hygiene promotion [3]	

Care should be taken with the disposal of urine of patients [4]

Epidemic measures : the source of infection should be determined and, if possible, dealt with [3]

Guinea-worm infection, Dracunculiasis, Dracontiasis

Guinea-worm is the only pathogen transmitted exclusively by drinking contaminated water (all other water-borne infections can be transmitted in several other ways). The infection can result in severe complications. In the past decade the number of infections in the world has reduced strongly.

Pathogen	: *Dracunculus medinensis* [15] (Helminth) The infection is caused by the female worm which can be over 1m long [2]
Distribution	: the WHO reports in 1999 the presence of guinea-worm in: Benin, Burkina Faso, Cameroon, Central African Republic, Chad, Côte d'Ivoire, Ethiopia, Ghana, Kenya, Mali, Mauritania, Niger, Nigeria, Senegal, Sudan, Togo, Uganda and Yemen [84]
Symptoms	: fever and localised complaints like swellings, itching, and local pains [2]. A blister containing a worm will appear [3], usually on the legs. Worms which are not removed will calcify in the body [2]. Most affected are people in the age group of 15 to 40 years [16]
Severity	: the infection can be the cause of severe illness and disability [44]. Worms entering in joints may cause arthritis. Adequate removal of the worm will reduce the risks of complications [2]. In up to 50% or more of the cases [16] secondary, potentially life-threatening infections of the blister can occur [2]
Incubation period	: around 12 months [3]
Duration	: several weeks if no complications occur
Communicability	: people who harbour the worm can contaminate water from the moment the blister bursts to (generally) 2 to 3 weeks after. Copepods are infective for around 3 weeks after infection, then they will die [3]

Transmission cycle [3]

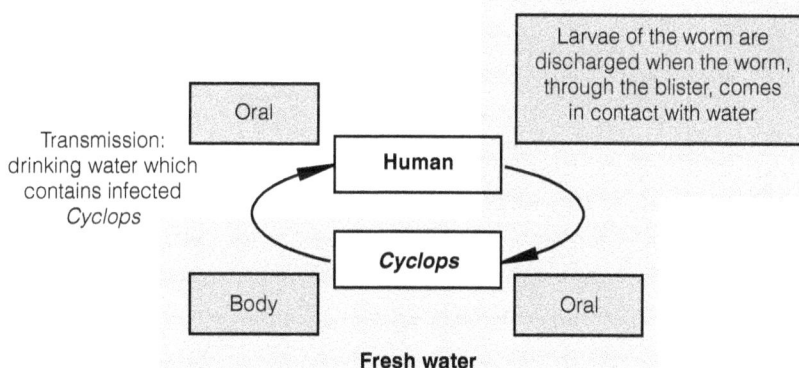

Transmission	: the blister containing the female worm will burst when in contact with water [16]. The worm emerges, and discharges its larvae into the fresh water. When these larvae are ingested by *Cyclops*, infection of the copepod can follow [73]. In *Cyclops* the pathogen has to go through a development of 12 to 14 days before it can infect humans [3]. People become infected when they drink water containing the infective *Cyclops* [73]. Most infections occur during a few months of the year [16]

169

Reservoir	:	humans are the only reservoir of the infection [3]
Vector/int. host	:	the intermediate hosts are copepods of the genus *Cyclops* [2]. These are small crustaceans (water fleas) which are barely visible to the eye.
Water-related	:	the intermediate host is water-based [73] and the pathogen is water-borne
Excreta-related	:	no
Environment	:	the infection is associated with small water sources in semi-arid countries [16]. Usually the pathogen is found in rural areas [44] where stagnant surface water is used as source of water [3]. Water sources where people have to stand in the water are particularly unsafe [2]. In arid regions transmission occurs in the rainy season when there is an availability of surface water. In wet regions transmission is most common in the dry season, when only a limited number of water-sources are available [16]
Risk in disaster	:	the infection is not a priority in a disaster. If the pathogen is present in the population, control of the infection could be started when the emergency phase is dealt with [47]
Remarks	:	the infection typically appears in the agricultural season [84]. As a large part of the farmers may be disabled by the infection, the agricultural production may be severely reduced because of the disease [16]. Progress is being made in the WHO programme of eradication of guinea-worm infection [2], therefore the geographical distribution of the infection is likely to change in the years to come. In 1989 the number of cases were estimated at 1,000,000; in 1997 it was estimated at less than 80,000 cases [84]

Preventative measures	Potential effect
Improving the quality of drinking water (the water can easily be filtered as *Cyclops* is rather large (a mesh size of 0.1mm is sufficient [3], the same side of the filter should always be 'up'))	(+++) [26]
Water sources for drinking water should not allow used or spilt water to flow back [73]	
Persons with the active infection should not enter into water used for drinking water [3]	
Control of *Cyclops* with the insecticide 'temefos' [3]	
Health and hygiene promotion [3]	

Epidemic measures : search for sources of infection and deal with them; health and hygiene promotion, assure drinking water quality [3]

Conjunctivitis

Infections which affect the eyes and are transmitted through direct contact. Large outbreaks are possible where the population has poor personal hygiene and lives in overcrowded conditions.

Pathogen : the infection can be caused by several types of bacteria (acute bacterial conjunctivitis); adenoviruses (adenoviral keratoconjunctivitis, adenoviral haemorrhagic conjunctivitis) and picarnoviruses (enteroviral haemorrhagic conjunctivitis)

Distribution : the infections occur worldwide [3]

Symptoms : acute bacterial conjunctivitis: irritation, purulent discharge from the eye [4], swelling of the eyelids. Children under 5 are most affected.
keratoconjunctivitis: sudden onset, swelling of the eyelids, pain, photophobia, and blurred vision.
haemorrhagic conjunctivitis: swollen eyelids, bleedings on the eyes [3], eye discharges are clear [4]

Severity : most infections are not severe [3]

Incubation period : acute bacterial conjunctivitis: 1 to 3 days
keratoconjunctivitis: 5 to 12 days or longer
haemorrhagic conjunctivitis: 12 hours to 12 days [3]

Duration : the conjunctivitis lasts between some days and some weeks [3]

Communicability : communicability of the infection is variable; normally up to 2 weeks, or as long as the infection lasts [3]

Transmission cycle [3]

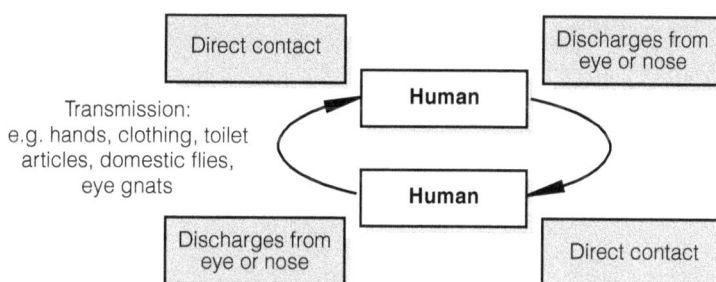

Transmission: e.g. hands, clothing, toilet articles, domestic flies, eye gnats

Direct contact → Human ← Discharges from eye or nose

Discharges from eye or nose → Human → Direct contact

Transmission : the pathogens leave the body through discharges of the eyes or nose. These discharges can transmit the infection to a susceptible person through hands, contaminated material (especially if used around eyes), or domestic flies and eye gnats. The importance of domestic flies or eye gnats in transmission is not entirely clear [3]. Epidemics can take place where the environment is favourable to transmission [73]. Attack rates of up to 50% in the population are possible [3,47]

Reservoir : humans are the only reservoir of the pathogens [3]

Vector/int. host : domestic flies and eye gnats can be mechanical vectors [3]

Water-related : the infections are water-washed [73]

Excreta-related : not directly; poor sanitation may increase the population of domestic flies

Environment : the infection occurs especially where crowding, poor personal hygiene (as well poor handwashing as inadequate hygiene of clothes and other materials), exposure to wind and dust, and poor sanitation (risk of domestic fly breeding) are found [47]

Risk in disaster : the infection will not be a priority in a disaster. Epidemics are possible where overcrowding is combined with poor personal hygiene [47]

Remarks : it may be necessary to provide separate treatment facilities during outbreaks [3].

Chlamydial conjunctivitis (which is not trachoma) is an infection which is transmitted sexually, or from mother to new-born baby. Obviously the transmission cycle and preventative measures of this infection will be different

Preventative measures	Potential effect
Improving water availability	(+++) [29]
Improve handwashing practise [3]	
Hygiene of clothes and other objects used around eyes [73]	
Improvement of sanitation	
Control of domestic flies or eye gnats (where these are suspected to play a role in transmission) [3] (for control of domestic flies, see Annexe 3)	
Children with active infection may have to be barred from school [3]	
Treatment of cases [3]	
If possible, overcrowding should be avoided [3]	
Health and hygiene promotion [3]	

Epidemic measures : make sure that people have access to water and soap to allow adequate personal hygiene. Cases and close contacts must be treated rapidly, if necessary in separate facilities. Health and hygiene promotion, and where appropriate, control of domestic flies [3]

Trachoma

An infection affecting the eye. The disease is the most common cause of preventable blindness in the world. Transmission is through direct contact with contaminated hands, domestic flies, clothing, or other objects.

Pathogen	: *Chlamydia trachomatis* [3] (Bacterium)
Distribution	: the infection occurs worldwide [3]
Symptoms	: the infection starts of as keratoconjuntivitis [73], followed by scarring of the conjunctiva. Severe cases can develop deformed eyelids. The eye-lashes are turned inward, which can, over time, lead to blindness [3]. The highest rate of infection is in young children [44]
Severity	: frequent reinfection is needed to create severe lifelong disease [3]
Incubation period	: 5 to 12 days [73]
Duration	: single infections can last for some years. The infection can be continuous through reinfection [3]
Communicability	: the period of communicability can be a few years [3]. The disease is not infectious in its later stages [73]

Transmission cycle [3]

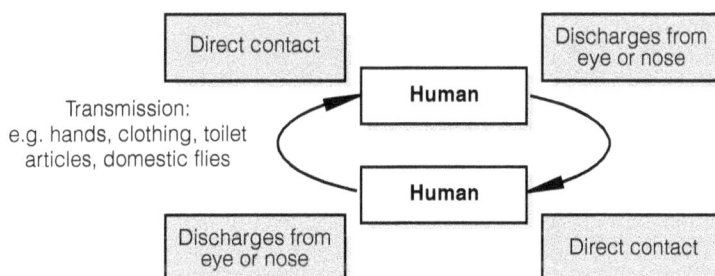

Transmission	: the pathogen is found in eye [73] or nasal discharges. Infection occurs through contact with these discharges [3]. Transmission of the infection is through hands, clothing or other objects, and domestic flies. A common way of transmission is rubbing infected eyes of a child with a cloth or hands. The pathogen is carried over when the cloth or hand is used on a susceptible person without proper cleaning or washing. Where the infection is endemic, up to 90% can be infected by the age of 3 years [73]
Reservoir	: humans are the only reservoir [3]
Vector/int. host	: domestic flies are a mechanical vector for the pathogen [16]
Water-related	: the infection is water-washed [73]
Excreta-related	: not directly; inadequate sanitation can increase the domestic fly population [16]
Environment	: the infection is most common in poor, rural communities [3]. The typical environment for trachoma is: poor personal hygiene, crowded conditions, a dry and dusty environment, and inadequate sanitation (human and animal) which results in a large domestic fly population [16]

Risk in disaster : the infection is not an urgent problem in case of a disaster [3]

Remarks : trachoma is the most important cause of preventable blindness in many regions in the world [44]. It is believed that 150,000,000 people are affected by the infection. Around 5,500,000 people are estimated to be blind, or at risk of becoming blind because of the infection [16]

Preventative measures	Potential effect
Improving water availability	(++) [29]
Improve handwashing practise and washing of face [3]	
Hygiene of clothes and other objects used around eyes [29]	
Improvement of sanitation	(+) [29]
Control of domestic flies [29]	
Search for cases and their treatment [4]	
Health and hygiene promotion [3]	

Epidemic measures : health and hygiene promotion in combination with improved water availability, improved sanitation, and mass treatment.

Yaws, Frambesia tropica

An infection which can be crippling and disfiguring. Transmission occurs when pathogens from the infectious skin papules of an infected person come in contact with abraded skin of a susceptible person.

Pathogen : *Treponema pallidum*, subspecies *pertenue* [3] (Bacterium)
Distribution : the infection occurs in Africa, Asia and South-America. The occurrence follows roughly the equator, with additional pockets in India and South-east Asia [73]
Symptoms : the infection starts with one papule (nipple-like structure) on the skin. The papule disappears, and after a period of weeks to months more papules emerge all over the body [73]. In 10 to 20% of untreated cases large destruction of skin and bones will occur 5 years or more after initial infection [3]. The infection affects mostly children between 2 and 15 years of age [16]
Severity : the disease is rarely fatal, but can be very crippling and disfiguring [3]
Incubation period : 2 to 8 weeks [73]
Duration : the disease will last years, with symptomatic and asymptomatic periods [3]. The effects of the disease can be lasting [73]
Communicability : the papules secrete a liquid which is highly contagious. Communicability will be as long as these papules exist [73]. In the later (destructive) phase of the disease, communicability has usually ceased [3]

Transmission cycle [3]

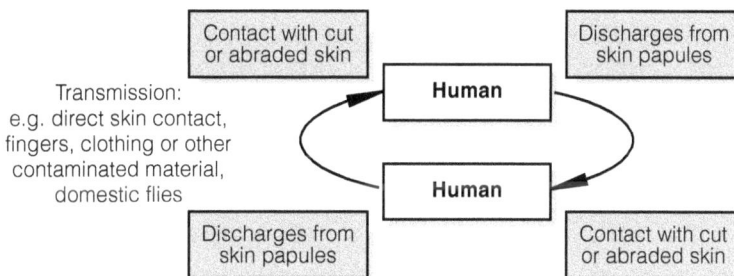

Transmission:
e.g. direct skin contact,
fingers, clothing or other
contaminated material,
domestic flies

Contact with cut or abraded skin — Human — Discharges from skin papules

Discharges from skin papules — Human — Contact with cut or abraded skin

Transmission : the pathogens are found in the liquid which is discharged from the papules. This liquid is highly contagious and infection can occur when it is brought in contact with damaged skin [73]. Transmission occurs either by direct skin contact, by infected material, or domestic flies. The pathogen can not penetrate intact skin [16]
Reservoir : reservoirs are humans and possibly primates [73]
Vector/int. host : domestic flies are possibly a mechanical vector [16]
Water-related : the infection is water-washed [73]
Excreta-related : not directly. Inadequate sanitation can increase the number of domestic flies
Environment : the infection is found in the warm and humid tropics. It is most common in rural areas [16] in large crowded families with poor personal hygiene [73]. In endemic zones infectious yaws is more common in the rainy season [16]
Risk in disaster : the infection will not be a priority in a disaster [3]
Remarks : -

Preventative measures	Potential effect
Improving water availability	(++) [29]
Improving handwashing practise	
Improve hygiene of body and clothes [73]	
Improvement of sanitation (reduction of domestic flies)	
Control of domestic flies [73] (see Annexe 3)	
Infected persons and their contacts should be treated [3]	
Health and hygiene promotion [3]	

Cases and their contacts should be searched for and treated. When the active disease occurs in over 10% of the population, treatment of the entire population is justified [3].

Epidemic measures : provide mass treatment and surveillance [3]

Leprosy, Hansen's disease

An infection which can potentially be very disabling and disfiguring. As the transmission route, and the role water plays in prevention of the infection are not clear, a summary listing is presented.

Pathogen	:	*Mycobacterium leprae* [3] (Bacterium)
Gen. description	:	an infection which occurs in Asia, tropical Africa, and South America [3]. The infection is often asymptomatic. If symptoms develop: nerve and skin damage [2]. Leprosy can result in serious disablement and disfigurement. The incubation period is 1 to 20 years. The infection is associated with poverty, crowding [2], close contact with infected persons [3], and poor personal hygiene [73]
Transmission	:	how transmission occurs is not entirely clear. Probably via close contact with infected persons [3] (50% of the cases have had close contact with an affected person [4]). Nasal discharges could play a role in transmission [3]. If there are more than 10 cases per 10,000 people, leprosy is seen as an important public health problem. Transmission in a population is believed to stop if there are less than 5 cases per 10,000 persons [2]
Reservoir	:	humans, in rare occasions armadillos [2]. *Mycobacterium* appears to be present in soil [4]
Water-related	:	the infection is possibly water-washed [29]
Risk in disaster	:	the treatment of leprosy takes years and should be continuous; disasters can disrupt the treatment scheme [2]
Remarks	:	in 1997 the WHO estimated the number of cases at 1,150,000 [84]

Preventative measures	Potential effect
Improving water availability is mentioned [29]	
Improved hygiene of the body is mentioned [73]	
Active detection of cases and their treatment [3]	
Health and hygiene promotion [3]	

Scabies, Sarcoptic itch, Acariasis

An infection which affects the skin. The disease is linked to poor personal hygiene and crowding. Transmission is through direct contact.

Pathogen	: *Sarcoptes scabiei* [3] (mite) The infection is caused by a mite of 0.3 to 0.4 mm long [16] which makes burrows in the skin [73]
Distribution	: the infection occurs worldwide [47]
Symptoms	: symptoms are small linear burrows dug by the mite [3], raised spots or small blisters on the skin (especially on wrists and hands), and itching [73]. Secondary infections are common [2]. 'Norwegian scabies' is a form of the infection with extensive scaling and crusting [3]. Children are most affected [16]
Severity	: though very uncomfortable, the infection itself is not severe [3]. Complications can be caused by secondary infections though [47]
Incubation period	: 2 to 6 weeks [73] for people infected for the first time. Persons who have been infected before will show symptoms 1 to 4 days after being infected [3]
Duration	: months
Communicability	: the infection is very contagious [47]. The infected person can spread the pathogen until treated successfully [3]

Transmission cycle [3]

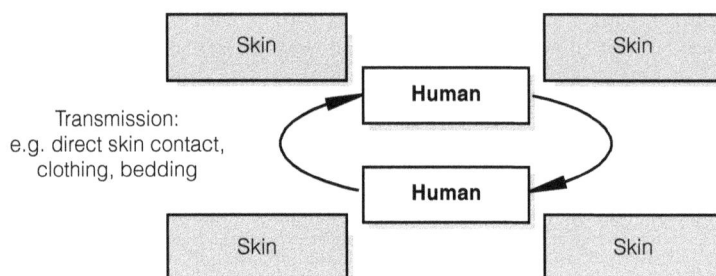

Transmission	: the infection is spread by a fertilised female mite [16]. The skin of an affected person is infective. Direct skin to skin contact will be the most common way of transmission. Transmission through clothing or bedding occurs, but is less common as the mites can only survive for a short period of time outside the human body [4]. An exception is 'Norwegian scabies', where the risk of transmission through clothes and bedding is high. It takes mites 2½ minutes to 'dig' into the skin [3]
Reservoir	: humans are the only reservoir [3]
Vector/int. host	: none
Water-related	: the infection is water-washed [73]
Excreta-related	: no

Environment	: the pathogen is most common in conditions of poverty, overcrowding [3], and poor personal hygiene. The infection occurs in all climates, but is widespread in the tropics [16]
Risk in disaster	: the infection is a potential problem, especially in conditions of overcrowding and poor personal hygiene [47]
Remarks	: A fully developed case of scabies may be infected with as little as 20 adult mites or even less [16]

Preventative measures	Potential effect
Improving water availability	(+++) [29]
Improving hygiene of body, clothes and bedding [73]	
Searching for cases and their contacts and treatment of these [3]	
Health and hygiene promotion [3]	

Treatment of individual cases is not enough, and all contacts (e.g. school, village) should be treated [73]. Where possible, 'Tetmosol soap' should be used [3].

Epidemic measures : mass treatment and health and hygiene promotion [3]. If the infection is an important public health problem distribution of soap may be useful [47]

Annexes

A1

Ringworm, Tinea (capitis, favosa, corporis, barbae), Dermatophytosis, Dermatomycosis

A fungal infection spread by direct and indirect contact.

Pathogen : *Microsporum* spp., *Trichophyton* spp., *Epidermophyton floccosum* [3] (Fungi) [73]

The infection is caused by several fungi (moulds) adapted to live on human skin [16]

Distribution : the infections occur worldwide [3]

Symptoms : asymptomatic infections do occur [44]. Tinea corporis (ringworm) is found on the body, with a growing, ring-shaped mark. Tinea capatis occurs on the scalp in the form of small raised spots [3], scaling, and baldness. Tinea favosa shows as yellowish, cup-like crusts. Tinea barbae occurs on bearded area [44] and results in scaling and baldness [3]

Severity : the infection is not severe

Incubation period : 4 to 14 days [73]

Duration : -

Communicability : as long as symptoms remain [3]

Transmission cycle [3]

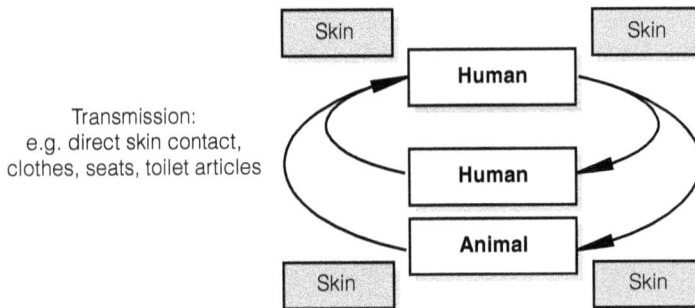

Transmission:
e.g. direct skin contact,
clothes, seats, toilet articles

Transmission : transmission occurs when the skin of a susceptible person comes into contact with the pathogen. Transmission can be direct through skin contact, or indirect through contaminated floors, seats, benches, toilet articles [3], or clothes [73]

Reservoir : reservoirs are humans, dogs, cats, cattle, other animals, and soil. Contaminated material can stay infectious for long periods [3]

Vector/int. host : none

Water-related : the infection is water-washed [73]

Excreta-related : no

Environment : common in most tropical countries. Especially in an environment with high humidity [16] and elevated temperatures [3].

Risk in disaster : the infection is not a priority in disasters [3]

Remarks : -

Preventative measures	Potential effect
Improving water availability	(++) [29]
Improved hygiene of body and clothes [29]	
Care in contact with domestic animals [3]	
Search for cases and treatment [3]	
Health and hygiene promotion [3]	

Epidemic measures : health and hygiene promotion and improvement of personal hygiene [3]

Yellow fever

An infection transmitted by mosquitoes. There are two transmission cycles, the first occurs in the jungle and involves monkeys and forest mosquitoes, people become infected incidentally. The second, epidemic, cycle can occur when infected persons or mosquitoes are introduced in an urban environment.

Pathogen	:	Yellow fever virus [73] (virus)
Distribution	:	sub-Sahara Africa, Southern and Central America [44]. Because of control of *Ae.aegypti*, epidemic urban yellow fever has not occurred in America since decades [16].
Symptoms	:	asymptomatic infections are common, especially where the infection is endemic [16]. Symptoms are fever, headache, backache, nausea, vomiting, and jaundice [3]. In severe cases internal bleedings can occur [73]. In endemic areas the infection occurs mainly in childhood [16]
Severity	:	where the infection is endemic the case fatality rate is under 5% [3]. In epidemics the case fatality rate can be 50% [73]
Incubation period	:	3 to 6 days [73]
Duration	:	a mild attack will last some days. The severe form may last up to 2 weeks [44]
Communicability	:	people are infective for mosquitoes during the first 3 to 5 days of the illness [3]. Lifelong immunity to the pathogen follows after infection [16]. Mosquitoes, once infected, remain infective for life [3]

Transmission cycle [73]

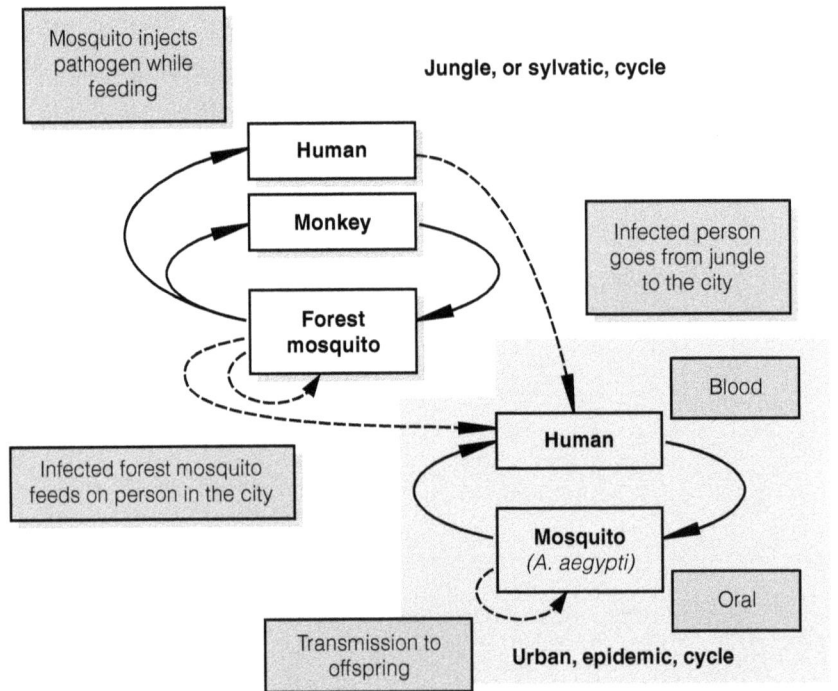

Two transmission cycles exist: the sylvatic cycle and the urban, epidemic, cycle. The sylvatic cycle occurs in the jungle. This cycle involves monkeys and forest mosquitoes. Monkeys are usually not affected by the infection (if monkeys start dying however, it could be an indication that the infection will spread to humans soon) [73]. Man does not play an essential role in the sylvatic cycle [3]. In this cycle people are infected incidentally when they get bitten by infected forest mosquitoes, either because they went into the jungle and got bitten (most common), or because forest mosquitoes leave the jungle [73]. When an infected person goes back to the city, or when infected forest mosquitoes infect someone in the urban environment, the urban, epidemic, cycle can begin. This cycle involves humans and the mosquito *Aedes aegypti* [3]. Large outbreaks can occur where *Aedes aegypti* is found in large numbers with many non-immune persons [16].

Transmission	:	mosquitoes are infected when they feed on the blood of a person or monkey who carries the infection [73]. At 37°C mosquitoes will become infective 4 days after biting an infected person; at 18°C this will be prolonged to 18 days [16]. Transmission to a person occurs through the bite of an infected mosquito [73].
Reservoir	:	monkeys are the reservoir for the rural cycle. The reservoir for the urban cycle are humans [73]. As infected mosquitoes can pass the pathogen to their offspring, they too are a reservoir of the pathogen. This transmission from mosquito to its young ensures that the infection can be passed on between the rainy seasons [83]
Vector/int. host	:	mosquitoes are the vector of the disease: in rural environment in Africa *Aedes* spp. serves as vector; while in America *Aedes* spp. and *Haemagogus* spp. are the main vectors. In urban environment *Aedes aegypti* is the main vector [73]
Water-related	:	the infection is spread by a water-related insect vector [15]
Excreta-related	:	no
Environment	:	the infection occurs in the tropics. In the rural, or sylvatic, cycle the infection is most common in males working in forested areas [3]. By cutting forests man encourages transmission of the infection to humans [16]. Epidemic or urban yellow fever can occur where the mosquito *Aedes aegypti* and enough non-immune people are present. The infection is linked to the rainy season [44]
Risk in disaster	:	the infection could be a problem in disasters [47]
Remarks	:	the WHO estimates that there are 200,000 cases of yellow fever per year resulting in 30,000 deaths [83] One confirmed urban case is considered an outbreak [83] and occurrence of the infection should be notified to the WHO [3].

Preventative measures	Potential effect
Urban epidemic yellow fever:	
Control of *Aedes aegypti* (see Annexe 3)	(+++) [2]
Immunisation [3]	
Patients should be isolated from mosquitoes [16]	
Health and hygiene promotion	
Rural of sylvatic yellow fever:	
Immunisation [3]	
Avoiding being bitten by mosquitoes [3]	
Patients should be isolated from mosquitoes [16]	
Health and hygiene promotion	

To prevent an epidemic, at least 80% of the population must be immunised [83].

Epidemic measures : mass immunisation and vector control [3]

Dengue fever, Dengue haemorrhagic fever, Breakbone fever

A mosquito-borne infection. The infection is seen as the most important Arbovirus (arthropod-borne virus) worldwide and can cause large, explosive outbreaks. Dengue fever is less dangerous than dengue haemorrhagic fever which can have a case fatality rate of 50%.

Pathogen
: Dengue virus [15] (virus)
There are 4 different serotypes of dengue viruses, which can all cause dengue fever and dengue haemorrhagic fever [3].
The cause of dengue haemorrhagic fever is not entirely clear as it is caused by the same viruses as dengue fever. It is believed that the disease occurs as a reaction of the body to a new serotype of dengue virus in people who have been infected with another serotype of virus before [2]

Distribution
: dengue fever occurs more or less worldwide
Dengue haemorrhagic fever occurs in South and South-east Asia, China, India, and Central and South America [3]

Symptoms
: asymptomatic infections are common [47]. Symptoms for dengue fever are fever, headache, severe joint/muscle pain [2], minor bleedings, and skin rashes [3]. In endemic areas the infection affects mostly children [16].
The symptoms of dengue haemorrhagic fever are fever, shock and bleedings [3]. The infection is most frequent in children under 10 years of age [4]

Severity
: Dengue fever is normally not fatal [4]. The disease is usually more severe in adults than in children.
Contrary to dengue fever, dengue haemorrhagic fever is a potentially fatal disease which, if untreated, can have a case fatality rate of up to 50%. With adequate treatment this can be brought down to 1 to 2% [3]

Incubation period
: 3 to 15 days [73]

Duration
: the infection normally lasts for up to some weeks [44]

Communicability
: people can infect mosquitoes as long as fever persists. After infection people become immune to the serotype which infected them, but not to the other serotypes. Mosquitoes, once infected, remain infective for life [3]

Transmission cycle [3]

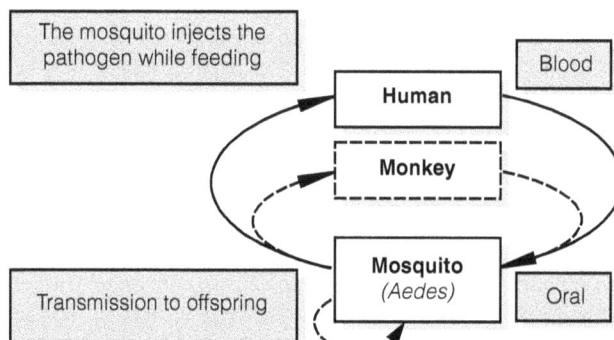

The mosquito injects the pathogen while feeding

Blood

Human

Monkey

Mosquito (*Aedes*)

Oral

Transmission to offspring

Transmission
: Mosquitoes become infective 8 to 12 days after feeding on a person carrying the virus [3]. People are infected through the bite of an infected mosquito [73]. Large, explosive, outbreaks are possible [3]. Especially where *Aedes aegypti*

occurs in urban zones with high population densities [2]. In epidemics attack rates of susceptible people are often 40 to 50%, but can be up to 90% [83]. As there are 4 serotypes of viruses which can all cause epidemics in a population, previous outbreaks do not necessarily mean that the population is immune to the infection [16]

Reservoir : humans are the main reservoir of the pathogen [2]. Monkeys can be reservoirs in South-east Asia and West Africa [3]. It seems that mosquitoes can transmit the pathogen to their offspring, but the role of this in the transmission of the pathogen is not clear [16]

Vector/int. host : Mosquitoes are the vector of the infection. Different species of *Aedes* are vectors, with *Aedes aegypti* being the most important [3]. *Ae.albopictus* and *Ae.scutellaris* are other important vectors of the infection [73]

Water-related : the infection is spread by a water-related insect vector [15]

Excreta-related : no

Environment : transmission occurs throughout the year. In many areas there is an increase of cases in the rainy season [16]. Outbreaks are possible where the vectors are present in a susceptible population. Outbreaks occur as well in urban as in rural environment [3]

Risk in disaster : the infection can be a risk in case of a disaster [47]

Remarks : the WHO estimates the number of cases per year at 50,000,000 [83]. Dengue fever is seen as the most important arthropod-borne viral disease (Arboviral infection) of the moment. It is expected that in the future the number of cases will increase [47]

Preventative measures	Potential effect
Control of *Ae.aegypti* [16] (see Annexe 3)	
Patients should be isolated from mosquitoes [16]	
Health and hygiene promotion [3]	

Epidemic measures : control of mosquitoes [3]

Filariasis, Bancroftian filariasis, Malayan filariasis, Elephantiasis

A mosquito-borne infection. Severe infections can result in elephantiasis.

Pathogen	:	*Wuchereria bancrofti* causes bancroftian filariasis *Brugia Malayi* causes Malayan filariasis [15] (Helminths)
		The worms causing the infections are up to 10 cm long and live in the lymphatic system [2]
Distribution	:	*W.bancrofti* : the infection occurs in Asia, Africa, the Pacific islands, South and Central America [3]
		B.Malayi : the infection can be found in India, South-east Asia and China [15]
Symptoms	:	asymptomatic infections are common [3]. Symptoms are intermittent attacks of fever, enlarged lymph nodes, and swellings that do not recede. Severe cases can develop elephantiasis (permanent enlargement of scrotum, leg, breast, or arm) [2]
Severity	:	the infection is rarely fatal, but can cause severe disability. Malayan filariasis is usually less severe than bancroftian filariasis [2]
Incubation period	:	3 to 12 months [73]
Duration	:	the life span of the worms is up to 12 years [73], but 20 years is mentioned [16]. The disease can cause permanent disfigurement and disablement [2]
Communicability	:	the time the worms continue to shed microfilariae is not clear. Periods mentioned are from 2½ years [73] to 20 years (it is the microfilariae which infect the mosquitoes) [16]

Transmission cycle [73]

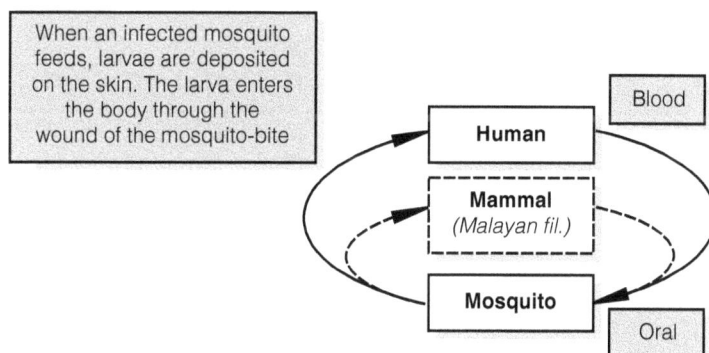

Transmission	:	the worms in the lymphatic system produce microfilariae which are present in the blood of an infected person. When a mosquito ingests microfilariae in a blood meal, it will become infected [73]. The mosquito becomes infective to people from 10 days after the infective blood meal [16] up to 21 days in colder temperatures. When an infected mosquito bites a person, the larva of the worm will emerge and be deposited on the skin. The larva will have to find its way (generally through the wound of the mosquito bite) in the human body. It is estimated that around 15,500 infective bites are needed to result in a reproducing couple of worms [73].

	In general no more than 40 to 50% of the population is infected [16]
Reservoir	: *W.bancrofti* : humans are the only reservoir [3]
	B.Malayi : reservoirs are humans, rodents, monkeys [15], and cats [3]
Vector/int. host	: mosquitoes are the vector of the infection.
	W.bancrofti : in the urban environment the main vector is *Culex quinque-fasciatus* [2]. In rural environment in Asia and Africa *Anopheles* is the main vector. In the South pacific islands *Aedes* is an important vector [16].
	B.Malayi : the main vector is *Mansonia*. In towns *Anopheles* plays a role in transmission [2]. *Aedes* plays a role in the transmission of the infection too [3]
Water-related	: the infection is transmitted by a water-related insect vector [15]
Excreta-related	: *W.bancrofti* : one of the mosquitoes transmitting the infection is an excreta-related insect vector (*Culex quinquefasciatus*) [73]
Environment	: the infection occurs mainly in hot and humid climates [16]. The temperature range for transmission is between 17°C and 32°C, with an optimum of 26°C [73]. Pollution of freshwater and inadequate sanitation are favourable for the urban vector of bancroftian filariasis *Culex quinquefasciatus* [16]
Risk in disaster	: the infection will not be a priority in case of a disaster [3]
Remarks	: it is estimated that 250,000,000 people are infected with *W. bancrofti* worldwide [73]. 90% Of the infections occur in Asia [2]

Preventative measures	Potential effect
Installation of piped water supplies and its adequate maintenance	(+) [29]
Excreta in sanitary structures should be inaccessible to mosquitoes [73] (*C.quinquefasciatus* in bancroftian filariasis)	(+) [73]
Control of mosquitoes which are responsible for transmission [73] (see Annexe 3)	
Mass treatment is the main method of control [73]	
Health and hygiene promotion [3]	

Vector control methods will only show a reduction in infections after 2 to 3 years. Where *Anopheles* is the vector, mosquito control will have to be maintained for 10 years, or mass treatment for at least 5 years, for the infection to disappear.

Where *Culex* is responsible for transmission, control is more difficult. This because *Culex* is more easily infected with the pathogen than *Anopheles*. A limited reduction in exposure to mosquitoes can be effective in reducing infection in a population [73].

Epidemic measures : mass treatment and vector control [16] (it will take time before the effects will show) [3]

Encephalitis (Mosquito-borne arboviral): Japanese encephalitis/ Murray Valley encephalitis/ St. Louis encephalitis/ Rocio encephalitis/ Eastern equine encephalitis/ Western equine encephalitis/ Venezuelan equine encephalitis

A group of mosquito-borne infections. The infections can be severe, and can present as encephalitis.

Pathogen : several arboviruses (arthropod-borne viruses) named after the infection they cause [3]

Distribution : Japanese encephalitis (J.E.): South-east Asia, East Asia, India, Sri Lanka, former USSR [73], and the Pacific islands.
Murray valley encephalitis (M.V.E.): Australia and New Guinea.
St. Louis encephalitis (S.L.E.): Trinidad, Jamaica, Panama, Brazil, and North America.
Rocio encephalitis (R.E.): Brazil [3].
Eastern equine encephalitis (E.E.E.): North America, Central America, South America, and the Caribbean islands.
Western equine encephalitis (W.E.E.): North America, Central America, and South America.
Venezuelan equine encephalitis (V.E.E.): northern South America, Central America, the Caribbean, and the USA [73]

Symptoms : most infections are asymptomatic. In J.E.: 1 infection in 1,000 is symptomatic [44]; E.E.E.: in adults 1 out of 4-50 infections are symptomatic, in children this is 1 out of 2-8; W.E.E. in adult less than 1 in 1,000 infections are symptomatic, in children 1 in 8-50 [16].
Symptoms are headache, high fever, and coma [73]. Severe cases will develop encephalitis [3]

Severity : the case fatality rate for J.E. can be up to 50% [16], M.V.E. up to 60% [73], for E.E.E. it can be 50 to 80% [44], while for W.E.E. the case fatality rate is 10% [16]. Children and older people are most at risk [73]. V.E.E. can be fatal, and the infection is especially dangerous in the malnourished [16]

Incubation period : all infections have incubation periods of 5 to 15 days except for V.E.E. which has an incubation period of 2 to 6 days [3,73]

Duration : V.E.E. usually lasts 3 to 5 days [3]

Communicability : only in V.E.E. will people be infectious to mosquitoes. For all these infections mosquitoes remain infective for life [3]

Transmission cycle [3]

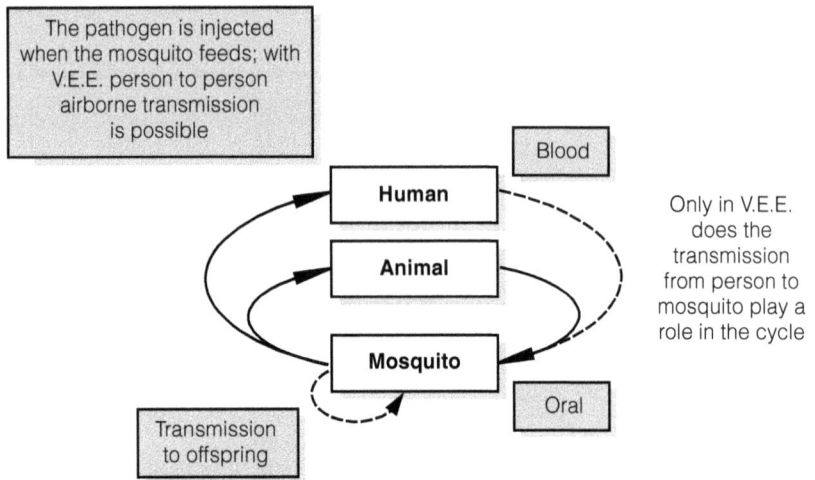

Transmission : mosquitoes are infected by feeding on an infected host, or by receiving the pathogen from their parents [3]. The normal transmission cycles of all these infections are between animals and mosquitoes [2]. Infections in persons are accidental, as are infections in horses for J.E., E.E.E., W.E.E., and V.E.E. [16]. With all infections, except V.E.E., it is unusual that humans (or horses) infect mosquitoes [3]. In J.E. birds can spread the infection from the rural to the urban environment. Human infection occurs if there is a high density of mosquitoes. In W.E.E. outbreaks in horses often precede outbreaks in humans [16].

The pathogens are transmitted to people when an infected mosquito takes a blood meal.

With V.E.E. mosquitoes can be infected by people and horses, and transmission is possible from person to person through air-borne droplets [3]

Reservoir : J.E.: birds and pigs [3]
M.V.E.: birds
S.L..E.: birds
R.E.: not certain, possibly birds [73]
E.E.E.: wild and domestic birds [16] and rodents [73]
W.E.E.: wild and domestic birds [16]
For these infections humans do not play a role as reservoirs. For J.E., E.E.E., and W.E.E. horses can develop the infection, but are not important as reservoir [3].

V.E.E.: mainly rodents. Contrary to the other infections, people and horses do play a role as reservoir for the pathogen for this infection [3]. Over 150 animal species can be infected with the pathogen [16]

Vector/int. host : Mosquitoes are the vectors of the infection.
J.E.: *Culex tritaeniorhynchus* is the main vector of the infection in North Asia and Japan. In the eastern parts of the former USSR the main vector is *C.pipiens*, in Malaysia *C.gelidus*, and in India *C.vishnui* [16]
M.V.E.: *Culex annulirostris*

S.L..E.: *Culex tarsalis*, other species of *Culex*

R.E.: probably mosquitoes [73]

E.E.E.: *Culiseta melanura, c.morsitans, Aedes sollicitans, Ae.taeniorhynchus* [16], and species of *Culex* [73]

W.E.E.: *Culex tarsalis*, and *Culiseta melanura* where *C.tarsalis* does not occur [16]

V.E.E.: species from *Culex, Anopheles* [16], and others [3]

Water-related	: the infection is transmitted by a water-related insect vector [73]
Excreta-related	: some *Culex* spp. are excreta-related insect vectors
Environment	: J.E. is associated to rice fields and to keeping pigs [73]. E.E.E. has been linked to a presence of salt marches and swamps [16]
Risk in disaster	: the infections are probably not a risk in disasters [3]
Remarks	: E.E.E. can cause a high mortality in wild and domestic birds. Most infected horses die within a few days [16]

Preventative measures	**Potential effect**
Control of mosquitoes [3] (see Annexe 3)	
Keeping domestic animals at a distance from living quarters (birds, pigs) [3]	
For J.E. immunisation is possible [47]	
For J.E. immunisation of pigs is a possibility [3]	
For V.E.E. immunisation of horses could be an option [3]	
Health and hygiene promotion [3]	

Epidemic measures : vector control [3]

Arboviral fevers mosquito-borne: Rift valley fever/ West Nile fever/ Bwamba virus disease/ Group C virus fever/ Oropouche virus disease

Mosquito-borne infections. The infections usually present themselves as fevers. Some of these infections can result in outbreaks.

Pathogen	: the infections are caused by arboviruses specific to the infection [3]
Distribution	: Rift valley fever (R.V.F.): Africa [73]
	West Nile fever (W.N.F.): Africa, South-east Asia, and France [2]
	Bwamba virus disease (B.V.D.): Africa
	Group C virus fever (G.C.V.F.): occurs in the tropical parts of South America, Panama, and Trinidad [3]
	Oropouche virus disease (O.V.D.): South America and Trinidad [73]
Symptoms	: asymptomatic infections are common [3]. General symptoms are headache, fever and, malaise [73]. Often a light form of conjunctivitis will occur. Infections of R.V.F. may show eye problems, meningitis, and bleedings [3]. In W.N.F. a skin rash is common; and inflammation of the brain and its membranes (meningoencephalitis) may occur. Meningoencephalitis is possible in O.V.D.. In endemic areas the infections are most common in children [73]
Severity	: variable [3]
Incubation period	: 3 to 12 days [73]
Duration	: usually up to one week [3]
Communicability	: mosquitoes remain probably infected for life [3]

Transmission cycle [3]

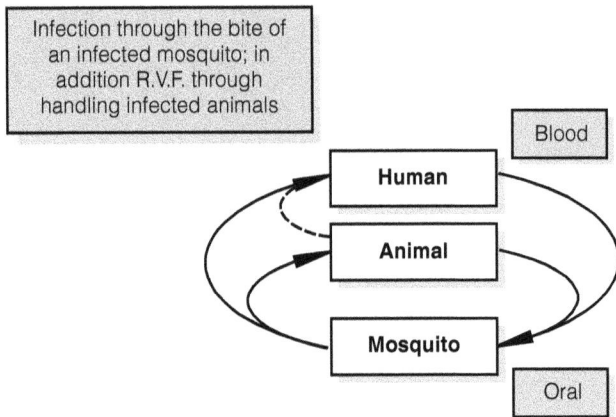

Infection through the bite of an infected mosquito; in addition R.V.F. through handling infected animals

Blood — Human — Animal — Mosquito — Oral

Transmission	: people get infected through the bite of an infective mosquito. R.V.F. and O.V.D. can cause larger outbreaks [3]
Reservoir	: R.V.F.: domestic animals [73] (e.g. sheep) [3]
	W.N.F.: birds [73]
	B.V.D.: unknown
	G.C.V.F.: rodents [3]
	O.V.D.: monkeys, sloths, and birds [73]
Vector/int. host	: the vectors of these infections are mosquitoes: R.V.F.: several species of *Aedes* (*Ae.caballus* [73], *Ae.mcintoshi* [3]), and *Culex* (*C.quinquefasciatus, C.theileri*) [73]

Annexes

A1

W.N.F.: *Culex* spp. [73]
B.V.D.: *Aedes* spp.
G.C.V.F.: species of *Aedes* and *Culex* [3]
O.V.D.: possibly *Culicoides* [73]

Water-related	:	the infections are transmitted by water-related insect vectors [3]
Excreta-related	:	*Culex quinquefasciatus* is an excreta-related insect vector
Environment	:	the infections are most common in rural areas; though outbreaks have occurred in urban areas with R.V.F. and O.V.D.. R.V.F. is often linked to the butchering of infected animals [3]
Risk in disaster	:	usually the infections will not be a risk in disasters [3]
Remarks	:	-

Preventative measures	Potential effect
Control of mosquitoes [3] (see Annexe 3)	
Cases should be isolated from mosquitoes [3]	
For R.V.F.: care should be taken in handling infected animals [3]	
For R.V.F.: sheep, goats and cattle can be immunised [3]	
Health and hygiene promotion [3]	

Epidemic measures : control of mosquitoes; for R.V.F. immunise sheep, goats and cattle [3]

Annexes

A1

Arboviral arthritis mosquito-borne: Chikungunya virus disease/ O'nyong-nyong/ Sindbis virus disease, Ockelbo virus disease/ Mayaro virus disease/ Ross river fever

Mosquito-borne infections. Typical symptoms of these infections are fever and arthritis.

Pathogen : arboviruses specific to the infections [3]

Distribution : Chikungunya virus disease (C.V.D.): Africa, India, Sri Lanka, South-east Asia [73], and the Philippines [3].
O'nyong-nyong (O.N.N.): sub-Saharan Africa [2].
Sindbis virus disease (S.V.D.): throughout the old world and Australia.
Mayaro virus disease (M.V.D.): occurs in the northern parts of South America [3].
Ross river fever (R.R.F): the Pacific islands, Australia and New Zealand [73]

Symptoms : symptoms are fever with arthritis (inflammation of the joints). Skin rashes are common. In India and South-east Asia C.V.D. can cause bleedings [3]

Severity : -

Incubation period : 3 to 12 days [73]

Duration : the arthritis can last days to months [3]

Communicability : mosquitoes are infective for life [2]

Transmission cycle [3]

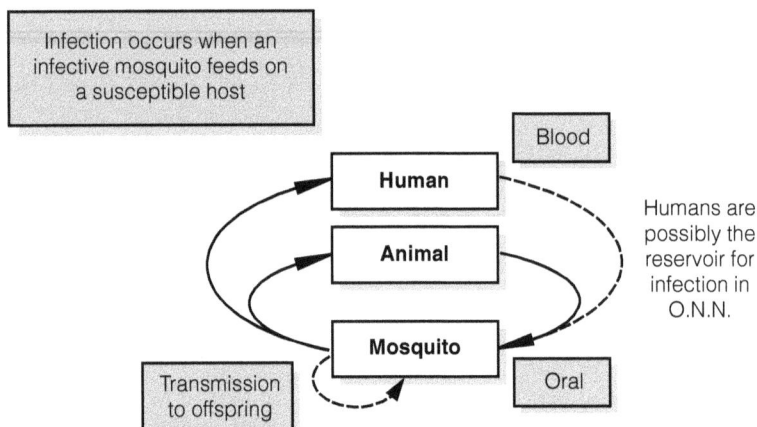

Transmission : mosquitoes either receive the pathogen from their parents, or are infected when feeding on an infected host. People are infected when bitten by an infective mosquito. R.R.F. can cause major outbreaks [3]

Reservoir : C.V.D.: rodents, baboons, monkeys and bats
O.N.N.: possibly humans [73]
S.V.D.: birds [3]
M.V.D.: -
R.R.F.: rodents [73]

with most of these infections mosquitoes can transmit the infections to their offspring, which makes them reservoirs of the pathogens [3]

Vector/int. host	: the vector of these infections are mosquitoes: C.V.D.: *Aedes aegypti, Ae.africanus, Ae.luteocephalus, Culex* spp. [73] O.N.N.: species of *Anopheles* [3] (*A.gambiae, A.funestus*) [73] S.V.D.: *Culex* spp. M.V.D.: *Mansonia* spp. and *Haemagogus* spp. R.R.F.: *Culex annulirostris, Aedes vigilax, Ae.polynesiensis,* and other *Aedes* spp. [3]
Water-related	: the infections are transmitted by water-related insect vectors [3]
Excreta-related	: some may be excreta-related insect vectors
Environment	: where the right mosquito vector is found
Risk in disaster	: these infections will not be a priority in case of a disaster [3]
Remarks	: -

Preventative measures	Potential effect
Control of mosquitoes [3] (see Annexe 3)	
Health and hygiene promotion [3]	

Epidemic measures : control of mosquitoes [3]

Malaria

A mosquito-borne infection. Every year an estimated 300,000,000 cases occur [73]. Large outbreaks are possible in non-immune populations.

Pathogen : *Plasmodium falciparum (P.falc.), Plasmodium vivax (P.viv.), Plasmodium malariae (P.mal.),* and *Plasmodium ovale (P.oval.)* (protozoa) [73]

Distribution : *P.falc.:* worldwide in the tropics and subtropics [3].

P.viv.: worldwide in temperate zones, the subtropics, and the tropics [73]. The infection is rare in sub-Sahara Africa [16].

P.mal.: in most areas where malaria occurs [16]. The pathogen is most common in Africa [44].

P.oval.: rare outside West Africa [16]

Symptoms : where malaria is common, people will have built a resistance to the pathogen, and many infections will be light or asymptomatic. Some of the general symptoms of a malaria attack are shivering, peaks of fever, anaemia, enlarged spleen, and jaundice.

P.falc. can cause severe jaundice, delirium, convulsions [2], shock, and coma. Infections of *P.viv., P.mal.,* and *P.oval.* show recurrent peaks in fever with 1,2, or 3 day intervals [3].

If untreated, relapses can occur. Attacks of *P.falc.* can reoccur in the year following the initial infection. Relapses are possible for over 30 years with *P.mal.*. Relapses of *P.viv.* and *P.oval.* may occur for up to 5 years, even if the infection was treated [2]

Severity : attacks of *P.falc.* are usually the most severe, and almost all deaths and severe illnesses are caused by this pathogen [16]. Most at risk are young children who have not yet developed an immunity, pregnant women, and non-immune people [73]. In non-immune persons the case fatality rate for *P.falc.* is over 10% [3]. Severe disease with *P.viv., P.mal.,* and *P.oval.* are unusual [16]; still, fatal infections can occur in weakened people [3]

Incubation period : *P.falc.:* 7 to 14 days [3].

P.viv.: 12 to 17 days. In temperate climates the incubation period may be prolonged to up to 9 months.

P.mal.: 18 to 40 days [73].

P.oval.: usually 8 to 14 days. The incubation period may be delayed with 10 months or longer [3]

Duration : usually the illness will last for one week to one month. Relapses can occur though [3], especially if the infection was not treated [2]

Communicability : mosquitoes can be infected by humans for a relatively long period if the infection was not treated: *P.falc.* for up to 1 year, *P.viv.* for 1 to 2 years, *P.mal.* for up to 3 years. Mosquitoes remain infective for life [3]

Transmission cycle [73]

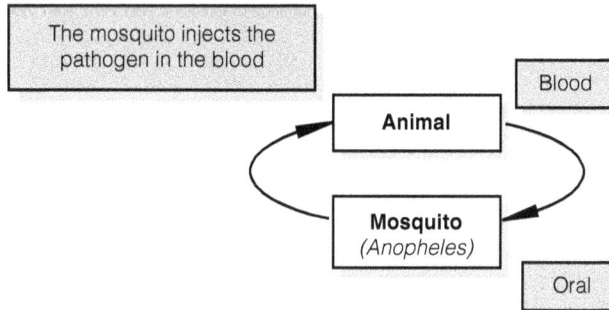

Transmission	: *Anopheles* mosquitoes pick the pathogen up when feeding on an infected person. The time it takes before the mosquito becomes infective varies with temperature. The colder the environment, the longer the mosquito takes to become infective:

Transmission : *Anopheles* mosquitoes pick the pathogen up when feeding on an infected person. The time it takes before the mosquito becomes infective varies with temperature. The colder the environment, the longer the mosquito takes to become infective:

P.falc. takes 9 days at 30°C and 20 days at 20°C.

P.viv. takes 7 days at 30°C and 16 days at 20°C.

P.mal. takes 15 days at 30°C and 30 days at 20°C.

This should be compared to the average life expectancy of a mosquito which is shorter than 30 days [73].

A person is infected when bitten by an infective mosquito.

People will build up a resistance to severe malaria if they are regularly exposed [2]. Where transmission rates of *P.falc.* are high, local adults will never develop severe malaria. Where transmission rates are lower, severe illness will occur at all ages [16]. The immunity which is built up will be lost in some years if the individual does not come into contact with the pathogen during this time [2]. If transmission is possible all year round, endemic malaria will occur. If transmission is only possible every few years (e.g. because of exceptional climatic circumstances), there will be a large risk of outbreaks [73]

Reservoir : people are the only important reservoir for malaria [3]

Vector/int. host : the vectors of the infection are *Anopheles* mosquitoes [3].

How effective the mosquito is in transmitting the pathogen depends on its length of survival, its preferred source of blood (only man, or preferably animal and incidentally man) and other factors. All anopheles feed at night-time, making this the dangerous period. Mosquitoes can adapt to long-term changes in environment, like lighting and use of insecticides [73].

Water-related : malaria is transmitted by a water-related insect vector [73]

Excreta-related : no

Environment : transmission occurs only at temperatures between 16°C and 33°C and at altitudes below 2,000 metres [16]. Temperatures below which the pathogen can not be maintained: *P.falc.* below 19°C, *P.viv.* below 17°C, *P.mal.* below 20°C [73]. High humidity is favourable to the vector. Malaria is often a seasonal infection with a peak in the rainy season. If the rains are too intense the number of mosquitoes will reduce though. Transmission of malaria is influenced by many factors related to the population, the vectors, and the environment. Changes in use of land and deforestation can have important effects on transmission [16]

Risk in disaster : the infection is a risk in case of disasters [3]

Remarks : every year an estimated 3,000,000 people are killed by malaria [73]. Most of these deaths are children in Africa. The number of cases of malaria in the world is increasing [16]. *P.falc.* has in many areas built up a resistance to commonly used anti-malarial drugs [44].

Preventative measures	Potential effect
Installing piped water and maintenance of the system	(+) [29]
Control of mosquitoes (see Annexe 3)	(+++) [47]
Health and hygiene promotion [73]	

The most effective measures of vector control will depend on the mosquitoes which transmit malaria, the environment in which transmission occurs, and the population affected. A good understanding of the local circumstances will be needed to plan an appropriate mosquito control programme [73].

Epidemic measures : vector control and treatment of cases [3]

Trypanosomiasis (African), Sleeping sickness

Infections transmitted by the tsetse fly. Two types of infections exist, a more chronic infection which is found in tropical western and Central Africa, and an acute infection found in tropical eastern and southern Africa. Both infections will lead to death if untreated.

Pathogen	:	*Trypanosoma brucei gambiense* (*T.b.gam.*) and *Trypanosoma brucei rhodesiense* (*T.b.rhod.*) [3] (Protozoa)
Distribution	:	*T.b.gam.*: occurs usually in tropical western and Central Africa [3]. *T.b.rhod.*: is found in tropical eastern and southern Africa [2]
Symptoms	:	*T.b.gam.* is a more chronic disease than *T.b.rhod.*, which is an acute infection [73]. Sometimes there is a boil resulting from an inflammation at the site of the bite (less common in *T.b.gam.*). Symptoms of *T.b.gam.* are fever, enlarged lymph glands, change in behaviour, restlessness followed by almost continuous sleeping, coma, and death. *T.b.rhod.* shows similar symptoms, but evolves much quicker [2]
Severity	:	with both infections the host will die of the illness if not treated [3]
Incubation period	:	*T.b.gam.*: several months to years. *T.b.rhod.*:3 days to some weeks [3]
Duration	:	*T.b.gam.*: sometimes the infected person dies after a short period [2], but usually death comes after years [47] *T.b.rhod.*: death will follow in weeks to months [44]
Communicability	:	as long as the pathogen can be found in the blood, the fly can become infected when feeding on a host. The fly becomes infective 12 to 30 days after the infective bite. The tsetse fly remains infective for life [3]

Transmission cycle [3,73]

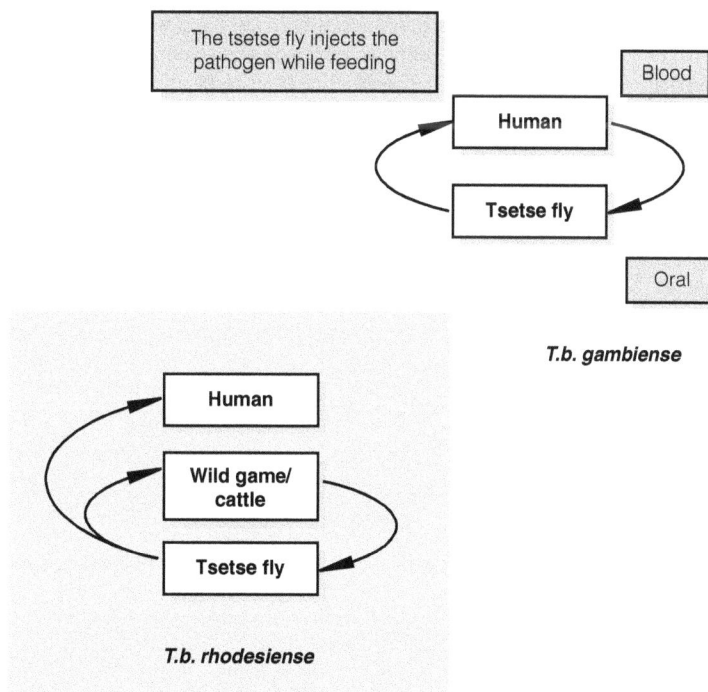

T.b. gambiense

T.b. rhodesiense

Annexes

A1

Transmission : when a tsetse fly feeds on an infected person or animal, it can become infected. When the fly feeds on a susceptible person, the pathogen will be transmitted [73].

In endemic regions 0.1 to 2% of the population can be infected. In epidemics this can be up to 70%. Outbreaks can occur when infected persons or flies move into a new zone, or when contact between humans and tsetse flies is intensified [3]. Outbreaks in *T.g.rhod.* are less common [2], but an indication that one is developing is when children and women start being affected [73].

Reservoir : *T.b.gam.*: humans are the main reservoir. Pigs and other animals are possible reservoirs, but their role in transmission is minor [2].

T.b.rhod.: the normal reservoir are wild game and cattle. Humans are less important as reservoirs [3]

Vector/int. host : the vector for the infections is the tsetse fly (*Glossina* spp.) [3].

T.b.gam.: is transmitted by tsetse flies which breed and live in forest which edges rivers; the riverine tsetse flies of the *Glossina palpalis* group [2]. People or animals coming close to the river are attacked.

T.b.rhod.: is transmitted by tsetse flies that move in open forest and savannah; mainly *Glossina morsitans*, which are not confined to water.

The percentage of infected flies is usually small [73]

Water-related : *T.b.gam.* has a water-related insect vector [16]

Excreta-related : no

Environment : *T.b.gam.*: is usually linked to rivers (water collection points, washing sites, river crossings) [16], or lakes. The flies occur in forest galleries (up to 20 metres from the river banks) along rivers, streams or lakes [2]. Women are often most affected because of their contact to this zone (e.g. washing clothes) [73]. Transmission occurs particularly at the end of the dry season.

T.b.rhod.: is linked to open forest and savannah [16]. Most affected are people who are in contact with forest and savannah; usually men who work there [73]

Risk in disaster : the infection could be a problem when people move into a place where the vector and the pathogen are present [73]

Remarks : the total number of cases of African trypanosomiasis (*T.b.gam.* and *T.b.rhod.* totalled) is estimated at 20,000 to 50,000 per year [16]

Preventative measures	Potential effect
Reducing the need for people to come in contact with the river (install a convenient alternative source of water). Only effective against *T.b.gam.*	(+++) [29]
Active search for cases and their treatment [2] This is more effective in outbreaks of *T.b.gam.* than in outbreaks of *T.b.rhod.* as the infection is less acute	(++) [2]
Control of tsetse flies (see Annexe 3)	
Health and hygiene promotion [47]	

Epidemic measures : active case finding and treatment, and control of tsetse flies [3]

Leishmaniasis cutaneous and muco-cutaneous (Oriental sore)/ Visceral leishmaniasis (Kala-azar)

Infections transmitted by sandflies.

Pathogen	:	*Leishmania* spp. [3] (Protozoa)
		Different species of *Leishmania* will cause different types of leishmaniasis. The types of leishmaniasis are cutaneous leishmaniasis (cut.l.), muco-cutaneous leishmaniasis (muc.l) and visceral leishmaniasis (vis.l.) [73]
Distribution	:	cut.l.: Africa, South and Central America, southern Europe, Middle-East to India [73], and China [3].
		muc.l.: Central and South America [73].
		vis.l.: Africa, India, Bangladesh, Pakistan, South and Central America, China, southern Europe, and the southern parts of ex-USSR [2]
Symptoms	:	cut.l.:a papule which turns into an ulcer [3].
		muc.l.: the disease evolves out of cutaneous leishmaniasis [3] and affects the mucous membranes in the nose [73].
		vis.l.: fever, sweating, enlargement of spleen and liver, anaemia [2], and progressive weakness [3]
Severity	:	cut.l. and muc.l.: the infections can result in disfigurement [73].
		vis.l.: has a case fatality rate of 90% if not treated. If treated, the case fatality rate drops to below 10% [4]
Incubation period	:	cut.l. and muc.l. : have an incubation period of one week to months.
		vis.l.: the incubation period is usually 2 to 6 months [3], but can be anything between 2 weeks and years [2]
Duration	:	cut.l. and muc.l.: the infection can last for years [3,73]
		vis.l.: persons can survive for over 2 years [2]
Communicability	:	untreated persons can be infective to sandflies for up to 2 years, or as long as the infection lasts [3]

Transmission cycle [3]

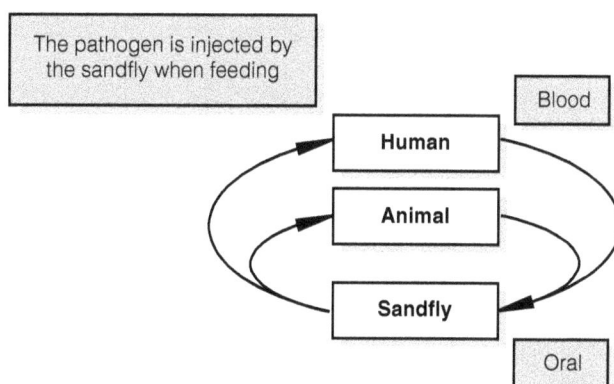

Transmission	:	the sandfly takes up the pathogen when feeding on an infected animal or person. It takes a minimum of 8 days for the sandfly to become infective [3]. A person will be infected by the bite of an infective sandfly. Sandflies usually bite in the period between dusk and dawn [2], or in shady or overcast conditions [73].
		The infection is usually sporadic [73] but outbreaks do occur [2]

Reservoir	: reservoirs are humans, rodents, dogs, jackals, foxes [73], and sloths [3]. The importance of the reservoir in the transmission cycle varies from region to region [2]
Vector/int. host	: the vector of the infection is the sandfly; in Africa, Asia and Europe: *Phlebotomus* spp., in South and Central America: *Lutzomyia* spp.. Adult sandflies live for around 2 weeks. Sandflies stay low to the ground, and can not fly in windy conditions [73]. Sandflies breed in moist and dark places (like cracks in masonry, caves, termite mounds, rubble) [2]. Usually they will not be found more than 200 m from their breeding place [2], but wind can take them further [16]
Water-related	: no
Excreta-related	: no
Environment	: the infection is more linked to a rural environment than to an urban environment. In Central and South America the disease is connected to people working or living in forested areas [3]
Risk in disaster	: can be a problem if a population enters an endemic region [47]
Remarks	: Every year there are an estimated 1,500,000 cases of cutaneous leishmaniasis and 500,000 cases of visceral leishmaniasis [85]

Preventative measures	Potential effect
Adequate solid waste management (in Africa, Asia and Europe) [3]	
Control of sandflies [3] (see Annexe 3)	
Control of reservoir animal (dog, rodents) [3]	(+++) [16,73]
Systematic case finding and treatment	(+++) [16]
Health and hygiene promotion [3]	

Sandflies are very susceptible to residual insecticides.
Like other vector-borne infections, occurrence of leishmaniasis in the population is the result of a dynamic interaction between persons, vectors, reservoir animals, and the environment. Control of the disease by active case finding and treatment has been very effective in some areas, and unsuccessful in others [16]. Control of dogs or rodents have proven very effective in some places [3,73], but may be inappropriate in others. A good understanding of the dynamics of transmission will be needed before effective control of the infection is possible.

Epidemic measures : treatment of cases, and control of sandflies and animal reservoirs [3]

Bartonellosis, Oroya fever, Verruga peruana, Carrión disease

An infection transmitted by sandflies. The infection occurs in Colombia, Peru, and Ecuador in mountain valleys. The infection has two distinctive forms.

Pathogen : *Bartonella bacilliformis* [3] (Bacterium)

Gen. information : the infection occurs in Colombia, Peru and Ecuador [16] in mountain valleys of the Andes [3] at altitudes between 800 and 3,000 metres above sea level. The infection is most common between January and April [16]. Asymptomatic infections do occur. The illness is milder in children than in adults [3].
The disease can show itself in two distinctive forms. Oroya fever, with as symptoms malaise, anaemia, and severe pains in head, joints, and bones [16]. The case fatality rate of Oroya fever is 10 to 90% [3]. The other form is Verruga peruane, which often follows Oroya fever. The symptoms are severe pains, fever, and eruptions of the skin [16]. Verruga peruane is rarely fatal [3]. The two forms of disease can occur at the same time [16]. The incubation period is usually 16 to 22 days [73], but can be as much as 4 months. People can be infective to sandflies for years [3]

Transmission cycle [3]

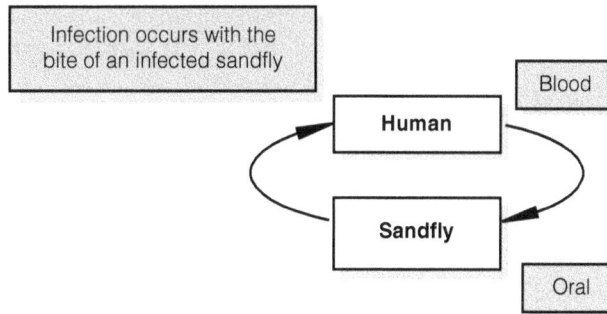

Infection occurs with the bite of an infected sandfly

Human

Blood

Sandfly

Oral

Transmission : the sandflies are infected when biting a person carrying the pathogen. The pathogen is transmitted when the sandfly feeds on a person [3]. Outbreaks of the infection can occur [16]

Reservoir : humans are the only reservoir. Where the infection is endemic, 5% of the population may be asymptomatic carrier of the pathogen [3].

Vector/int. host : the vector of the infection is the sandfly (*Lutzomyia* spp.). The flies feed at night [16]

Risk in disaster : could be a problem if people are placed in an endemic area [16]

Preventative measures	Potential effect
Avoiding endemic areas at night [3]	
Control of sandflies [3] (see Annexe 3)	
Infected persons should be isolated from sandflies [3]	
Health and hygiene promotion	

Epidemic measures : search for cases and control of sandflies [3]

Arboviral fevers sandfly-borne: Sandfly fever, Phlebotomus fever/ Changuinola virus disease/ Vesicular stomatitis virus disease

Infections transmitted by sandflies. The illnesses last only some days and are not fatal. Outbreaks are possible if non-immune people enter endemic areas.

Pathogen : several arboviruses [3]

Gen. description : the infections occur in the Mediterranean, the Middle-east [16], Africa, Asia towards Myanmar and China, and Central and South America. They can be found in the (sub)tropics with hot and dry seasons [3]. The infections occur in the warm period [45]. The incubation period is 3 to 6 days [73], and the period of illness usually last 2 to 4 days [44]. Symptoms are fever, malaise, nausea, headache, and pains in limbs and back. The local population is relatively resistant to the infections [3]. The infections are not fatal [16]

Transmission cycle [3]

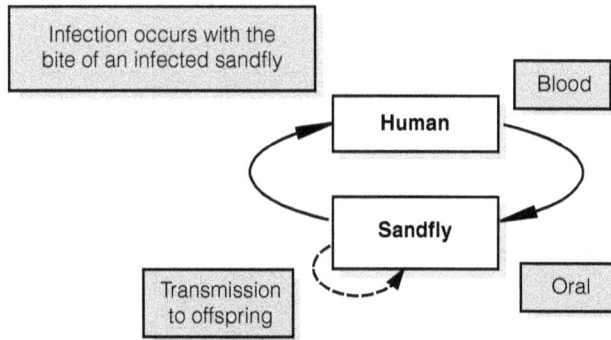

Transmission : sandflies are infected either through biting an infected person, or by receiving the infection from its parents [16]. Sandflies become infective one week after biting an infected person. People are infected by the bite of an infective sandfly [3]. Outbreaks can occur when non-immune people enter into an endemic area [16]

Reservoir : the main reservoirs are humans and sandflies. Sandflies can transmit the pathogens to their offspring [16]. Rodents can be potential reservoirs [3]

Vector/int. host : the main vector is the common sandfly (*Phlebotomus papatasi*). This sandfly bites at night. The sandfly *Sergentomyia* spp. is a probable vector. In Central and South America the vectors are sandflies belonging to *Lutzomyia*. Sandflies remain infective for life (up to one month) [3]

Preventative measures	Potential effect
Adequate solid waste management (in Africa, Asia and Europe) [3]	
Control of sandflies [3] (see Annexe 3)	
Health and hygiene promotion	

Epidemic measures : control of sandflies and health and hygiene promotion [3]

Onchocerciasis, River blindness

An infection transmitted by blackflies. The infection is associated with fast-flowing rivers. The pathogen can cause blindness. The socio-economic consequences of the disease are important as it has pushed people to abandon fertile areas.

Pathogen : *Onchocerca volvulus* [15] (Helminth)
The worms are up to 50 cm long and live under the skin, either free-living or in nodules [2]

Distribution : the infection occurs in tropical Africa, southern Mexico, Guatemala, Venezuela, Colombia, Ecuador, Brazil, and Yemen [3]. More than 95% of the cases occur in Africa, and over 30% in Nigeria [16]

Symptoms : adult worms will usually not cause any symptoms other than creating nodules. It is the microfilariae shed by the worms which cause symptoms. Mild infections may be asymptomatic. Symptoms are itching and skin rash; heavy infections will lead to loss of pigment and loss of elasticity of skin [2]. Infections can result in blindness, but this may take up to 20 to 30 years before it occurs. Not every case will develop damage to the eye [44].
Men in working age are most affected [16]

Severity : the infection can cause blindness [3]

Incubation period : 6 to 12 months [73]

Duration : worms can survive for up to 20 years [2]

Communicability : man can be infective to the blackfly for up to 15 years [3]

Transmission cycle [73]

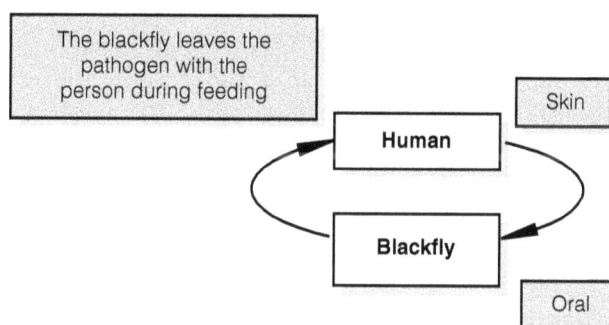

Transmission : the adult worms shed microfilariae which are found in the skin of the host. When blackflies feed on a person microfilariae will infect the vector [3]. It will take around 7 days before the fly will become infective to humans [16]. When an infective fly feeds on a person infection can take place [3]

Reservoir : humans are the only reservoir of importance [3]

Vector/int. host : the vector of the infection is the blackfly (*Simulium* spp.) [73]. The flies lay their eggs in fast-flowing, oxygenated rivers (turbulent, 'white' rivers). And can travel long distances, normally 5 to 10 km from the river. The chances of being bitten are largest close to breeding sites. The flies feed at dusk and dawn [16]

Water-related : the infection is transmitted by a water-related insect vector

Excreta-related : no

Environment   : close to turbulent streams. During the rainy season flies may search for new sites to breed. In the dry season they stay close to permanent streams [16]

Risk in disaster   : the infection will not be a priority in a disaster [3]

Remarks   : it is estimated that around 18,000,000 people are infected, with around 360,000 people permanently blinded by the disease. Up to 15% of the population living near fast flowing rivers may be infected [16]. The disease has a big socio-economic impact on society as it has often pushed people to abandon fertile soils [3].

Preventative measures	Potential effect
Supply the population with an alternative source of water (avoid contact to river)	(+) [29]
Control of blackflies [73] (see Annexe 3)	
Search for cases and treatment [3]	
Health and hygiene promotion [3]	

As the blackfly can travel great distances (up to 80 km in a day), control measures using chemical vector control will need to cover large areas and be conducted over longer periods to have a lasting effect [2,16].

Epidemic measures : treatment of cases, control of blackflies [3]

Annexes

A1

Loiasis, Loa loa infection, Eye worm disease, Calabar swelling

A mild infection transmitted by tabanid flies. The public health importance of the pathogen is limited.

Pathogen : *Loa loa* [15] (Helminth)

Gen. description : loiasis is an infection caused by 30 to 70 mm long worms which live under the skin [2]. The infection is found in West and Central Africa [73]. The infection is relatively mild [2], with usual symptoms being localised itching and transient swellings ('Calabar swelling') [3]. Occasionally the worm can be seen passing through the eye under the conjunctiva (which is harmless) [73]. The incubation period is usually years, but can be 4 months [3]. Worms can survive in the body for 17 years or more [16], and can be infective for *Chrysops* for the same time [3]

Transmission cycle [3]

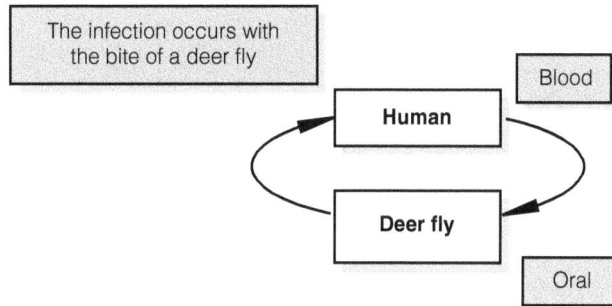

Transmission : *Chrysops* is infected when it feeds on the blood of a person carrying microfilariae shed by a fertilised worm. After 10 to 12 days the fly becomes infective to humans. Human infection occurs when the pathogens enter the body through a bite of the fly [3]

Reservoir : humans are the only reservoir [3]

Vector/int. host : the vector of the pathogen is the tabanid fly [73] or deer fly (*Chrysops* spp.) [3]. Breeding sites of the flies are linked to forest streams. Biting will generally be within 200 m of the breeding site. The flies attack during the day but not in the open sun [2]

Water-related : the vector is a water-related insect vector [2]

Environment : it is a rural disease [73], occurring in rain forests, or swamp forest areas [16]

Remarks : In some villages in the Congo River basin up to 90% of the population is infected with the pathogen [3]

Preventative measures	Potential effect
Control of the flies (chemical vector control is usually not efficient, control by avoidance of the flies is more effective) [3,16]	
Health and hygiene promotion [3]	

Trypanosomiasis (American), Chagas disease

An infection spread by reduviid bugs. The infection is associated with poor quality housing (poverty). The pathogen only occurs in Central and South America. The disease commonly results in disability and death.

Pathogen	: *Trypanosoma cruzi* [15] (Protozoon)
Distribution	: Central and South America [73]
Symptoms	: asymptomatic infections are common [2]. Symptoms are fever, malaise, affected lymph system, and enlarged liver and spleen [3]. Many people will initially not show any symptoms, but will develop complications years after the infective bite occurred [2]
Severity	: the infection commonly results in disability or death [73]
Incubation period	: 5 to 14 days [3]
Duration	: the duration of the infection is variable; months to years [44]
Communicability	: as long as the infection lasts the bug can take up the pathogen. Infected bugs remain infective for life. The bugs can live for up to 2 years [3]

Transmission cycle [3]

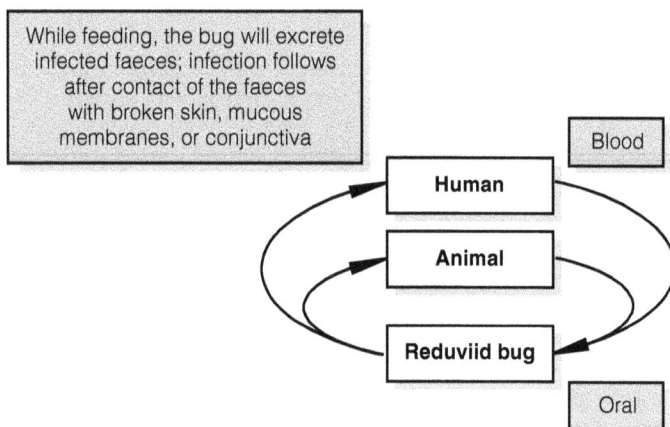

While feeding, the bug will excrete infected faeces; infection follows after contact of the faeces with broken skin, mucous membranes, or conjunctiva

Blood

Human

Animal

Reduviid bug

Oral

Transmission	: A bug becomes infected when feeding on a host. The reduviid bug will become infective to people 10 to 30 days after biting the host. When feeding, the bug will excrete, and it is in these excreta that the pathogens are found. Infection occurs when the excreta of the infected bug come in contact with broken skin (e.g. the bite wound), mucous membranes, or conjunctiva [3]. It is possible that excreta from bugs are infective when ingested [73], this route of transmission will not be very common though
Reservoir	: reservoirs are humans and many wild or domestic animals. Dogs can introduce the pathogen from the 'wild cycle' which occurs outside the house to the 'domestic cycle' which occurs inside the house. In Central America the rat is an important reservoir [73]. In Argentina goats may play a role in transmission. Animals which can be infected, but whose role in the transmission cycle are limited, are cats, pigs, cattle, and horses [16]

Vector/int. host	: the vector is the reduviid bug (*Reduviidae* spp.), also called kissing bug or assassin bug [2]. The bugs live in rural (poor) houses; cracked mud walls and thick palm roofs are ideal hiding places [16]. One single hut may contain thousands of reduviid bugs [2]
Water-related	: no
Excreta-related	: no
Environment	: the infection is linked to poverty [73]. The quality of the housing and the presence of bugs are related. Walls with cracks, thatched roofs [16], and reservoir animals living in or close to the house [73] are all risk factors
Risk in disaster	: the infection will normally not be a priority in disasters [3]
Remarks	: it is estimated that 10,000,000 people are infected with the pathogen [44]

Preventative measures	Potential effect
Control of reduviid bugs [3] (see Annexe 3)	
Control of reservoir animals living close to man (dogs, rats) [73]	
Adapt housing of people [2]	
Health and hygiene promotion [3]	

Epidemic measures : control of reduviid bugs and reservoir animals [3]

Plague, Yersinia pestis

A flea-borne infection. The disease is severe, and outbreaks can occur. In many regions the disease is naturally present in a wild rodent–flea cycle, where this cycle is disturbed, people can get infected.

Pathogen : *Yersinia pestis* [3] (Bacterium)
Distribution : southern, eastern, and western Africa, Asia, South America, USA [73]
Symptoms : asymptomatic infections do occur. Different forms of plague exist [47]:
Bubonic plague (Bub.P.): fever, chills, pains in muscles, formation of bubo (inflamed lymph nodes) which swell, are tender, and may burst and discharge pus [3]. 90% Of the cases with plague will develop this type of infection [16]. About 5% of those who develop Bub.P. will progress into pneumonic plague [73].

Pneumonic plague (Pne.P.): affects the lungs.
Septicemic plague (Sep.P.): can evolve out of other types of infections, the infection affects other organs through blood [3]
Severity : Bub.P. :
has a case fatality rate of 50 to 60% [3]; with adequate treatment this can be reduced to below 5% [4].
Pne.P. and Sep.P. are always fatal if untreated [47]
Incubation period : 1 to 7 days [3]
Duration : death follows after some days in Pne.P. and Sep.P. [73]
Communicability : pus coming out of bubo is infective. Fleas can remain infective for months [3]

Transmission cycle [3,73]
Transmission : the normal transmission cycle takes place between wild resistant rodents

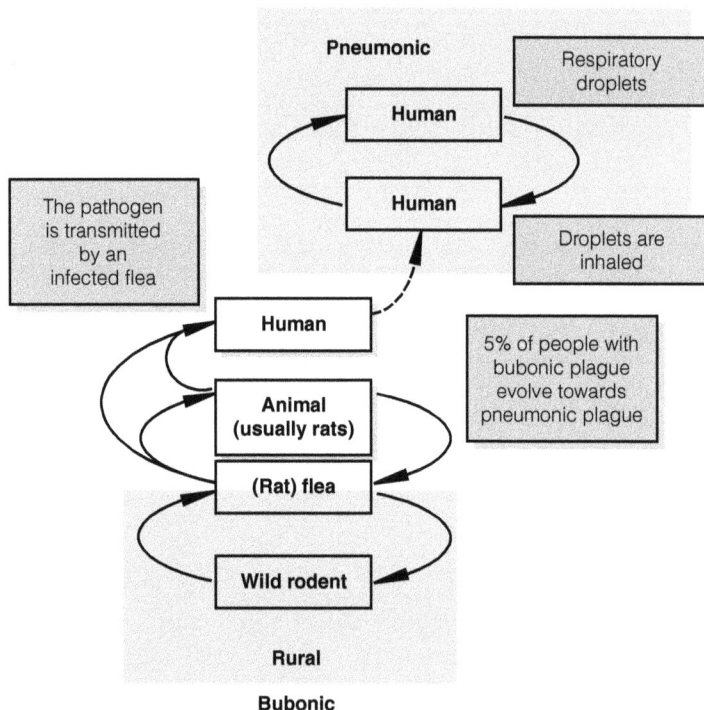

and fleas, this is the sylvatic or rural cycle [3]. When domestic rats enter into this cycle, infected fleas can colonise them. As these rats are less resistant to the infection than wild rodents, they will die, leaving the fleas without a source of food [73] (a sudden die-off of domestic rats can be an indication that a human outbreak is going to occur) [16]. Domestic rats live normally close to humans, and the infective fleas will search for new sources of blood, transmitting the infection to people when feeding on them [73].

Domestic animals may take wild rodent fleas into the human environment [3]. Another way of transmitting the infection is through direct contact with body tissues of infected animals [3]. Pne.P. can be spread through air-borne transmission and is highly contagious [47]

Reservoir : the domestic black rat (*Rattus rattus*) and the brown sewer rat (*R.norvegicus*) are the main reservoirs which transmit the infection to humans [16]. Other animals which can play a role as reservoir are mice, other rodents, dogs, camels, monkeys, rabbits [73], cats, and wild carnivores [3]. Over 340 animal species can be infected with the pathogen [73].

The pathogen can survive for months in the cool, damp environment of animal burrows. In dry conditions they may survive for a few days, but longer in dried blood or secretions. They are killed after being for 15 minutes at 56°C or by being exposed to direct sunlight for 4 hours [16]

Vector/int. host : fleas are the vector of the infection. The most important is *Xenopsylla cheopsis* (a rat flea) [3], though *X.brasiliensis* and *X.astia* are implied too [73]. In the Andes region in South America the human flea (*Pulex irritans*) plays a role in transmission [3].

Water-related : the infection is water-washed [73]

Excreta-related : no

Environment : presence of the pathogen in the rural cycle is obviously a risk factor [73]. The infection is more likely to occur in rural areas. Crowding and unhygienic conditions are risk factors, as are occupations like hunting or trapping [3]. The disease is associated with war and civil disturbance [73]. Most cases occur in the warm and dry season [16]

Risk in disaster : the infection is a risk where the disease is endemic, in conditions of overcrowding and poor environmental hygiene [3]

Remarks : the infection should be notified to the WHO [3]. Sporadic cases in endemic areas do not necessarily indicate an outbreak. The pathogen occurs in the rural cycle between wild rodents and fleas in many regions. In some of these regions, humans are not infected while in others outbreaks have occurred [73]

Preventative measures	Potential effect
Improving water availability	$(++)$ [29]
Improving hygiene of body and clothes [73]	
Control of fleas [47] (see Annexe 3)	
When dealing with refugees or displaced people, new arrivals should be dusted against fleas (people and their luggage) [47]	
Cases and contacts of cases should be dusted with insecticide against fleas [47]	
Control of rats (after successful flea control! If rats carrying infected fleas are killed, the disease can spread easily to people) [73] (see Annexe 3)	
Improving solid waste management and storage of food (rat control) [3]	
Care in handling dead animals that could be infected [3]	
People or animals that died or are suspected to have died of plague should be buried or burnt, and handled in a safe way [73]	
Persons with pneumonic plague should be strictly isolated [3]	
Contacts of people with pneumonic plague should receive treatment [47]	
Workers at risk should be protected against fleas [3]	
Health and hygiene promotion [73]	

Epidemic measures : search for cases and treat them, health and hygiene promotion, flea control, control of rats after successful control of fleas, protection and/or treatment of contacts, protection of workers against fleas [3]

Typhus (murine) fever, Flea-borne typhus, Endemic typhus fever

A flea-borne infection which should not be confused with epidemic louse-borne typhus fever or scrub typhus. The infection is generally endemic, and has a low mortality.

Pathogen	:	*Rickettsia mooseri* [73] (Rickettsia)
Distribution	:	the pathogen is found worldwide [3]

Symptoms	:	fever, rash [73], headache, and chills [3]
Severity	:	the case fatality rate is 1% to 2% [16]
Incubation period	:	1 to 2 weeks [73]
Duration	:	the illness lasts 7 to 10 days [73]
Communicability	:	infected fleas remain infective for life (fleas can live for up to 1 year) [3]

Transmission cycle [3,73]

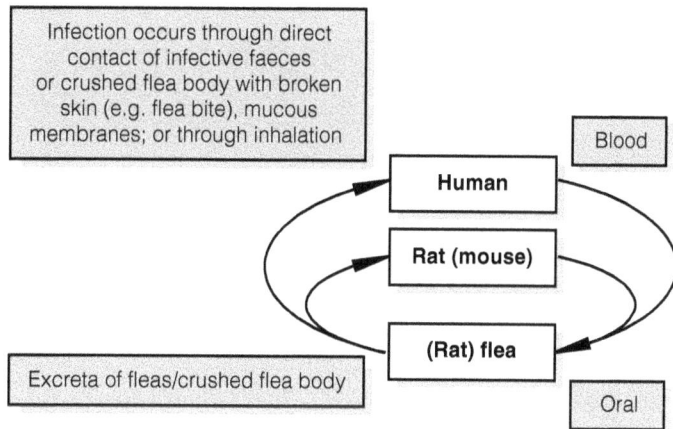

Infection occurs through direct contact of infective faeces or crushed flea body with broken skin (e.g. flea bite), mucous membranes; or through inhalation

Blood

Human

Rat (mouse)

(Rat) flea

Excreta of fleas/crushed flea body

Oral

Transmission	:	fleas become infected by feeding on a host [73]. It is the excreta of the fleas which contain the pathogen. The infective excreta can infect a person by contaminating the flea bite or other wound [3], mucous membranes, or conjunctiva. The faeces are infective too if inhaled by a person. Which transmission route is most common is not clear. In addition, the body of the flea is infective, and crushed fleas are as dangerous as their faeces. Crushing fleas between teeth can result in infection [73].
		The infection is generally an endemic infection, with sporadic cases occurring [3]
Reservoir	:	the main reservoirs of the pathogen are the domestic black rat (*Rattus rattus*) and the sewer brown rat (*R. norvegicus*) [73]. Mice can play a role as a reservoir for human infection. Rodents do not suffer seriously from the infection [16]. In addition to rodents, the infection occurs in cats, opossums, shrews, and skunks, their role as a reservoir of the infection is minor though [73]
Vector/int. host	:	the main vector of the infection is the rat flea (*Xenopsylla cheopsis*) [3]. Other vectors which have been found to carry the pathogen are the human flea (*Pulex irritans*), lice (this is not epidemic louse-borne typhus), mites (this is

not scrub typhus), and ticks. These will generally not be very important in the transmission of the infection [73]. In some places cat fleas (*Ctenocephalides felis*) could be the vector of a similar infection, the importance of this vector will be limited though [3]

Water-related : the infection is water-washed [73]

Excreta-related : no

Environment : the infection is linked to an urban environment [73] where people and rats (or mice) live in close association [3]. People in close contact with rats or mice are most at risk (e.g. workers in granaries, food stores, breweries, shops, or garbage workers). The domestic environment may be a risk too [16]

Risk in disaster : where people and rats live closely together cases are likely to occur [3]. The infection will not be a priority in the initial emergency phase [47]

Remarks : -

Preventative measures	Potential effect
Improving water availability	(++) [73]
Improving hygiene of body and clothes [73]	
Control of fleas [3] (see Annexe 3)	
After successful flea control, control of rats and mice [3] (see Annexe 3)	
Buildings should be rat-proof [73]; especially grain-stores and other food-stores [16]	
Workers at risk should be protected against fleas (e.g. garbage workers) [16]	
Health and hygiene promotion [3]	

Epidemic measures : control of fleas [3], after successful control of fleas, control of rats/mice [73]

Typhus (epidemic louse-borne) fever, Louse-borne typhus, Classic typhus fever

A louse-borne infection with a high case fatality rate. Where people live in crowded conditions, have poor personal hygiene, and are infested with lice, the infection can cause outbreaks. Where these conditions exist, preventative measures should be taken before an outbreak occurs. The infection should not be mistaken for endemic typhus fever or scrub typhus.

Pathogen   : *Rickettsia prowazekii* [3] (Rickettsia)
Distribution   : the infection occurs worldwide [3]
Symptoms   : mild infections do occur [3]. Symptoms are headache, continuous high fever, shivering, general pains [73], and skin rash [3]
Severity   : the severity of the disease ranges from mild to fatal [3]. Untreated cases have a case fatality rate of 10 to 60% [44]
Incubation period   : 1 to 2 weeks, shorter if the infecting dose is large [73]
Duration   : the duration of the illness is around 2 weeks [3]
Communicability   : people are infective to lice probably up to 2 to 3 days after fever has disappeared [3]. Long-term carriers of the pathogen probably exist [16] in the form of recurrent typhus, or Brill-Zinsser disease. The infected person can be a carrier for decades [73].
The lice will die of the infection 2 weeks after the infective bite [3]

Transmission cycle [73]

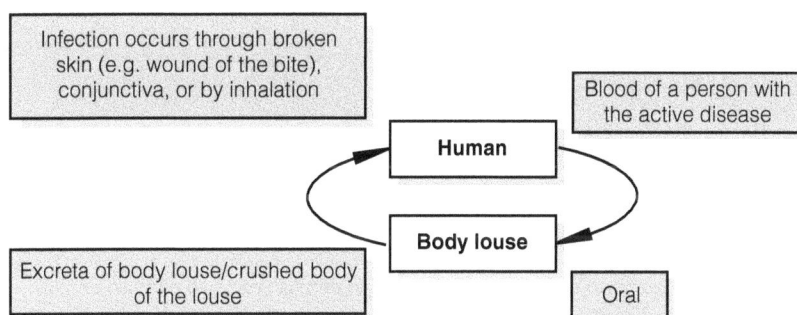

Infection occurs through broken skin (e.g. wound of the bite), conjunctiva, or by inhalation

Blood of a person with the active disease

Human

Body louse

Excreta of body louse/crushed body of the louse

Oral

Transmission   : lice are infected when feeding on a person with the active disease. As well the excreta as the body of the louse are infective. If infective louse faeces, or crushed lice, come in contact with broken skin (e.g. the biting wound), infection can follow [3]. Crushing lice between teeth is dangerous. Inhaling dried faeces of lice is a potential transmission route, as is contact of the conjunctiva with the infective excreta of the lice [73]
Reservoir   : humans are probably the only reservoir [73].
Rickettsia in dead lice can remain infective for weeks [3]. The pathogen can remain viable for over 100 days in louse faeces [73]

Vector/int. host	: the main vector transmitting the infection is the body louse (*Pediculus humanus corporis*). Other lice (*Phthirus pubis* and *Pediculus humanus capitis*) are possibly involved in transmission. Body lice live between underclothing and body, and lay eggs in the seams of clothing. Adult lice which have no access to a blood meal die within 10 days, and clothes which have not been worn for 1 month will be free of adults and eggs. Body lice can not survive if clothes are frequently washed or changed. Ironing, and washing clothes at over 60°C, will kill the lice. Lice do not support high ambient temperatures [73]
Water-related	: the infection is water-washed [3]
Excreta-related	: no
Environment	: epidemic louse-borne typhus fever is a risk where a combination of crowding [84], cold weather (people wear more clothes), poor personal hygiene, and infestation of the population with body louse occurs [3]. The infection is associated with mountainous areas (cold weather) [15], war, and famine [3]
Risk in disaster	: the infection is a serious risk in circumstances of overcrowding, poor personal hygiene, and if body louse is present in the population. If people carry body louse, the population should be treated against the vector before the first cases occur [47]
Remarks	: the infection is under surveillance by the WHO [73]

Preventative measures	Potential effect
Improve water availability	(++) [29]
If appropriate, soap can be made available [47]	
Improve hygiene of clothes and body [73]	
Control of body louse [3] (see Annexe 3)	
If displaced people are infested with lice they should be treated with residual insecticides. This should be done before cases occur [47]	
Refugees and displaced people entering camps should be checked for lice if the risk of an outbreak is present [47]	
Cases, contacts, and their clothes and houses should be deloused [221, 241]	
If possible, contacts of cases should be put under observation [3]	
People at risk can, if appropriate, receive preventative treatment [16]	
Health and hygiene promotion [3]	

Epidemic measures : control of body louse, search for the source of the outbreak [3]

Relapsing louse-borne fever

A louse-borne infection. The infection usually occurs in outbreaks and can have high case fatality rates. The infection is a risk in places of overcrowding, poor personal hygiene, and where the population carries lice. Preventative measures against lice should be taken before an outbreak occurs. The infection should not be mistaken for tick-borne relapsing fever.

Pathogen : *Borrelia recurrentis* [15] (Bacterium)

Distribution : the infection occurs in Africa, Asia, and South America [3]. Endemic areas are the highlands of Ethiopia, Burundi, North-west Africa, East Africa, China, India, Peru, and Bolivia [16]

Symptoms : asymptomatic infections do occur [16]. Symptoms are chills, high fever, headache, and vomiting [4]. If the infection is not treated relapses can occur [44] (normally 1 to 2) [2]

Severity : the case fatality rate in untreated persons is usually 2 to 9%, though in epidemics case fatality rates of up to 70% have occurred [16]

Incubation period : 5 to 15 days, usually 8 days [3]

Duration : the total duration of the illness is 13 to 16 days [3]

Communicability : lice remain infective for life (which can be up to 40 days) [3]

Transmission cycle [73]

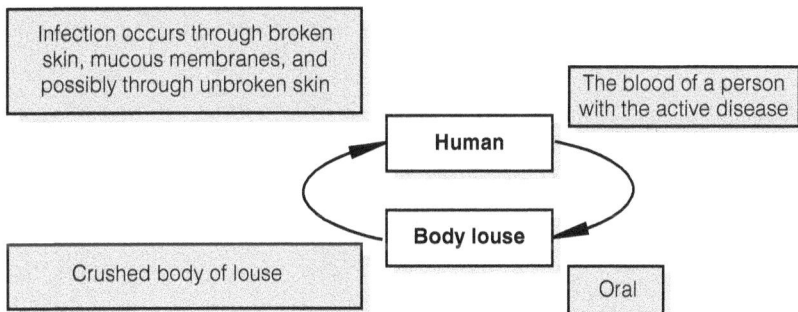

Transmission : Lice take up the pathogen by feeding on a person who is ill [73]. Lice will become infective 4 to 5 days after biting the host [3]. The pathogen is present in the body of the louse, which must be crushed and brought in contact with the bite wound, an abrasion [3], or mucous membranes for infection to take place. Possibly the pathogen can cause infection through unbroken skin. Crushing lice between teeth or fingernails is dangerous.

Outbreaks of louse-borne relapsing fever occur under similar circumstances as outbreaks of epidemic louse-borne typhus, and sometimes the two infections occur at the same time [73].

If relapsing fever is transmitted by lice, it is usually epidemic (contrary to tick-borne relapsing fever which is endemic) [3]. Endemic occurrence of the infection is possible though [2]

Reservoir : humans are the only reservoir [3]

Vector/int. host	:	the main vector is the body louse (*Pediculus humanus corporis*) [2]. Body lice are maintained between clothing and body. Eggs are deposited in the seams of clothing. Body lice will not survive if clothes are frequently washed or changed. Ironing clothes and washing them at over 60°C will kill the lice. Body louse does not support high ambient temperatures [73]. The head louse (*Pediculus humanus capitis*) can play a role in transmission [16], but this is rare [2]
Water-related	:	the infection is water-washed [47]
Excreta-related	:	no
Environment	:	the infection is one of overcrowding, poor personal hygiene, and cold climate (people wearing clothes). In the tropics it is encountered in mountainous areas [16]
Risk in disaster	:	the infection is a major risk in disasters. If people carry body lice, the population should be treated against lice before the first cases occur [47]
Remarks	:	the infection is under surveillance by the WHO [3]

Preventative measures	Potential effect
Improve water availability	(++) [29]
If appropriate, soap can be made available [47]	
Improve hygiene of clothes and body [73]	
Control of body louse [3] (see Annexe 3)	
If displaced people are carrying lice: treatment with residual insecticides. This should be done before cases occur [47]	
Refugees and displaced people entering camps should be checked for lice if the risk of an outbreak is present [47]	
Cases, contacts, and their clothes and houses should be deloused [3]	
People at risk can, if appropriate, receive preventative treatment [16]	
Health and hygiene promotion [3]	

Epidemic measures : control of body louse [73]

Trench fever

A usually fairly mild louse-borne infection. Occurrence of the disease is an indication of a risk for outbreaks of epidemic louse-borne typhus or louse-borne relapsing fever.

Pathogen : *Bartonella quintana (Rochalimaea quintana)* [3] (Bacterium) [73]

Distribution : the infection is found in Ethiopia, Burundi, North Africa [3], Mexico [16], Bolivia, Canada, Poland, former USSR [3], China, and Japan [16]

Symptoms : mild infections are common. Symptoms are fever, headache, malaise, pains, enlarged liver and spleen, and sometimes a skin rash [3]. Recurring attacks may occur for up to 10 years [4]

Severity : the severity of the infection is variable [3] but usually fairly mild [16]. The disease is not fatal [3]

Incubation period : 7 to 30 days [73]

Duration : the duration of the illness varies, and relapses are possible [3]

Communicability : humans can infect lice for years. Body lice stay infective for life (lice live approximately 5 weeks after hatching) [3]

Transmission cycle [3,4]

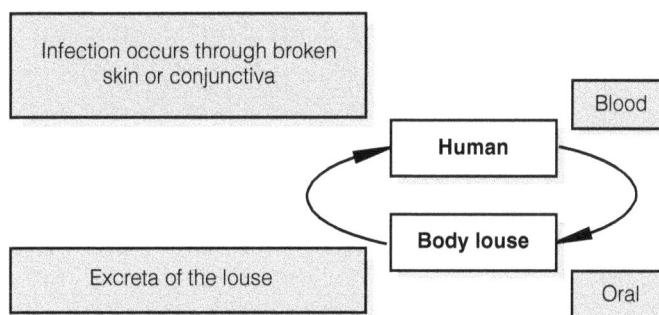

Transmission : lice are infected by ingesting blood containing the pathogen. Their excreta become infective 5 to 12 days after their infective blood meal. People are infected when infective louse-faeces come in contact with broken skin (e.g. the bite-wound) [3], or the conjunctiva [4]

Reservoir : humans are the reservoir of the pathogen [3]. Though it is possible that rodents act as a reservoir [16]

Vector/int. host : the vector of the pathogen is the human body louse [16] (*Pediculus humanus corporis*) [3]

Water-related : the infection is water-washed [73]

Excreta-related : no

Environment : the infection occurs where people have poor personal hygiene, live in overcrowded circumstances, and are carriers of body louse [3]

Risk in disaster : there is a risk where louse-infested people live in crowded conditions [3]

Remarks : -

Preventative measures	Potential effect
Improving water availability	(++) [29]
Improving hygiene of clothes and body [73]	
Control of body louse [3] (see Annexe 3)	
Health and hygiene promotion	

If trench fever occurs in a population, there is a risk of outbreaks of epidemic louse-borne typhus fever and louse-borne relapsing fever [3]. If body louse is a problem in a population, a rapid control of the vector is very important [47]

Epidemic measures : control of body louse [3]

Typhus (mite-borne) fever, Scrub typhus, Tsutsugamushi disease, Rural typhus

An infection transmitted by the larvae of mites. The infection occurs in Asia, and is generally very localised in 'typhus islands'. The infection is often severe and can cause large outbreaks if susceptible people are brought into these 'typhus islands'.

Pathogen : *Rickettsia tsutsugamushi (Rickettsia orientalis)* [3] (Rickettsia)
Distribution : the pathogen occurs in Central, eastern, and South-east Asia [3], and Australia [44]
Symptoms : a skin ulcer will form where the larval mite was attached. Other symptoms are fever, malaise, headache, enlarged spleen, conjunctivitis, rash, delirium, and deafness [2]
Severity : the case fatality rate in untreated cases is 1 to 60 % [3]
Incubation period : 1 to 3 weeks [73]; usually 10 to 12 days [3]
Duration : around 2 weeks [3]
Communicability : mites remain infective over several generations [2]

Transmission cycle [73]

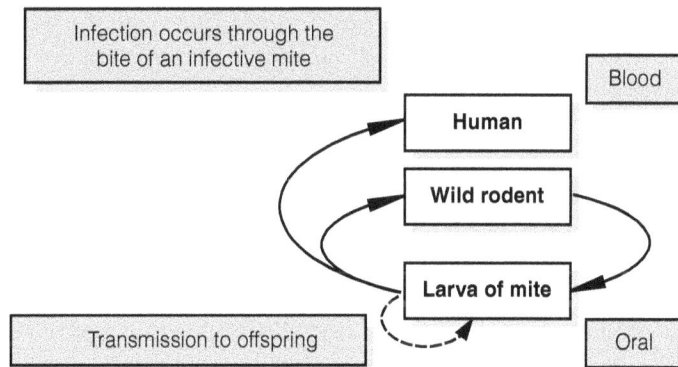

Transmission : mites acquire the pathogen either from their parents, or by feeding on an infected rodent [73]. The rodents and mites live together in specific zones: 'typhus islands' [3]. The extent of this 'community' is limited to where the rodents are present [73]. When people enter into these zones they can get infected if bitten by the infective larva of the mite [2]. In military operations up to 50% of the soldiers have been infected [3]
Reservoir : reservoirs for the pathogens are wild rodents [16]. Mites are important as reservoirs as they can pass the infection to their offspring. The infection can be maintained in mites without reinfection from an infected rodent for several generations [2]
Vector/int. host : the vector of the infection are the larvae of mites (*Leptotrombidium akamushi, L.deliensis* and related species) [3]. The mites live in transitional or fringe zones [73]

Water-related : no
Excreta-related : no
Environment : the infection occurs in rural zones where the pathogen, mites, and rodents coexist. These areas can be small (measured in some square metres) [3] or large. They are almost always created by human activity [73]; e.g. where jungle has been cut and been replaced by scrub [2] (jungle grass) [16]. Infection occurs to an altitude of up to 3,500 metres above sea level [3]
Risk in disaster : the infection is a risk if people are placed close to 'typhus islands' [3]
Remarks : -

Preventative measures	Potential effect
Avoiding known 'typhus islands' [47]	
Personal protection against the mites (wearing covering clothing impregnated with insecticides or repellents [73], repellents to skin [3])	
If a 'typhus island' must be rendered safe, the undergrowth or scrub should be cleared and burnt; and left to dry completely [73] or treated with residual insecticides [2]	
Health and hygiene promotion	
Control of rodents does not have a direct effect as the mite transmits the pathogen to its offspring [2]	

Epidemic measures : control of mites by personal protection and clearing of areas containing the mites [3]

Annexes

A1

Relapsing tick-borne fever

A tick-borne infection which should not be confused with louse-borne relapsing fever. The infection is endemic in Africa.

Pathogen	:	in Africa caused by *Borrelia duttoni*; elsewhere other species are responsible [2] (Rickettsia)
Distribution	:	the infection occurs in the whole of tropical Africa [3], where the infection is endemic [73]. The infection occurs in foci in northern Africa, the Middle-east, and Central Asia up to China, Central America, South America, Spain, Portugal [16], and northern America [3]
Symptoms	:	infections may be asymptomatic [2]. Symptoms are fever and headache, usually lasting 4-5 days. An attack of fever will reoccur after an interval of 2 days to 3 weeks [16] (usually 7 to 10 days) [73]. These attacks will repeat themselves 3 to 6 times (in Africa up to 11 times) [16]. Where the infection is endemic, it is mainly a disease of babies, young children, and pregnant women [73]
Severity	:	the case fatality rate of the infection is low [16]
Incubation period	:	3 to 10 days [73], though may be up to 14 days [16]
Duration	:	illness lasts for as long as relapses occur
Communicability	:	ticks remain infective for life [3] (they can live for over 5 years [73])

Transmission cycle [73]

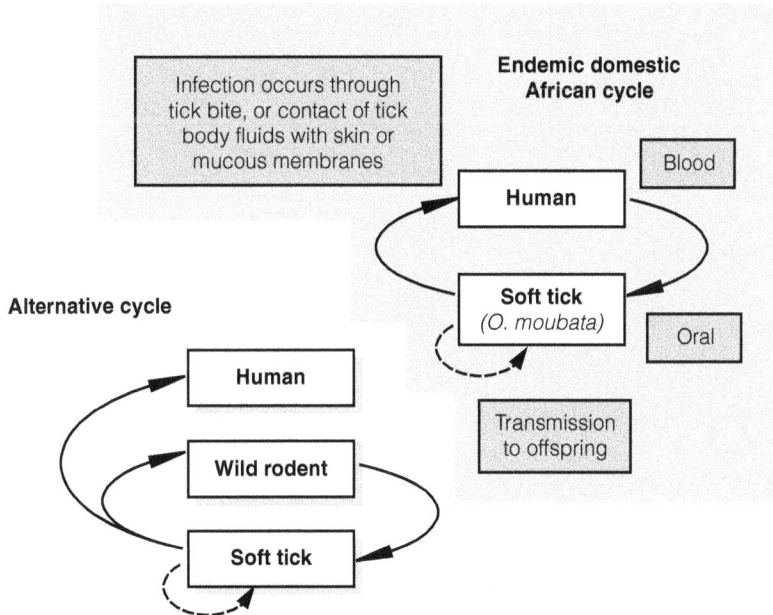

two transmission cycles occur: in Africa the infection is endemic and the cycle is between people and domestic ticks. Elsewhere an alternative cycle exists; the infection is normally transmitted between rodents and ticks, and people are infected by chance. If contact becomes more intense a cycle similar to the African endemic cycle may occur [73].

Transmission : Ticks are infected by feeding on infected blood, or receive the infection from their parents [73]. The infection is transmitted to humans through the bite of an infective tick [3]. Body fluids of the ticks are infective too, and infection can occur through contact with mucous membranes, conjunctiva, or intact skin [16]. Limited outbreaks are possible [16]

Reservoir : in the endemic domestic African cycle reservoirs are humans and ticks [73]. In the alternative cycle the normal reservoirs are wild rodents and ticks. The ticks transmit the pathogen to their offspring [3], and the infection can be maintained in ticks for at least 5 generations [2]

Vector/int. host : in the endemic domestic African cycle the vector is the soft tick *Ornithodorus moubata* which lives in cracks and fissures in houses. The ticks can survive 5 years without blood, which means that empty houses can remain infested with ticks for years [73].
For the alternative cycle; in Africa: *O.hispanica*; in the Near East and Middle East: *O.tholozani*; in Central and South America: *O.rudis* and *O.talaje*; and in the USA: *O.hermsi* and *O.turicata*. The ticks usually feed at night [3]

Water-related : no
Excreta-related : no
Environment : in the endemic domestic African cycle the infection occurs in houses which allow ticks to hide in cracks in walls and floors. In the alternative rodent-tick cycle people become infected in caves or shelters which are inhabited by rodents, or close to rodent burrows [73]

Risk in disaster : the infection is not a priority in a disaster [47]
Remarks : -

Preventative measures	Potential effect
Chemical and environmental control of ticks [3,47]	
Using personal protection methods (repellents [3], mosquito net [73])	
Structures should be made rodent-proof to prevent rodents and their ticks from settling [3]	
Houses of cases should be treated against ticks [73]	
Health and hygiene promotion [3]	

Once ticks have infested a house it is very difficult to get rid of them [73]

Epidemic measures : control of ticks [3]

Typhus – African tick, Boutonneuse fever, Kenya tick typhus, India tick typhus, Mediterranean tick typhus, Mediterranean spotted fever/ Siberian tick typhus, North Asian tick fever/ Queensland tick typhus

Infections spread by ticks.

Pathogen	: African tick typhus (Afr.T.T.): *Rickettsia conorii* and closely related *Rickettsia*. Siberian tick typhus (Sib.T.T.): *Rickettsia sibirica*. Queensland tick typhus (Que.T.T.): *Rickettsia australis* [3] (Rickettsia)
Distribution	: Afr.T.T.: Africa, the Mediterranean, the Middle-east, India [16], and possibly Mexico. Sib.T.T.: the Asian parts of the former USSR, Mongolia, and China. Que.T.T.: Australia [3]
Symptoms	: mild infections do occur. Occasionally a small black ulcer is visible where the tick was attached [3]. Other symptoms are a skin rash and fever [2]
Severity	: the infections have a negligible case fatality rate [210,221]
Incubation period	: Afr.T.T.: usually 5 to 7 days. Sib.T.T.: 2 to 7 days. Que.T.T.: 7 to 10 days [3]
Duration	: in some cases the illness can last up to 2 weeks [3]
Communicability	: the ticks remain infective for life (about 18 months) [3]

Transmission cycle [3]

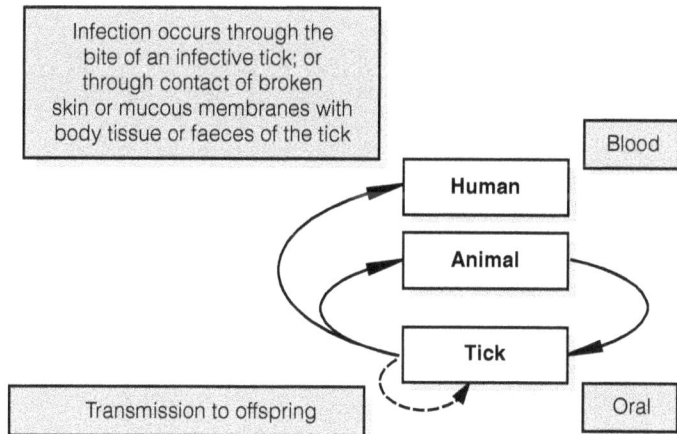

Infection occurs through the bite of an infective tick; or through contact of broken skin or mucous membranes with body tissue or faeces of the tick

Blood

Human

Animal

Tick

Transmission to offspring

Oral

Transmission	: the tick can either receive the infection from its parents, or by feeding on an infected animal. People are usually infected when a tick bites. Crushed ticks, or tick excreta, can cause infection when in contact with broken skin or mucous membranes. The tick must be attached for at least 4 to 6 hours before the pathogen is able to cause infection [3]
Reservoir	: the reservoirs for all infections are rodents [2,3], dogs [3,16], and other animals. Ticks are a reservoir as they can transmit the infection to their offspring [3]

Vector/int. host	:	the vectors for these infections are ticks:
		Afr.T.T.: *Haemaphysalis leachi, Amblyomma hebraeum, Rhipicephalus appendiculatus, Boophilus decoloratus, Hyalomma aegyptium.* In the Mediterranean the vector is the brown dog tick (*Rhipicephalus sanguineus*).
		Sib.T.T.: *Dermacentor* spp. and *Haemaphysalis* spp..
		Que.T.T.: *Ixodes holocyclus* [3]
Water-related	:	no
Excreta-related	:	no
Environment	:	where people are at risk of ticks
Risk in disaster	:	the infections will normally not be a problem in disasters [3]
Remarks	:	-

Preventative measures	**Potential effect**
Control of ticks [3]	
The entire body should be searched every 3 to 4 hours in a risk area [3]	
Clothing should cover skin, repellents can be used [3]	
Avoiding areas with many ticks [3]	
Removing ticks from dogs [3]	
Health and hygiene promotion [3]	

Epidemic measures : control and avoidance of ticks [3]

Typhus (tick-borne) fever, Rocky mountain spotted fever

An infection transmitted by ticks. The pathogen causes a potentially dangerous illness. The infection only occurs in South, Central, and North America.

Pathogen : *Rickettsia rickettsii* [3] (Rickettsia) [73]
Distribution : the infection can be found in South, Central, and North America [73]

Symptoms : sudden onset of fever, malaise, headache, muscle pains, and skin rash [73]
Severity : the case fatality rate is between 13 and 25%; with adequate treatment this can be brought down to below 5% [3]
Incubation period : 3 to 13 days [73]
Duration : the illness lasts several weeks [44]
Communicability : ticks remain infective for life [3]

Transmission cycle [3,73]

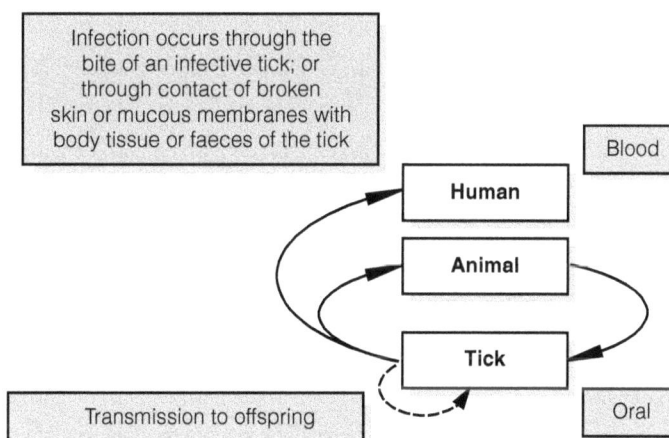

Infection occurs through the bite of an infective tick; or through contact of broken skin or mucous membranes with body tissue or faeces of the tick

Blood

Human

Animal

Tick

Transmission to offspring

Oral

Transmission : ticks can pass the pathogen to their offspring, and are either infected in this way, or when feeding on a host [73]. Humans are infected by the bite of a tick (a tick must be attached for at least 4 hours to transmit the pathogen), or through contact of tick faeces, or a crushed tick, with broken skin or mucous membranes [3]
Reservoir : rodents and other small mammals are the main reservoir [45]. Dogs are a potential reservoir [3]. As the ticks transmit the infection to their offspring they serve as a reservoir to the pathogen [16]
Vector/int. host : the vector of the infection are ticks: in Central and South America the main vector is *Amblyomma cajennense* [3]; in Mexico: *Rhipicephalus sanguineas* [44]. In the USA, the American dog tick (*Dermacentor variabilis*), the Rocky Mountain wood tick (*D. andersoni*) and occasionally the Lone Star tick (*Amblyomma americanum*) play a role in transmission [3]
Water-related : no
Excreta-related : no
Environment : where contact with ticks is likely

Risk in disaster : the infection is not a priority in a disaster [3]
Remarks : -

Preventative measures	Potential effect
Avoidance of tick-infested areas [73]	
Search the entire body regularly when in an area at risk [3]	
Control of ticks [3]	
Control of dogs [73]	
Health and hygiene promotion [3]	

Epidemic measures : control of ticks [3]

Haemorrhagic fevers: (Tick-borne arboviral), Crimean-Congo haemorrhagic fever, Central Asian haemorrhagic fever/ Omsk haemorrhagic fever/ Kyasanur forest disease

Infections transmitted by ticks. Severe cases can show bleedings.

Pathogen : Crimean-Congo haemorrhagic fever virus, Omsk haemorrhagic fever virus and Kyasanur forest disease virus [3]

Distribution : Crimean-Congo haemorrhagic fever (C.C.H.F): tropical and South Africa, the former USSR, the southern parts of eastern Europe, Middle-east, Pakistan, and China [3].
Omsk haemorrhagic fever (O.H.F.): the Omsk region in Siberia [16].
Kyasanur forest disease (K.F.D.): the Kyasanur forest in India [3]

Symptoms : C.C.H.F.: asymptomatic infections do occur [16]. Symptoms are fever, malaise, pains, skin rash, possibly bleeding from gums, nose and intestines [3]. In Africa cases with bleeding are rare [16]
O.H.F. and K.F.D. : symptoms are chills, headache, fever, pains, conjunctivitis is common, diarrhoea, and vomiting. Severe cases may develop bleeding. Cases of K.F.D. sometimes develop problems in the central nervous system [3]

Severity : C.C.H.F.: the case fatality rate is between 2% [3] and 30% to 50%. The higher fatality rates tend to occur in outbreaks. In Africa deaths due to the infection are uncommon.
O.H.F.: the case fatality rate is 1% to 3% [16].
K.F.D.: the case fatality rate is estimated at 1% to 10% [3]

Incubation period : C.C.H.F.: transmission through a tick-bite: 1 to 3 days (with a maximum of 9 days); transmission through contact with infected blood, secretions, or body tissues: 5 to 6 days (with a maximum of 13 days) [83].
O.H.F.: usually 3 to 8 days [3].
K.F.D.:3 to 12 days [73]

Duration :the illnesses may last for weeks. Complete recovery may take a long time [3]

Communicability : ticks remain infective for life [3]

Transmission cycle [3,16]

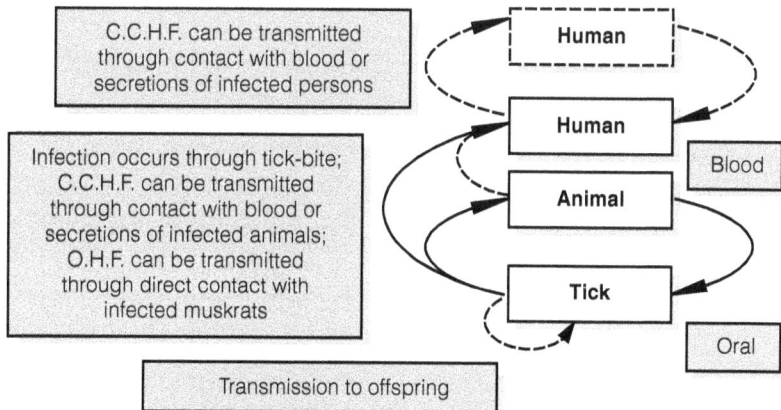

C.C.H.F. can be transmitted through contact with blood or secretions of infected persons

Infection occurs through tick-bite; C.C.H.F. can be transmitted through contact with blood or secretions of infected animals; O.H.F. can be transmitted through direct contact with infected muskrats

Transmission to offspring

Human

Human

Animal

Tick

Blood

Oral

Transmission	:	ticks are infected either through their parents, or by feeding on an infected host. The infections are transmitted to people through the bite of an infective tick. C.C.H.F. can be transmitted through contact with blood and secretions of infected persons or reservoir animals [3]. Persons commonly acquire O.H.F. through direct contact with infected muskrats. The possibility of air-borne transmission is suspected with C.C.H.F. and O.H.F..
		Outbreaks are possible with all of the infections. Epidemics of C.C.H.F. can occur in endemic areas. For O.H.F. there is risk of an outbreak if there is a high mortality in muskrats [16]
Reservoir	:	C.C.H.F.: hares, birds, and domestic animals (sheep, goats, cattle) [3].
		O.H.F.: the main reservoir is the muskrat, but other rodents serve as reservoirs too [16].
		K.F.D.: probably rodents, shrews, and monkeys [3].
		Ticks transmit the pathogens to their offspring, and are therefore reservoirs [3,16]
Vector/int. host	:	ticks are the vector of these infections:
		C.C.H.F.: *Hyalomma marginatum, H.anatolicum*, possibly other ticks [3].
		O.H.F.: *Dermacentor pictus* and *D.marginatus* [16].
		K.F.D.: probably *Haemaphysalis spinigera* [3]
Water-related	:	no
Excreta-related	:	no
Environment	:	C.C.H.F.: most cases occur in persons working closely with animals, medical personnel working with infected persons, and close contacts of cases [3].
		O.H.F.: most at risk are trappers and people working in water-courses [16].
		K.F.D.: the infection occurs mainly in the dry season in young men who come in contact with the forest [3]
Risk in disaster	:	the infections will not be a priority in disasters [3]
Remarks	:	-

Preventative measures	Potential effect
Avoidance of tick-infested areas [3]	
Search the entire body regularly when in an area at risk [3]	
Control of ticks [3]	
With C.C.H.F. people at risk can be vaccinated [73]	
Patients with C.C.H.F. must be kept in strict isolation [16]	
Health and hygiene promotion [3]	

Epidemic measures : control of ticks [3]

230

Encephalitis (Tick-borne arboviral): Far eastern tick-borne encephalitis, Russian spring-summer encephalitis / Central European tick-borne encephalitis/ Powassan virus encephalitis

Infections transmitted by ticks. The pathogens occur in the former USSR, Europe, and northern America

Pathogen   : a group of closely related arboviruses [3]
Distribution   : Far eastern tick-borne encephalitis (F.E.E.): mainly in the far eastern parts of the former USSR.
Central European tick-borne encephalitis (C.E.E.): mainly in Europe.
Powassan virus encephalitis (P.V.E.): Russia, the USA, and Canada [3]
Symptoms   : symptoms are fever, headache, disorientation, and meningitis. F.E.E. can result in epilepsy and paralysis [3]
Severity   : F.E.E.: the case fatality rate can be up to 30%.
C.E.E.: the case fatality rate is around 3% [16].
P.V.E.: has a case fatality rate of around 10% [3]
Incubation period : 7 to 14 days [73]
Duration   : illness will last several weeks [3]
Communicability   : infected ticks remain infective for life [3]

Transmission cycle [3]

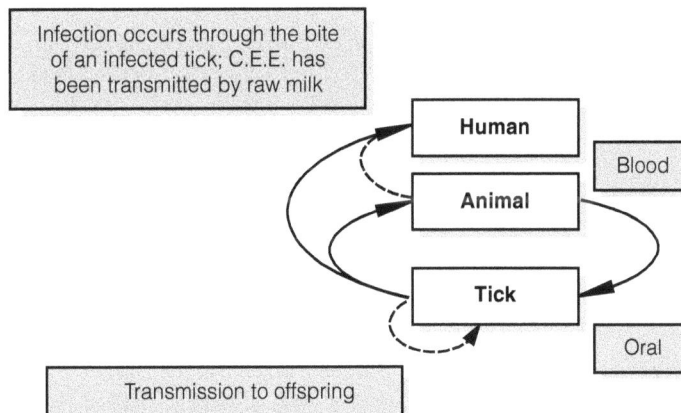

Infection occurs through the bite of an infected tick; C.E.E. has been transmitted by raw milk

Human
Blood
Animal
Tick
Oral
Transmission to offspring

Transmission   : ticks are infected either by receiving the pathogen from their parents, or by feeding on an infected host. Humans are infected when an infective tick feeds on them. C.E.E. has been transmitted by ingesting raw milk [3]. Outbreaks can occur after periods in which voles have been numerous [16]
Reservoir   : the reservoirs of the infections are rodents, other mammals, and birds [3]. Infected ticks can pass the pathogens to their offspring and are therefore a reservoir [221, 241]
Vector/int. host : the vectors of the infections are ticks: in the eastern parts of the former USSR mainly *Ixodes persulcatus*, in the western parts of the former USSR and Europe the main vector is *I.ricinus*, and in the USA and Canada *I.cookei* [3]

Water-related : no

Excreta-related : no

Environment : F.E.E. occurs mainly in spring and early summer, and is an infection of the forest and taiga. C.E.E. is associated with forests and occurs in late spring to early autumn [16]. P.V.E. can mainly be found in rural or forested zones [3]

Risk in disaster : the infections will not be a priority in a disaster [3]

Remarks : -

Preventative measures	Potential effect
Avoidance of tick-infested areas [3]	
the entire body should be regularly searched for ticks when in an area at risk [3]	
Control of ticks [3]	
Immunisation is possible [3]	
Where C.E.E. occurs milk should be pasteurised [3]	
Health and hygiene promotion [3]	

Epidemic measures : control of ticks [3]

Lyme disease, Lyme borreliosis

An infections transmitted by ticks. The pathogen occurs in the former USSR, China, Japan, Europe, and northern America.

Pathogen	: *Borrelia burgdorferi* [3] (Bacterium)
Gen. description	: an infection which occurs in the former USSR, China, Japan, Europe, and northern America. Symptoms are: an expanding red mark (ring-shaped) at the place of the tick-bite, malaise, fever, headache, and pains in muscles. Weeks to months after the bite, problems in the nervous system may arise [3]. Intermittent arthritis will occur in 60% of the cases [45]. The incubation period (for the red mark) is 3 to 30 days [73]. If untreated, the infection can last for years and result in severe chronic health problems [3]

Transmission cycle [3]

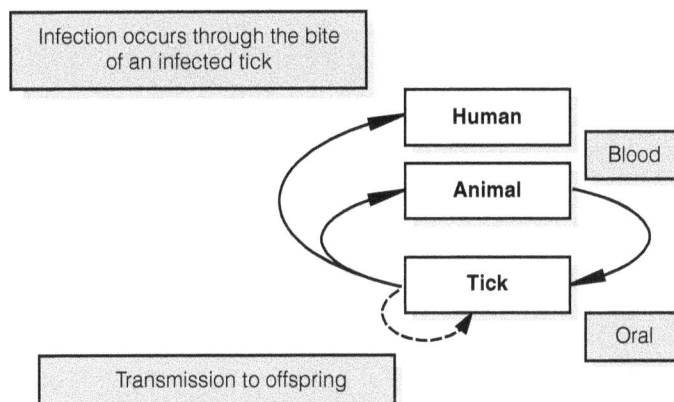

Transmission	: ticks are infected either through their parents or by feeding on an infected host. Humans are infected through an infective tick-bite. In tests ticks had to be attached for over 24 hours to animals before transmission of the pathogen occurred [3]
Reservoir	: the reservoirs of the infection are rodents and other animals. Dogs, cattle, and horses can develop the illness. Ticks serve as reservoirs as they can transmit the pathogen to their offspring [3]
Vector/int. host	: the vectors of the infections are ticks: in Asia *Ixodes persulcatus*, in Europe *I.ricinus*, and in the USA *I.pacificus* and *I.scapularis* [3]
Environment	: infection usually occurs in summer (when the ticks are most active) [3]

Preventative measures	Potential effect
Avoidance of tick-infested areas [3]	
Regularly search the entire body for ticks when in an area at risk [3]	
Control of ticks [3]	
Health and hygiene promotion [3]	

Epidemic measures : control of ticks [3]

Annexe 2

Summary tables of infections related to water and environmental sanitation
(excluding vector-borne infections)

Table A2.1: Faecal-oral infections

Infection	Occurrence				Measures of control							
	Africa	Asia	Central and/or S. America	Animal reservoir	Improving water quality	Improving water availability	Improving handwashing	Improving sanitation	Control of food hygiene	Control of domestic animals	Control of domestic flies	Additional measures
Faecal-oral diseases	✓	✓	p	++	+++	++	++	++	p	p	p	
Diarrhoeal diseases	✓	✓	p	++	+++	++	++	++	p	p	p	
Campylobacter enteritis	✓	✓	✓	++	+++	++	++	++	++	–	–	
Bacterial enteritis*	✓	✓	p	++	+++	+	++	–	–	–	–	
Salmonellosis	✓	✓	✓	++	+++	++	++	n.s.	n.s.	–	–	
Yersiniosis	✓	✓	✓	++	+++	+	++	n.s.	n.s.	–	–	
Bacillary dysentery	✓	✓	–	++	+++	++	++	–	–	–	n.s.	
Cholera	✓	✓	–	+++	+++	+++	++	–	–	–	n.s.(a)	care in handling, and burial, of the dead

+ + +: very effective; ++: effective; +: some effect; n.s.: extent of effectiveness is not specified; p: possible, depending on the pathogen; –: no, or not effective

(a): where contaminated wastes are present

*caused by E.coli

Table A2.1: Faecal-oral infections (continued)

Infection	Occurrence			Measures of control								
	Africa	Asia	Central and/or S. America	Animal reservoir	Improving water quality	Improving water availability	Improving handwashing	Improving sanitation	Improving food hygiene	Control of domestic animals	Control of domestic flies	Additional measures
Rotaviral enteritis	✓	✓	–	?	?	?	?	?	–	?		
Epidemic viral gasteroenteropathy	✓	✓	–	n.s.	+?	n.s.?	+	+	–	–		
Amoebiasis	✓	✓	–	n.s.	++	++	++	+	–	n.s.		
Giardiasis	✓	✓	–	++	++	++	+	+	–	–		
Cryptosporidiosis	✓	✓	✓	n.s.	n.s.	n.s.	n.s.	n.s.	n.s.	–		
Balantidiasis	✓	✓	✓	n.s.	n.s.	n.s.	n.s.	n.s.	n.s.	–		
(para-) typhoid fever	✓	✓	–	+++	+++	++	++	++	–	n.s.		control of food handlers
Hepatitis A and E	✓	✓	–	n.s.	+?	n.s.?	+	+	–	–		
Poliomyelitis	✓	–	–	–	+?	n.s.?	+	+	–	–		immunisation: +++

+ + +: very effective;   + +: effective;   +: some effect;   n.s.: extent of effectiveness is not specified;   ?: uncertain   - : no, or not effective

Annexes

A2

Table A2.1: Faecal-oral infections (continued)

Infection	Occurrence				Measures of control							Additional measures
	Africa	Asia	Central and/or S. America	Animal reservoir	Improving water quality	Improving water availability	Improving handwashing	Improving sanitation	Improving food hygiene	Control of domestic animals	Control of domestic flies	
Hymenolepiasis	✓	✓	–	n.s.	+	+	?	n.s.	n.s. (a)	–		
Pinworm infection	✓	✓	–	–	+	+	n.s.	–	–	–		hygiene of bedding and clothes
Hydatid disease	✓	✓	✓ (b)	–	++	++	n.s. (b)	n.s.	n.s. (b)	–		
Cysticercosis	✓	✓	–	–	++	++	n.s.	n.s.	n.s.	–		

+++: very effective;   ++: effective;   +: some effect;   n.s.: extent of effectiveness is not specified;   – : no, or not effective

(a): possibly mice
(b): dogs

Table A2.2: Water-based helminths (schistosomiasis and water-based helminths with 2 intermediate hosts)

Infection	Occurrence				Measures of control						
	Africa	Asia	Central and/or S. America	Animal reservoir	Reducing water contact	Improving sanitation	Improving food preparation	Control of freshwater snails	Control of domestic animals	Mass treatment	Additional measures
Schistosomiasis	✓	✓	✓[a]	+++	+	–	n.s.	–	n.s.		
Fasciolopsiasis	–	✓	–	–	+[b]	+++	–	n.s.[b]	–		
Fascioliasis	✓	✓	✓	–	n.s.[c]	n.s.	n.s.	n.s.	–		
Clonorchiasis/Opisthorchiasis	–	✓	–	–	+	+++	–	n.s.	–		
Diphyllobothriasis	✓	✓	✓	–	+	+++	–	–	n.s.		
Paragonimiasis	✓	✓	✓	–	+	+++	n.s.	n.s.	–		care in disposal of sputum

+++: very effective; ++: effective; +: some effect; n.s.: extent of effectiveness is not specified; –: no, or not effective

[a]: for S.japonicum
[b]: pigs
[c]: domestic animals

Annexes

A2

Table A2.3: Soil-transmitted helminths

Infection	Occurrence			Measures of control							Additional measures
	Africa	Asia	Central and/or S. America	Animal reservoir	Improving water availability	Improving handwashing	Improving sanitation	Improving food hygiene	Wearing closed shoes	Mass treatment	
Hookworm disease	✓	✓	–	–	+++	–	+++	–	+++	+++	
Strongyloidiasis	✓	✓	–	–	+++	–	+++	–	+++	–	
Roundworm infection	✓	✓	–	++	+++	+	+++	+++	–	+++	
Trichuriasis	✓	✓	–	+	+	+	+	+	–	n.s.	

+ + +: very effective; + +: effective; +: some effect; n.s.: extent of effectiveness is not specified; –: no, or not effective

Table A2.4: Beef and pork tapeworm

Infection	Occurrence				Measures of control			Additional measures
	Africa	Asia	Central and/or S. America	Animal reservoir	Improving sanitation	Improving food hygiene	Meat inspection	
Beef tapeworm	✓	✓	✓	–	+++	+++	+	
Pork tapeworm	✓	✓	✓	–	+++	+++	+	Measures against cysticercosis can be found under faecal-oral infections

Table A2.5: Leptospirosis and guinea-worm infection

Infection	Occurrence				Measures of control				Additional measures
	Africa	Asia	Central and/or S. America	Animal reservoir	Improving water quality at source	Reducing water contact	Improving food hygiene	Control of domestic animals	
Leptospirosis	✓	✓	✓	+++	++	++	–	n.s.	control of rodents
Guinea-worm infection	✓	(a)	–	–	+++	n.s.	–	–	control of Cyclops spp.

+++: very effective; ++: effective; +: some effect; n.s.: extent of effectiveness is not specified; –: no, or not effective

(a): in Yemen

Annexes

A2

Table A2.6: Infections transmitted through direct contact

Infection	Occurrence				Measures of control						
	Africa	Asia	Central and/or S. America	Animal reservoir	Improving water availability	Improving handwashing	Care in dealing with clothes and hygiene of body	Control of domestic animals	Control of domestic flies	Treatment of cases	Additional measures
Conjunctivitis	✓	✓	✓	–	+++	n.s.	n.s.	–	n.s.	n.s.	
Trachoma	✓	✓	✓	–	++	n.s.	n.s.	–	n.s.	n.s.	
Yaws	✓	✓	✓	–	++	–	–	–	n.s.	n.s.	
Leprosy	✓	✓	✓	–	p	–	p	–	–	n.s.	
Scabies	✓	✓	✓	–	+++	–	n.s.	n.s.	–	n.s.	
Tinea	✓	✓	✓	✓	++	–	n.s.	n.s.	–	n.s.	

+ + +: very effective; + +: effective; +: some effect; - : no, or not effective
n.s.: extent of effectiveness is not specified; p: possibly effective

Annexe 3

Summary tables of vector-borne infections, vectors and their control

A3 **Annexes**

Table A3.1: Vector-borne infections with their vectors [3,73]

Infection	Mosquito	Tsetse fly	Sandfly	Blackfly	Deer fly	Reduviid bug	Flea	Body louse	Mite	Tick
Yellow fever	Ae									
Dengue fever	Ae									
Filariasis	Ae;Cu; Ma;An									
Mosquito-borne arboviral encephalitis	Cu									
Mosquito-borne arboviral fevers	Ae;Cu									
Mosquito-borne arboviral arthritis	Ae;Cu; Ma;An									
Malaria	An									
Sleeping sickness		✓								
Leishmaniasis			✓							
Bartonellosis			✓							
Sandfly-borne arboviral fevers			✓							
River blindness				✓						
Loiasis					✓					
American trypanosomiasis						✓				

Mosquito: Ae (Aedes spp.); Cu (Culex spp.); Ma (Mansonia spp.); An (Anopheles spp.)

Table A3.1: Vector-borne infections with their vectors (continued) [3,73]

Infection	Mosquito	Tsetse fly	Sandfly	Blackfly	Deer fly	Reduviid bug	Flea	Body louse	Mite	Tick
Plague							✓			
Murine typhus fever							✓	Oc.	Oc.	
Louse-borne typhus fever							Oc.	✓		
Louse-borne relapsing fever							Oc.	✓		
Trench fever							Oc.	✓		
Scrub typhus								Oc.	✓	
Tick-borne relapsing fever										✓
... tick typhus										✓
Tick-borne typhus fever										✓
Tick-borne arboviral haemorrhagic fever										✓
Tick-borne arboviral encephalitis										✓
Lyme disease										✓

... tick typhus: African tick typhus, Siberian tick typhus, Queensland tick typhus
Oc.: occasional transmission is possible.

Annexes

A3

Annexes

A3

Table A3.2: The vectors and their characteristics (rats have been included) (from 61,67,77,80)

Vector	I/O[a]	D/N[b]	Breeding sites	Resting sites	Range	Additional information
Mosquito Aedes spp.	I/O	D	water bodies with fluctuating water levels, containers in refuse, water storage tanks, usually clean water	most species outdoors, but Aedes aegypti in and around houses	0.1-0.8 km	eggs can withstand desiccation for months.Generation cycle: 8-10 days
Mosquito Culex spp.	I/O	N	organically polluted water: latrines, septic tanks, blocked drains	indoors and outdoors in sheltered, shaded places	0.1-0.8 km	Generation cycle: 8-10 days
Mosquito Mansonia spp.	I/O	N	water bodies with permanent vegetation: swamps, ponds, canals	usually outdoors	?	
Mosquito Anopheles spp.	I/O	N	lakes, pools, puddles, slow-flowing streams; often in sunlight and with vegetation, clean water	indoors and outdoors in sheltered places	2 km	Generation cycle: 10-14 days
Tsetse fly (Glossina spp.)	O	D	in shaded moist soil: under bushes, logs, stones, leaf litter	in shaded places in forests, vegetation	2-4 km	Generation cycle: 60 days
Sandfly (Phlebotomus spp.; Lutzomyia spp.)	I/O	D/N	humus-rich damp soil; deep cracks in soil, rodent burrows, termite hills	shaded, sheltered, humid places	200 m	Generation cycle: 6-8 weeks
Blackfly (Simulium spp.)	O	D	fast-flowing, shallow, 'white water' in rivers and streams	outdoors	10 km	Generation cycle: 2-3 weeks
Reduviid bug (Triatoma spp.)	I	N	cracks in walls, other indoor hiding places	cracks in walls or floors, furniture, thatched roofs	10-20 m	The bugs can survive for up to 4 months without a blood meal. Generation cycle: 6-24 months

[a] I/O: the biting place is indoors (I) or outdoors (O)
[b] D/N: the time of activity is during the day (D) or during the night (N)
n/a: not applicable

Table A3.2: The vectors and their characteristics (continued) (from 61,67,77,80)

Vector	I/O[a]	D/N[b]	Breeding sites	Resting sites	Range	Additional information
Flea (*Xenopsylla* spp.; *Pulex irritans*)	I	D/N	close to sleeping and resting place of the host; in cracks in walls or floors, animal burrows	animals, beds, clothing	n/a	vector fleas are associated with rats; may survive for up to 1 year in vacant houses. Generation cycle: 8 weeks
Body louse (*Pediculus humanus corporis*)	n/a	D/N	seams in clothing	clothes	n/a	can only survive for up to 1 week off people. Generation cycle: 3 weeks
Mite (*Leptotrombidium* spp.)	O	D	often artificially created environments: where jungle has been replaced by scrubs, jungle grass	often artificially created environments: where jungle has been replaced by scrubs, jungle grass	n/a	
Tick (many different types)	I/O	D	depending on the sort	indoors: cracks in walls, floors and furniture; outdoors: sheltered places	n/a	different ticks can act as vector of different diseases
Domestic fly (*Musca* spp.)	n/a	D	organic material: faeces, corpses, food	outdoors and indoors	5 km	domestic flies are mechanical vectors. Generation cycle: 7-14 days
Cockroach (several types)	n/a	N	sheltered, warm and damp places	sheltered, warm and damp places	?	Generation cycle: 2-3 months
Rat (*Rattus* spp.)	n/a	N	buildings, burrows, sewers, refuse dumps	buildings, burrows, sewers, refuse dumps	50-80 m	Generation cycle: 3-4 months

[a] I/O: the biting place is indoors (I) or outdoors (O)
[b] D/N: the time of activity is during the day (D) or during the night (N)
n/a: not applicable

Annexes

A3

247

Annexes

A3

Table A3.3: Preventative measures against vectors (rats have been included) [adapted from 21,61,67,73,77,78]

Vector	Use of repellents, protective clothes	Use of bednets	Improve personal hygiene	Improve sanitation	Improve drainage	Improve solid waste management	Improve food storage	Improve housing	Clear land vegetation	Clear aquatic vegetation	Changing flow velocity	Chemical control	Traps	Additional measures
Mosquito: Aedes	++	–	+	++	++	++	–	+	+	+[1]	++	–	(a)	
Mosquito: Culex	++	–	++	++	++	++	–	+	+	+[1]	++	–		
Mosquito: Mansonia	++	–	–	+	–	++	–	–	++	+[1]	–	–	(b)	
Mosquito: Anopheles	++	–	–	++	–	++	–	+	+	+[1]	++	–	(b), (c)	
Tsetse fly	+	–	–	–	–	–	–	++	–	–	+	++		
Sandfly	++	–	n.s.	n.s.	n.s.	++	–	++	–	–	++	–	(d)	
Blackfly	++	–	–	–	–	–	–	–	–	+[2]	++	–	(e)	

++ : effective; + : limited effect; n.s. : extent of effectiveness is not specified; – : not effective

[1]: increasing velocities in streams, rivers, channels
[2]: modifying streams so that the creation of 'white', turbulent water is avoided
(a): fill up, remove, cover or repair all 'vessels' in the domestic area (e.g. old tyres, buckets, domestic water storage reservoirs, barrels, gutters, holes in construction blocks, old cars or machines)
(b): introduce larvivorous fish
(c): it is sometimes possible to divert mosquitoes to domestic animals
(d): destruction of rodent colonies; avoiding places where sandflies rest or breed
(e): avoidance of areas where the blackfly is abundant (e.g. rapids in streams)

Table A3.3: Preventative measures against vectors (continued) (adapted from 21,61,67,73,77,78)

Vector	Use of repellents, protective clothes	Use of bednets	Improve personal hygiene	Improve sanitation	Improve drainage	Improve solid waste management	Improve food storage	Improve housing	Clear land vegetation	Clear aquatic vegetation	Changing flow velocity	Chemical control	Traps	Additional measures
Reduviid bug	–	+	–	–	n.s.	–	++	n.s.	–	–	–	++	–	
Flea	++	–	–	–	++	–	++	–	–	–	–	++	–	(f)
Body louse	–	–	++	–	–	–	–	–	–	–	–	++	–	(g)
Mite	++	–	–	–	–	–	–	+	–	–	–	++	–	(h)
Tick	++	++[3]	–	n.s.	++	–	n.s.[3]	n.s.	–	–	–	++	–	(i)
Domestic fly	–	++[4]	++	n.s.	++	n.s.	+	–	–	–	–	++	++	
Cockroach	–	++[4]	n.s.	n.s.	++	n.s.	+	–	–	–	–	n.s.	n.s.	
Rat [5]	–	–	n.s.	n.s.	++	n.s.	++[a]	n.s.	–	–	–	++	++	

++ : effective; + : limited effect; n.s. : extent of effectiveness is not specified; – : not effective

[3]: only effective against soft ticks (the vector of tick-borne relapsing fever) which live in the house
[4]: correct use of fly-nets will prevent flies and cockroaches from reaching food or babies
[5]: where flea-borne infections (plague, murine typhus fever) are present, or a risk, fleas must be successfully controlled before rat control begins
(f): improve hygiene of the house
(g): clothing has to be cleaned and treated with insecticide; mass treatment is necessary; treatment of bedding
(h): avoid 'mite islands'
(i): check body after visiting tick-infested areas; treating domestic animals with insecticide

Annexes

A3

Annexe 4

Chlorination of drinking-water

Chlorination of drinking water

In this annexe we will show how the chlorine demand of water can be determined, and how to calculate the amount of chlorine that should be added in the treatment of a batch of water, and in a continuous supply.

Materials needed:
- Turbidity tube (preferably)
- Chlorine-generating product (e.g. HTH)
- Tablespoon (or other object which contains around 15 ml)
- Measuring jug
- Non-metallic vessels (e.g. plastic buckets) with a volume of 5 litres or more
- Syringe (without needle)
- Pooltester with DPD1 tablets
- A watch
- Possibly a calculator

Assessing whether the raw water can be chlorinated directly

The water which is going to be treated should be relatively limpid (transparent). Suspended matter in the water can protect pathogens from the effect of chlorine, and chlorination will only be effective if the water contains little suspended material.

The amount of suspended matter in the water can be determined by measuring its turbidity. This can be done with a turbidity tube. A turbidity tube is a closed tube with a mark on the bottom. The tube is completely filled with water and the mark is observed through the water in the tube. The water is tipped out in small quantities until the mark is just visible. The turbidity of the water is determined by reading up to where the water comes on the scale on the side of the tube.

If no turbidity tube is available, the turbidity is probably acceptable if a small black cross on a white background is visible through about 0.6 metres of water (this is a turbidity of roughly 5 NTU).

Although chlorination is relatively effective at a turbidity of up to 20 NTU, the water should normally have a turbidity below 5 NTU [21]. If the turbidity of the water is higher, than some form of treatment (e.g. sedimentation, rough filtration, coagulation) will be necessary to remove the suspended material.

It should be remembered that the turbidity of surface water will normally fluctuate with the seasons.

The mother solution and chlorine-generating products

The most appropriate way of chlorinating water is usually by adding a mother solution to the raw water. A mother solution is a solution with a specific percentage of chlorine. Often a mother solution with a chlorine content of 1% (containing 10 grams of chlorine per litre) is used.

The mother solution is made by mixing the chemical which generates chlorine with water. How much of the chemical is needed to make a 1% solution will depend on its chlorine content. Table A4.1 present some common chlorine-generating products with their form, their chlorine content in percentage, and how 1 litre of mother solution of 1% chlorine can be made.

Table A4.1. Common chlorine-generating products with some of their characteristics			
Product	Form	Chlorine content	How to make 1 litre of mother solution
High Test Hypochlorite (HTH)	granules	± 70 %	Mix 15 gram (± 1 tablespoon [a]) with 1 litre of water
Bleaching powder	powder	± 30 %	Mix 33 grams (± 2 tablespoons [a]) with 1 litre of water
Liquid laundry bleach	liquid	± 5 %	Mix 200 ml of liquid bleach with 800 ml of water

[a]: 1 tablespoon has a volume of 15 ml

If other chlorine-generating products are used, the quantity of product needed to make one litre of a 1% mother solution can be calculated with the formula:

$$Qty = 10 \times \left(\frac{100}{Cl_{cont}} \right)$$

Qty : amount of product needed to make 1 litre of a 1% mother solution (in grams or ml)

Cl_{cont} : chlorine content of the product (in %)

Thus if stabilised tropical bleach would be used with a chlorine content of 25%, the amount that would have to be dissolved in 1 litre of water to make a 1% mother solution is (10 x 100/25) = 40 grams.

Chlorine-generating products do not support being exposed to light, air, metal, or high temperatures. They should therefore be stored in dark, covered, non-metallic containers in a cool place. As they can emit chlorine gas, the storage room should be well ventilated.

Determining the chlorine demand of the raw water

The amount of mother solution that is needed to chlorinate the raw water will have to be determined by experimentation.

A number of non-metallic vessels (e.g. plastic buckets or jerrycans) are filled with a known amount of the raw water (e.g. 4 buckets filled with 10 litres of water). Specific amounts of mother solution are added to each of the buckets with a syringe (e.g. 0.5 ml, 1.0 ml, 1.5 ml and 2 ml). The water is well mixed, and left for 30 minutes.

After 30 minutes no more chlorine should be lost to consumed or combined residual chlorine, and the content of free residual chlorine of the water can be determined with a pooltester. A DPD1 tablet is added to the water in a pooltester, and the tester is closed and vigorously shaken to dissolve the tablet. Chlorine in the water will turn the water pink; the more chlorine there is, the darker the colour. The content in free residual chlorine is determined by comparing the colour of the water with a colour scale. We are looking for the dose which results in a free residual chlorine content of 0.2-0.5 mg/l.

Imagine that our series would give the results:

Bucket	Mother solution added to 10 litres	Free residual chlorine (in mg/l)
1	1.5 ml	0 mg/l
2	2.0 ml	0 mg/l
3	2.5 ml	0.1 mg/l
4	3.0 ml	0.5 mg/l

In this case a dose of 2.7 ml to 3.0 ml of mother solution per 10 litres of raw water would normally be adequate to reach a free residual chlorine content of 0.2-0,5 mg/l.

This method gives a rough indication of the chlorine demand of the raw water. The free residual chlorine should be 0.2-0.5 mg/l at the point of distribution. As the content of free residual chlorine may reduce during distribution, we may want to have a higher content of free residual chlorine when the water leaves the treatment plant.

The content of the free residual chlorine in chlorinated water will have to be tested continuously to make sure that treatment is still adequate. The chlorine demand of the raw water will often not be constant over time.

Chlorinating a batch of water

If a batch of water has to be treated, the amount of mother solution that is needed can be calculated with the formula:

$$Ms_{bat} = \left(\frac{Vol_{bat}}{Vol_{test}} \right) \times Ms_{test}$$

Ms_{bat} : the amount of mother solution required to chlorinate the batch of raw water (in ml)

Vol_{bat} : the volume of the batch of water which has to be treated (in litres)

Vol_{test} : the volume of water that was used in the test (in litres)

Ms_{test} : the amount of mother solution which was required to chlorinate the water in the test (in ml)

Thus, if in our example we need a free residual chlorine content of 0.5 mg/l, and we want to treat the water in a reservoir of 15m³ (15,000 litres), the amount of mother solution we would have to add would be (15,000/10 x 3) = 4,500 ml (= 4.5 litres).

Chlorinating a continuous supply of water

If a continuous supply of water has to be chlorinated, the amount of mother solution that has to be added per unit of time can be calculated with the formula:

$$Rate_{Ms} = \left(\frac{Flow_{sup}}{Vol_{test}} \right) \times Ms_{test}$$

$Rate_{Ms}$: the rate at which mother solution has to be added to the supply (in ml/second)

$Flow_{sup}$: the flow of the supply of raw water (in litres/second)

Vol_{test} : the volume of water that was used in the test (in litres)

Ms_{test} :   the amount of mother solution which was required to chlorinate the water in the test (in ml)

If we would want to treat the raw water of our example in a system with continuous supply which has to deliver 1.67 litres/second (100 litres/minute), the mother solution would have to be added to the raw water at a rate of (1.67/10 x 3) = 0.5 ml/second.

Annexes

A4

Annexe 5

Sizing pits for pit latrines and determining their infiltration capacity

CONTROLLING AND PREVENTING DISEASE

Calculating the size of pits for latrines, and assessing their infiltration capacity

In this annexe we will look at how we can calculate the size of a pit of a pit latrine, and we present a method for assessing how much liquid could be discharged in the pit.

Materials needed:
- Ruler which allows to measure in mm
- A transparent jar with cover
- A watch which indicates seconds
- Possibly a calculator

Determining the required size of a pit

The liquids in the pit will normally infiltrate into the soil, and excreta and anal cleansing material will decompose over time. What stays behind in the pit are decomposed solids.

To determine what volume a pit will have to be, we have to know how much of these solids (sludge) will accumulate during its period of use. Table E.1 presents estimates on how much solids will accumulate in pits used under different circumstances. These are the sludge accumulation rates.

Table A5.1. Approximate sludge accumulation rates in pit latrines [30]		
Anal cleansing material	**Wet pit** [a]	**Dry pit** [b]
Water	40 l/p/y (0.04 m³/p/y)	60 l/p/y (0.06 m³/p/y)
Solid material (e.g. stones, corncobs)	60 l/p/y (0.06 m³/p/y)	90 l/p/y (0.09 m³/p/y)

[a] : a pit in which the excreta are in the (ground)water
[b] : a pit in which the excreta are not in liquid
l/p/y : litres per person per year
m³/p/y : cubic metres per person per year

The values presented in table A5.1 are values that can be used when designing a latrine which will be used for several years.

It takes time for the solids to decompose, and the sludge will accumulate at a higher rate over the short term. If a latrine is designed for short term use, the accumulation rates from table E.1 will have to be multiplied by 1½.

The volume of the sludge that will accumulate over the design life (i.e. the total time over which the pit will be used) can be calculated with the formula [30]:

$$V_s = R \times P \times N$$

V_s : approximate volume of sludge that will be produced (in m³)
R : estimated sludge accumulation rate per person (see table E.1 (in m³/p/y))
P : the average number of people using the latrine over the design life
N : the design life of the pit (in years)

> A family of 6, who would build a latrine with a dry pit, and who would use water for anal cleansing, would accumulate over a period of 15 years a volume of around (0.06 x 6 x 15) = 5.4 m³.

Two additional things have to be taken into account when sizing the pit that has to be dug: the pit should be taken out of use when the level of the sludge in the pit has reached 0.5 metres below the slab [57], and if the pit needs to be lined, the lining may take an important volume.

> Thus, if in our example a rectangular pit would be dug of 1.6 x 1.4 metres, and it would have to be lined from the bottom to the top[1] with blocks 0.1 metres wide, the pit would only have an effective size of around 1.4 x 1.2 metres (we lose the width of the blocks on two sides). The horizontal surface of the pit would be (1.4 m x 1.2 m) = 1.68 m². To be able to contain 5.4 m³ of sludge, the pit would need to be (5.4 m³/1.68 m²) = 3.2 metres deep. As the top 0.5 metres of the pit can not be used, the total depth of the pit should be (3.2 m + 0.5 m =) 3.7 metres.

Determining the infiltration capacity of the pit

To avoid that a structure will flow over, the infiltration capacity of the pit needs to be sufficient to allow all the liquid to seep away. The infiltration capacity of a pit depends mainly on the type of the liquid, the surface area which allows infiltration, and the soil type.

The liquid that seeps out of a latrine pit will cause a partial blockage of the pores in the soil. This means that the infiltration capacity of a pit used for excreta will be

---

[1] Only the top 0.5 metres of a lining should be completely sealed. Below this, the lining should have sufficient openings to allow the liquid to seep into the surrounding soil

much lower than the infiltration capacity of an identical pit used for clean water. The figures we present here take into account this reduced capacity of infiltration of the soil.

The bottom of the pit will most probably clog up and become impermeable. Therefore only the vertical sides of the pit will be used to calculate the infiltration capacity [30].

The area of the pit which allows infiltration is the surface area of the bare soil. An impermeable lining (e.g. bricks, blocks, concrete) hinders infiltration. Only the openings in the lining should therefore be used to determine the surface of the infiltration area.

Liquid infiltrates into the soil because its hydraulic gradient is higher than that of the water in the surrounding soil. Therefore only the surface of the pit above the water table should be used to calculate the infiltration area [57].

In other words, the effective infiltration area is all bare soil on the vertical sides of a pit which are above the groundwater table (and below 0.5 metres under the slab).

In our example the actual size of the pit is 1.4 x 1.2 x 3.7 metres. As the top 0.5 metres of the pit should not be used, the effective depth of the pit is 3.2 metres. The pit will thus have two sides of 1.4 x 3.2 metres, and two sides of 1.2 x 3.2 metres. This gives a total surface area of ((2 x (1.4 x 3.2)) + (2 x (1.2 x 3.2))) = 16.6 m². If the blocks are laid in a honeycomb structure which leaves ¼ of the soil exposed, the effective area of infiltration will be (¼ x 16.6 m²) = 4.2 m². As the pit is dry, all this area is used.

(However, if during the wet season there is 1.5 metres of water in the pit, the effective depth of the pit would be (3.2 – 1.5 m) = 1.7 metres. The effective size of the pit would be ((2 x (1.4 x 1.7)) + (2 x (1.2 x 1.7))) = 8.8 m², and the area of infiltration (¼ x 8.8 m²) = 2.2 m²).

To estimate the potential infiltration capacity of the soil the following method can be used.

A transparent jar is half filled with soil, and topped up to three quarters with water. The jar is shaken vigorously to bring all soil in suspension and to break up all soil (no lumps of soil should be left). The jar is placed on a flat surface and the time taken. A mark is made to where the particles have settled after 25 seconds; this part are stones and sand. A second mark is made after 60 seconds, this part is silt. After 24 hours, clay will have settled out.

If the sample contains sand, silt and clay, three layers will have been identified. An estimate of the percentages of the different categories of particles can be found with the formula:

$$Per_{lay} = \left(\frac{Th_{lay}}{Th_{tot}} \right) \times 100 \%$$

Per_{lay} : percentage of the specific category of particles
Th_{lay} : thickness of the specific layer (in mm)
Th_{tot} : total thickness of all layers (in mm)

There are four possibilities (adapted from 249,268,281):

Sand	Silt	Clay	Infiltration capacity (in litres per m² per day)
-	-	over 40%	under 10 l/m²/d
-	over 50%	20-40%	around 10 l/m²/d
over 50%	under 50%	under 20%	around 25 l/m²/d
over 90%	-	-	around 33 l/m²/d

- : percentage is unimportant

If we would find in our test a layer of sand of 31 mm, silt 20 mm, and clay 6 mm (total thickness of all layers: 57 mm), than the percentages of the different particles would be: sand ((31/57 mm) x 100%) = 54%; silt ((20/57 mm) x 100%) = 35%; and clay ((6/57 mm) x 100%) = 11%. This would mean that the infiltration capacity of our soil would probably be around 25 l/m²/d.

The infiltration capacity of a pit can be calculated with the formula:

$$Ic_{pit} = A_{pit} \times Ic_{soil}$$

Ic_{pit} : infiltration capacity of the pit (in litres/day)
A_{pit} : effective surface of infiltration of the soil (in m²)
Ic_{soil} : the infiltration capacity of the soil (in litres/m²/day)

In the latrine of our example, the pit could deal with a supply of around (4.2 m² x 25 l/m²/d) = 105 litres per day. This means that if the local water usage is around 15 litres per person per day, it would be acceptable for the 6 users to dispose of their wastewater in the latrine. If the water supply would be upgraded though, the latrine would probably not be able to cope with the wastewater.

Annexe 6

Designing a simple drainage system for stormwater

Designing a simple stormwater drainage system

In this annexe we present a method to estimate how much stormwater a catchment area will produce, and how a drain can be sized to remove this water.

This method can be used to design a simple drainage system, or to determine whether a proposed drainage system is realistic.

Materials needed:
- A map of the catchment area with gradient lines, or a study of the catchment area from which it is possible to calculate its gradients and boundaries
- Ruler
- Paper with gridlines
- A calculator with the option 'y to the power x' (y^x)
- Preferably the IDF-curves (intensity-duration-frequency curves) of the zone studied

Analysis of the catchment area

First the catchment area with its boundaries will have to be identified on the map. A catchment area is the entire surface that will discharge its stormwater to one point (the discharge point). As water always flows from high to low, it is possible to identify the catchment area on a map with the aid of the gradient lines. Once the catchment area is identified, its surface must be estimated. This can be done by transferring the contours of a catchment area on paper with gridlines, and counting the grids.

Now the average gradient in the catchment area has to be identified. This can be done on the map with the aid of the gradient lines and the horizontal distances. Figure A6.1 shows how to determine the gradient in a terrain. Usually the average gradient of the terrain can be taken.

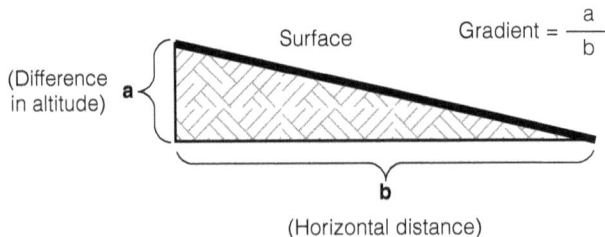

Figure A6.1. The gradient of a terrain

The next step is to assess the surface of the terrain. This information is needed to determine the runoff coefficient of the area. The runoff coefficient is that part of the rainwater which becomes stormwater; a runoff coefficient of 0.8 means that 80% of the rainfall will turn into stormwater. The runoff coefficient depends on the type of terrain, and its slope. Future changes in the terrain must be anticipated in the design of the drainage system to avoid problems at a later date. If no other values are available, the values from table A6.1 can be used.

Table A6.1. Runoff coefficients of different types of terrain (these values are approximate figures assuming a low soil permeability) [adapted from 49].

Terrain type	Runoff coefficient	
	Gradient < 0.05 (flat terrain)	Gradient > 0.05 (steep terrain)
Forest and pastures	0.4	0.6
Cultivated land	0.6	0.8
Residential areas and light industry	0.7	0.8
Dense construction and heavy industry	1.0	1.0

Determining the rainfall intensity for which the system is designed

If no local IDF-curves (intensity-duration-frequency curve) are available, a rainfall intensity of 100 mm per hour can be assumed (this value is for tropical countries, with catchment areas smaller than 150 ha) [17]. If no IDF curves can be found, the reader can skip directly to the section *Calculating the amount of water the catchment area will produce*

If the IDF curves of the area can be obtained, these should be used. IDF curves show the rainfall intensity (in mm per hour) against the duration of the rains (in minutes) for specific return periods. Several curves from different return periods may be presented in one graph. A curve with a return period of 1 year will show the worst storm that will on average occur every year, a curve with a return period of 2 years is the worst storm that can be expected in a 2 year period, and so on.

To know which value to take from the IDF curve, the time of concentration has to be calculated. The time of concentration is the time the water needs to flow from the furthest point in the catchment area to the point where it will leave the area (the discharge point). The time of concentration is determined with the formula [49]:

$$T_{con} = 0.02 \times (L_{max})^{0.77} \times (S_{av})^{-0.383}$$

T_{con} : the time of concentration (in minutes)
L_{max} : the maximum length of flow in the catchment (in metres)
S_{av}: the average gradient of the catchment area

If the furthest point of our catchment area is at a distance of 500 metres from the discharge point, and the difference in altitude between this point and the discharge point is 10 metres, than the time of concentration would be around $(0.02 \times (500)^{0.77} \times (10/500)^{-0.383} =)$ 11 minutes.

The curve with the appropriate return period is chosen (for residential areas often the curve with a 2 year return period [39]).

We look for the rainfall intensity on the chosen curve, at the duration of a storm equal to the time of concentration which we calculated.

Calculating the amount of water the catchment area will produce

The amount of stormwater the catchment will produce can be determined with the formula [adapted from 49]:

$$Q_{des} = 2.8 \times C \times i \times A$$

Q_{des} : the design peak runoff rate, or the maximum flow of stormwater the system will be designed for (in litres per second)
C : the runoff coefficient (see table F.1)
i : the rainfall intensity at the time of concentration read from the chosen IDF curve; if no IDF curves are available, a value of 100 mm/h can be taken (in mm/h)
A : the surface area of the catchment area (in ha (10,000 m²))

Thus, if our catchment area would be a residential area, with a surface of 12 ha, a gradient of 0.02, and a rainfall intensity of 100 mm/h, than the design peak runoff rate would be around $(2.8 \times 0.7 \times 100 \times 12 =)$ 2350 litres per second.

It should be remembered that this figure is not a fixed value. Every once in a while storms will occur which produce more water than the drainage system can deal with (normally, on average, periods just above the return period). The larger the capacity of the system (the longer the return period the system is designed for) the less often it will overflow, and the higher its costs.

Sizing a drain to cope with the design peak runoff rate

With the design peak runoff rate known, we will have to plan where the drains will be installed. A drainage system must be planned together with other structures like roads and buildings to assure they are all adapted to one another.

Unlined drains are at risk of erosion, and should therefore have a relatively low gradient to control the velocity of the stormwater. Gradients in unlined drains should probably not exceed 0.005 (1 metre drop in 200 metres horizontal distance). In less stable soil unlined drains should be made with a slope less steep than 1/2 (see figure A6.2), in more cohesive material a steeper slope could be used [17].

The size of the drain can be calculated with the formula [17]:

$$Q = 1000 \times \left(\frac{A \times (R)^{0.67} \times (S)^{0.5}}{N} \right)$$

Q : the capacity of discharge of the drain (in l/s)
A : the cross section of the flow (in m²)
R : the hydraulic radius of the drain (see figure F.3, in m)
S : the gradient of the drain
N : Manning's roughness coefficient: for earth drains, 0.025; brick drains,

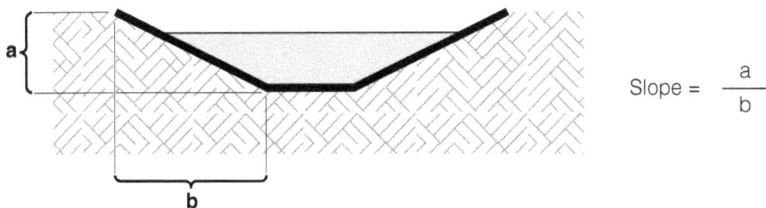

Figure A6.2. Section of an unlined drain in less stable soil

the hydraulic radius is the surface area of the cross section of the flow/the total length of the contact between water and drain;

Hydraulic radius = (a x b) / (a + b + c)

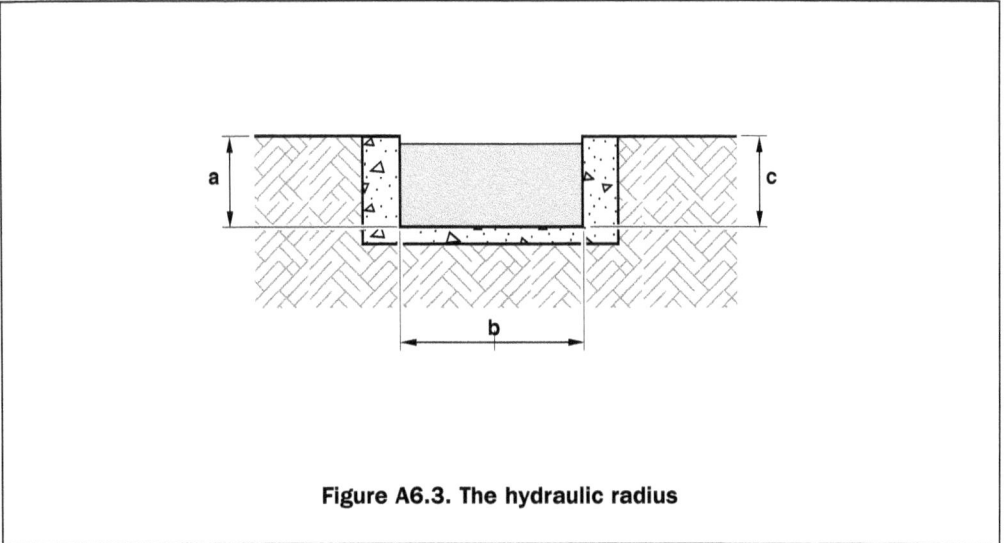

Figure A6.3. The hydraulic radius

A completely filled, rectangular, smooth concrete drain of 1.5 m by 0.7 m, with a gradient of 0.005, can in ideal circumstances discharge around $(1000 \times ((1.5 \times 0.7) \times ((1.5 \times 0.7/(1.5 + 0.7 + 0.7))^{0.67} \times (0.005)^{0.5}) / 0.015) = 2500$ litres per second.

This calculation will probably have to be repeated a number of times to find the adequate size of drain [17].

Some reserve will be needed so that the drain is not completely filled with water, and because the calculated discharge rate does not take into account deposited solids, and lack of maintenance, which will usually reduce the efficiency of the system [39].

Annexe 7

Minimum emergency standards

Annexes

Annexes

A7

Priorities and standards in emergency situations

In this annexe we present the requirements for survival, and the minimum standards in service in WES required by a population living in an unstable situation (e.g. after a natural disaster, internally displaced persons, refugees).

Survival level

Table A7.1 presents the minimum requirements so that healthy people can survive in the short term. This is an absolute minimum, and a rapid improvement, possibly within days, will be necessary to prevent a rapid deterioration of the health situation in a population. The survival levels do not cover the special needs of the sick, the wounded, or the undernourished.

Table A7.1. The minimum immediate requirements for survival of healthy people in an emergency

Water and personal hygiene	Sanitation	Environmental sanitation	Other possible needs
■ A water supply of 3 to 5 litres per person per day is needed, providing water of reasonable quality, accessible to all [21]. ■ Every household should have water containers which provide a storage capacity of 3 litres per person or more. If the water supply is unreliable, or access to water poor, people will need a larger storage capacity.		**Drainage** ■ People must be located so that stormwater or floodwater is not a direct threat to them.	■ Adequate protection from the elements (blankets, clothing, material to make shelters) [47]§ ■ Adequate supply of food ■ Cooking pots and fuel [66] ■ People must be located so that they are not under direct threat (e.g. hostile population, landmines) **Parallel to survival** ■ Setting up of a co-ordination system to deal with the emergency. ■ Assessment of the situation [47]

The minimum standards of service in emergencies

Certain standards of service must be provided to limit the health risks of people in an emergency. Table A7.2 presents the standards that should be aimed for in WES in an emergency. These standards must be achieved as quickly as the situation allows.

Medical personnel will have to set up a surveillance system of disease to identify oncoming epidemics and important health problems in the population. Emergency supplies needed in the case of epidemics have to be present locally, and local medical personnel have to be trained in advance on how to cope with outbreaks.

Table A7.2. The minimum standards in water and (environmental) sanitation in an emergency

Water and personal hygiene	Sanitation	Environmental sanitation
Water supply ■ Existing water sources must be protected. ■ A water supply of 15 litres per person per day should be accessible to all. The maximum distance to the water points should be <150 metres. The maximum number of people per tap should be: 200-250. The maximum number of taps per distribution point: 6-8. The maximum number of people per handpump: 500-750.	■ People must be discouraged from defecating in, or close to, streams, ponds, any other source of water, or on agricultural land with crops [64]. ■ Structures that deal with the excreta will have to be installed. Usually it is not possible to construct adequate structures in sufficient numbers immediately, and therefore the situation will have to be improved gradually.	**Drainage** ■ The site must have adequate drainage which rapidly removes stormwater [66]. ■ An adequate system of dealing with waste water from water points, leakage, domestic waste water and waste water from communal structures must be present. Waste water from water points can usually be led into vegetation.

Annexes

A7

Table A7.2. The minimum standards in water and (environmental) sanitation in an emergency (continued)

Water and personal hygiene	Sanitation	Environmental sanitation

■ The water quality must be reasonable to start with, and be improved as soon as possible.
It is often better to have enough water of intermediate quality than to have little water of high quality.At the beginning of the distribution system, a free residual chlorine content of 0.6–1.0 mg/litre is usually adequate to obtain water with a free residual chlorine content of 0.3–0.5 mg/litre at the distribution point [47].
 	
Water storage
■ Every household must have a minimum of 2 water collection vessels of 10–20 litres and an additional storage capacity of 20 litres. The vessels should have a narrow neck and be covered.
	■ The sanitary structures that can be used (in order of low preference (but ease to install) to high preference (but more demanding to install)):
	  – open defecation fields
	  – trench defecation fields
	  – communal trench latrines
	  – communal pit or borehole latrines
	  – household pit latrines [21]
	
	Gradually the structures will have to be improved, depending on the feasibility (e.g. start with trench defecation field, than communal pit latrines, than household pit latrines).
	In communal structures personnel for cleaning and maintenance will have to be employed.
	The sexes should be separated in communal structures, and the issues of safety to women must be addressed.
	Public latrines must be installed in public places.
	All structures need some kind of water source for handwashing, anal cleansing, cleaning of the structure and flushing.
		■ If waste water containing solids is led into a soakaway, it must be strained or led through a silt trap. If the waste water led into a soakaway contains grease or soap, it should be led through a grease-trap.
		■ No unwanted open water should be present close to, or in, the camp.
		■ Tools needed to maintain the drainage system should be provided [47].
		
		Solid waste management
		■ Where domestic refuse is not buried or burnt 'on-plot', waste will have to be collected every day, or every other day, to avoid attracting flies or rats.Every 10 households will need one container of 100 litres to collect and store the waste.
		The container should be within 15 metres of the dwelling. If a communal waste pit is used, it should not be more than 100 metres from the dwelling.
		■ There have to be adequate waste collection points on markets and slaughtering areas. These wastes should be collected daily [66].
		■ Wastes should be disposed of in a pit. Every day it should be covered by at least 0.15 metres of soil, and the ultimate layer of soil should be at least 0.5 metres thick.

Table A7.2. The minimum standards in water and (environmental) sanitation in an emergency (continued)

Water and personal hygiene	Sanitation	Environmental sanitation
Personal hygiene ■ A minimum of 250 grams of soap must be available per person per month. ■ If household bathing facilities are not available, communal facilities will be needed. These should be culturally acceptable, and the sexes must be separated. Communal laundry facilities may be required. Women must be able to wash undergarments and sanitary cloths in privacy. ■ A minimum of 1 washing basin per 100 people is needed [66]. *Other* ■ If diarrhoeal diseases are a risk, Oral Rehydration Therapy (ORT) units must be set up. The minimum is one ORT unit per health structure. In case of a diarrhoeal outbreak, decentralised ORT units are needed [47].	■ The latrines should be technically sound and acceptable to all users. Initially 1 latrine, or metre of trench, per 50 to 100 users must be installed [47], as soon as possible this must be improved to 1 latrine per 20 users. Latrines should if possible not be further away than 50 metres from dwellings [66]. Water sources used for drinking should not be at risk from sanitary structures. ■ Often anal cleansing material will have to be provided. In defecation fields, soil to cover faeces may have to be given to users.	■ Medical wastes must be properly disposed of by incineration and/or disposal in a deep protected pit. *Disposal of the dead* ■ Usually the health hazard associated with dead bodies is negligible [66], but during epidemics of cholera, plague, or louse-borne typhus fever, dead bodies must be dealt with adequately [21]. ■ Graveyards or mass graves should be located at least 30 metres from a groundwater source used for drinking. ■ Cemeteries should be planned early. Possibly cloth or other material needed for burial or cremation have to be provided to the family [66]. *Vector control* ■ Where the population is infested with body louse, they must be deloused. ■ Where possible the environment should be made unfavourable to vectors or intermediate hosts (e.g. through drainage and solid waste management). ■ If adequate and feasible, people have to be supplied with material that allows them to protect themselves against vectors (e.g impregnated mosquito nets) [47].

Annexes

A7

References

(1)   Agarwal, A.; Kimondo, J.; Moreno, G. and Tinker, J. (1983) *Water, Sanitation, Health - for all? Prospects for the International Drinking Water Supply and Sanitation Decade, 1981-90.* The International Institute for Environment and Development.

(2)   Bell, D.R. (ed.) (1995) *Lecture Notes on Tropical Medicine, 4th edition.* Blackwell Science Ltd.: Oxford (UK).

(3)   Benenson, A.S. (ed.) (1995) *Control of Communicable Diseases Manual, 16th edition.* The American Public Health Association: Washington (USA).

(4)   Berkow. R. (ed.) (1992) *The Merck Manual of Diagnosis and Therapy, 16th edition.* Merck Research Laboratories: Rahway (USA).

(5)   Birley, M.H. (-) *Guidelines for Forecasting the Vector-borne Disease Implications of Water Resources Development.* WHO Collaborating Centre: Environmental Management for Vector Control, Liverpool School of Tropical Medicine: Liverpool (UK).

(6)   Birley, M. and Lock, K. (1999) *The Health Impacts of Peri-Urban Natural Resource Development.* International Centre for Health Impact Assessment; Liverpool School of Tropical Medicine: Liverpool (UK)

(7)   Boot, M.T. and Cairncross, S. (eds.) (1993) *Actions Speak: The Study of Hygiene Behaviour in Water and Sanitation Projects.* IRC International Water and Sanitation Centre: The Hague (The Netherlands).

(8)   Bowry, T.R. (1984) *Immunology Simplified, 2nd edition.* Oxford University Press: Oxford (UK)

(9)   Brandberg, B. (1997) *Latrine Building: A Handbook for Implementing the SanPlat System.* Intermediate Technology Publications: London (UK).

(10)   Bres, P. (1986) *Public Health Action in Emergencies caused by Epidemics: A Practical Guide.* World Health Organization: Geneva (Switzerland).

(11)   Brown, V.; Moren, A and Paquet, C. (1996) *Evaluation Rapide de l'Etat de Sante d'une Population Deplacee ou Refugiee.* Médecins Sans Frontières: Paris (France).

(12)   Busvine, J.R. (1982) *Control of Domestic Flies, 7th edition.* Ross Institute of Tropical Hygiene Publication No.5: London (UK).

(13)   Cairncross, A.M. (1990) *Health Impacts in Developing Countries: New Evidence and New Prospects.* Journal of the Institution of Water and Environmental Managment: Vol.4, pp.571-577.

(14)   Cairncross, S.(1988) *Small Scale Sanitation. Ross Institute of Tropical Hygiene Bulletin No.8.* The Ross Institute: London (UK).

(15)   Cairncross, S and Feachem, R (1998) *Environmental Health Engineering in the Tropics: An Introductory Text, 2nd edition.* John Wiley & Sons: Chichester (UK).

(16)   Cook, G. (1996) *Manson's Tropical Diseases, 20th edition.* WB Saunders Company Ltd.: London (UK).

(17)   Cotton, A. and Franceys, R. (1991) *Services for Shelter: Infrastructure for Urban Low-Income Housing. Liverpool Planning Manual 3.* Liverpool University Press: Liverpool (UK).

(18)   Curtis, V. and Kanki, B. (1998) *Happy, Healthy and Hygienic: How to set up a Hygiene Promotion Programme. WES Technical Guidelines Series No.5.* United Nations Children's Fund: New York (USA).

(19)   Dale, R. (1998) *Evaluation Frameworks for Development Programmes and Projects.* Sage Publications: New Delhi (India)

(20)   Davis, J.; Garvey, G. and Wood, M. (1993) *Developing and Managing Community Water Supplies. Oxfam Development Guidelines No.8.* Oxfam: Oxford (UK).

(21)   Davis, J. and Lambert, R. (1995) *Engineering in Emergencies: A Practical Guide for Relief Workers.* Intermediate Technology Publications: London (UK).

(22)   Delmas, G. and Courvallet, M. (1994) *Public Health Engineering in Emergency Situation.* Médecins Sans Frontières: Paris (France).

(23)   Department for International Development (1998) *Guidance Manual on Water Supply and Sanitation Programmes.* WELL: London (UK).

(24)   Driscoll, F.G. (ed.) (1986) *Groundwater and Wells, 2nd edition.* U.S. Filter/Johnson Screens: St.Paul (USA).

(25)   Esrey, S.A. (1996) *Water, Waste, and Well-Being: A Multicountry Study.* American Journal of Epidemiology: Vol.143, No.6, pp.608-623.

(26)   Esrey, S.A.; Potash, J.B.; Roberts, L. and Shiff, C. (1991) *Effects of Improved Water Supply and Sanitation on Ascariasis, Diarrhoea, Dracunculiasis, Hookworm Infection, Schistosomiasis, and Trachoma.* Bulletin of the World Health Organization: 69(5), pp.609-621.

(27)   Feachem, R.G. (1984) *Interventions for the Control of Diarrhoeal Diseases among Young Children: Promotion of Personal and Domestic Hygiene.* Bulletin of the World Health Organization: 62(3), pp.467-476.

(28)   Feachem, R.F.; Bradley, D.J.; Garelick, H. and Mara, D.D. (1983) *Sanitation and Disease: Health Aspects of Excreta and Wastewater Management. World Bank Studies in Water Supply and Sanitation 3.* John Wiley & Sons: Chichester (UK).

(29)   Feachem, R.; McGarry, M. and Mara, D. (eds.) (1977) *Water, Wastes and Health in Hot Climates.* John Wiley & Sons: Chichester (UK).

(30)   Franceys, R.; Pickford, J. and Reed, R. (1992) *A Guide to the Development of On-Site Sanitation.* World Health Organization: Geneva (Switzerland).

(31)   Gerba, C.P.; Wallis, C. and Melnick, J.L. (1975) *Fate of Wastewater Bacteria and Viruses in Soil.* Journal of the Irrigation and Drainage Division; Proceedings of the American Society of Civil Engineers: Vol.101, No.IR.3, pp.157-174.

(32)   Han, A.M. and Hliang, T. (1989) *Prevention of Diarrhoea and Dysentery by Handwashing.* Transaction of the Royal Society of Tropical Medicine and Hygiene: NO.83, pp.128-131.

(33)   Hoque, B.A. and Briend, A. (1991) *A Comparison of Local Handwashing Agents in Bangladesh.* Journal of Tropical Medicine and Hygiene: Vol.94. pp.61-64.

(34)   House, S. and Reed, B. (1997) *Emergency Water Sources: Guidelines for Selection and Treatment.* Water, Engineering and Development Centre (WEDC); Loughborough University: Loughborough (UK).

(35)   Hoverd, C. and Brown, R. (1986) *Tropical Diseases: including Aspects of Hygiene, Malnutrition and Injuries.* MacMillan Publishers Ltd.: London (UK).

(36)   Hunter, J.M.; Rey, L.; Chu, K.Y.; Adekolu-John, E.O. and Mott, K.E. (1993) *Parasitic Diseases in Water Resources Development: The Need for Intersectoral Negotiation.* World Health Organization: Geneva (Switzerland).

(37)   Hurst, C.J. (ed.) (1996) *Modeling Disease Transmission and its Prevention by Disinfection.* Cambridge University Press: Cambridge (UK).

(38)   Kerr, C. (ed.) (1990) *Community Health and Sanitation.* Intermediate Technology Publications: London (UK).

(39)   Kolsky, P. (1998) *Storm Drainage: An Engineering Guide to the Low-Cost Evaluation of System Performance.* Intermediate Technology Publications: London (UK).

(40)   Koopman, J.S. (1978) *Diarrhea and School Toilet Hygiene in Cali, Colombia.* American Journal of Epidemiology: Vol.107, No.5, pp.412-420.

(41)   Kreier, J.P. and Mortensen, R.F. (1990) *Infection, Resistance, and Immunity.* Harper & Row: New York (USA).

(42)   Lewis, W.J.; Foster, S.S.D. and Drasar, B.S. (1980) *The Risk of Groundwater Pollution by On-Site Sanitation in Developing Countries: A Literature Review.* The International Reference Centre for Wastes Disposal: Duebendorf (Switzerland).

(43)   Macdonald, D.; Ahmed, K.M.; Islam, M.S.; Lawrence, A. and Khandker, Z.Z. (1999) *Pit Latrines - A Source of Contamination in Peri-Urban Dhaka?* Waterlines: Vol.17, No.4, pp.6-8.

(44)   Mahmoud, A.A.F. (ed.) (1993) *Tropical and Geographical Medicine: Companion Handbook, 2nd edition.* McGraw-Hill inc.: New York (USA).

(45)   Martin, E.A. (ed.) (1998) *Concise Colour Medical Dictionary, 2nd edition.* Oxford University Press: Oxford (UK).

(46)   Médecins Sans Frontières (1996) *Eau, Hygiene et Assainissement: Chimie des Eaux Guideline. Internal document from EHA MSF/B, Service Medical.* Médecins Sans Frontières: Brussels (Belgium).

(47)   Médecins Sans Frontières (1997) *Refugee Health: An Approach to Emergency Situations.* MacMillan Education Ltd.: London (UK).

(48)   Mintz, E.D.; Reiff, F.M. and Tauxe, R.V. (1995) *Safe Water Treatment and Storage in the Home: A Practical new Strategy to prevent Waterborne Disease.* The Journal of the American Medical Association: Vol.273, No.12, pp.948-953.

(49)   Morris, P. and Therivel, R. (eds.) (1995) *Methods of Environmental Impact Assessment.* University College London Press Ltd.: London (UK).

(50)   Moxon, E.R. (ed.) (1990) *Modern Vaccines: Current Practice and New Approaches; A Lancet Review.* Edward Arnold: London (UK).

(51)   Murray, C.J.L. and Lopez, A.D. (1997) *Global Mortality, Disability, and the Contribution of Risk Factors: Global Burden of Disease Study.* The Lancet: Vol.349, pp.1436-1442.

(52)   Murray, C.J.L. and Lopez, A.D. (1997) *Mortality by Cause for eight Regions of the World: Global Burden of Disease Study.* The Lancet: Vol.349, pp.1269-1276.

(53)   Reed, R.A. (1995) *Sustainable Sewerage: Guidelines for Community Schemes.* Intermediate Technology Publications: London (UK).

(54)   Perrin, P. (1996) *Handbook on War and Public Health.* International Committee of the Red Cross: Geneva (Switzerland).

(55)   Phoon, W.O. (ed.) (1985) *Epidemiology for the Health Officer: A Field Manual for the Tropics.* World Health Organization: Geneva (Switzerland).

(56)   Pickford, J. (ed.) (1991) *The Worth of Water: Technical Briefs on Health, Water and Sanitation.* Intermediate Technology Publications: London (UK).

(57)   Pickford, J. (1995) *Low-Cost Sanitation: A survey of Practical Experience.* Intermediate Technology Publications: London (UK).

(58)   Reed, R.A. (1998) *Low-Cost Sanitation: Unit 3: Pit Latrines-Components, Construction and Design. Distance Learning Module.* Water, Engineering and Development Centre (WEDC); Loughborough University: Loughborough (UK).

(59)   Robinson, D. (1981) 'Lecture Notes in Epidemiology and Communicable Disease Control' in Robinson, D. (ed.) (1985) *Epidemiology and the Community Control of Disease in Warm Climate Countries, 2nd edition.* Churchill Livingstone: Edinburgh (UK).

(60)   Rottier, E. (1999) *HeSaWa and Disease-prevention: The development of an Informative Tool on Holistic Disease-prevention. Unpublished MSc Project Report.* Water, Engineering and Development Centre (WEDC); Loughborough University: Loughborough (UK).

(61)   Rozendaal, J.A. (1997) *Vector Control: Methods for use by Individuals and Communities.* World Health Organization: Geneva (Switzerland).

(62)   Saywell, D. (1999) *Pollution from On-Site Sanitation - the Risks? What Risks?* Waterlines: Vol.17, No.4, pp.22-23.

(63)   Scott, T.M.E.; Gray-Donald, K. and Kalumba, O.N. (1996) *Multiple Infection with Plasmodium and Helminths in Communities of Low and relatively High Socio-Economic Status.* Annals of Tropical Medicine and Parasitology: Vol.90, No.3, pp.277-293.

(64)   Shaw, R.J. (ed.) (1999) *Running Water: More Technical Briefs on Health, Water and Sanitation.* Intermediate Technology Publications: London (UK).

(65)   Stanton, B.F. and Clemens, J.D. (1987) *An Educational Intervention for Altering Water-Sanitation Behaviors to Reduce Childhood Diarrhea in Urban Bangladesh: II. A Randomized Trial to Assess the Impact of the Intervention on Hygienic Behaviors and Rates of Diarrhea.* American Journal of Epidemiology: Vol.125, No.2, pp.292-301.

REFERENCES

(66)   The Sphere Project (2000) *Humanitarian Charter and Minimum Standards in Disaster Re-sponse.* The Spere Project: Geneva (Switzerland)

(67)   Thomson, M.C. (1995) *Disease Prevention through Vector Control: Guidelines for Relief Organisations.* Oxfam: Oxford (UK).

(68)   Twort, A.C.; Law, F.M.; Crowley, F.W. and Ratnayaka, D.D. (1994) *Water Supply, 4th edition.* Edward Arnold: London (UK).

(69)   UNICEF (1995) 'UNICEF strategies in Water and Environmental Sanitation' in Department for International Development (1998) *Guidance Manual on Water Supply and Sanitation Programmes.* WELL: London (UK).

(70)   VanDerslice, J. and Briscoe, J. (1995) *Environmental Interventions in Developing Countries: Interactions and their Implications.* American Journal of Epidemiology: Vol.141, No.2, pp.135-144.

(71)   Vaughan, J.P. and Morrow, R.H. (eds.) (1989) *Manual of Epidemiology for District Health Management.* World Health Organization: Geneva (Switzerland).

(72)   Veer, de T. (1998) *Beyond Sphere: Integral Quality System for the Operation of Water and Sanitation Programs in Camps, unpublished draft report.* De Veer Consultancy: Leiden (the Netherlands).

(73)   Webber, R. (1998) *Communicable Disease Epidemiology and Control.* CAB International: Wallingford (UK).

(74)   Werner, D.; Thuman, C. and Maxwell, J. (1992) *Where There is no Doctor: a Village Health Care Handbook, revised English edition.* The Hesperian Foundation: California (USA).

(75)   Withers, B. and Vipond, S. (1974) *Irrigation: Design and Practice.* B.T. Batsford Limited: London (UK).

(76)   World Bank, the (1993) 'World Development Report' in Webber, R. (1998) *Communicable Disease Epidemiology and Control.* CAB International: Wallingford (UK).

(77)   World Health Organization (1980) *Environmental Management for Vector Control. WHO Technical Report Series 649.* World Health Organization: Geneva (Switzerland).

(78)   World Health Organization (1981) *Drinking-water and Sanitation 1981-1990: A Way to Health.* World Health Organization: Geneva (Switzerland).

(79)   World Health Organization (1990) *WHO Expert Committee on Environmental Health in Urban Development.* World Health Organization: Geneva (Switzerland).

(80)   World Health Organization (1991) *Insect and Rodent Control through Environmental Management: A Community Action Programme.* World Health Organization: Geneva (Switzerland).

(81)   World Health Organization (1993) *The Urban Health Crisis: Strategies for Health for All in the Face of Rapid Urbanisation.* World Health Organization: Geneva (Switzerland).

(82)   World Health Organization (1997) *Guidelines for Drinking-Water Quality: Volume 3, Surveillance and Control of Community Supplies. 2nd edition.* World Health Organization: Geneva (Switzerland).

(83)   World Health Organization (1999) World Health Organization Fact Sheets. <http://www.who.int/inf-fs/en/>: 20.08.1999.

(84)   World Health Organization (1999) World Health Organization Fact Sheets. <http://www.who.int/inf-fs/en/>: 15.09.1999.

(85)   World Health Organization (1999) World Health Organization. <http://www.who.int/emc/diseases/leish/>: 20.08.1999.

(86)   Wright, R.C. (1986) *The Seasonality of Bacterial Quality of Water in a Tropical Developing Country (Sierra Leone).* The Journal of Hygiene: Vol.96, pp.75-82

(87)   Yeager, J.G. and O'Brien, R.T. (1979) *Enterovirus Inactivation in Soil.* Applied and Environmental Microbiology: Vol.38, pp.694-701.

(88)   Zaidi, S.A. (1988) *Poverty and Disease: Need for Structural Change.* Social Science and Medicine: Vol.27, No.2, pp.119-127.

Alphabetical index of diseases

Other titles in this series

Emergency Sanitation
Assessment and programme design

Peter Harvey, Sohrab Baghri and Bob Reed

This book is designed to assist those involved in planning and implementing emergency sanitation programmes. The main focus of the book is a systematic and structured approach to assessment and programme design. It provides a balance between the hardware (technical) and software (socio-cultural, institutional) aspects of sanitation programmes, and links short-term emergency response to long-term sustainability. The book is relevant to a wide range of emergency situations, including both natural and conflict-induced disasters, and open and closed settings. It is suitable for field technicians, engineers and hygiene promoters, as well as staff at agency headquarters. Included free with each book is a mini CD and an 'aide-memoire' to the process of planning and implementation.

384pp. (250/176)   **2002**
Price: £29.95   **ISBN:** 1 84380 005 5
http://www.lboro.ac.uk/wedc/publications/es.htm

Emergency Vector Control Using Chemicals

Christophe Lacarin and Bob Reed

The control of vectors that transmit diseases in emergencies is critical to the prevention of epidemics. This handbook describes how such vectors can be identified and controlled using chemicals. Aimed at non-specialists such as logisticians, engineers and health workers, it provides advice on identifying the responsible vector, selecting the appropriate control chemical and the means of application, together with advice on planning an implementation programme.

134pp. (250/176)   **1999**
Price: £19.95   **ISBN:** 0 906055 65 2
http://www.lboro.ac.uk/wedc/publications/evc.htm

Emergency Water Sources
Guidelines for selection and treatment

Sarah House and Bob Reed

These guidelines have been designed to help those involved in the assessment of emergency water sources to collect relevant information in a systematic way, to use this information to select a source or sources and to determine the appropriate level of treatment required to make the water suitable for drinking. The book is relevant to a wide range of emergency situations, including both natural and conflict-induced disasters.

320pp. (250/176)   **2000**
Price: £25.95   **ISBN:** 0 906055 71 7
http://www.lboro.ac.uk/wedc/publications/ews.htm

Out in the Cold
Emergency water supply and sanitation for cold regions

Mark Buttle and Michael Smith

During the 1990s, events in the Balkans, countries of the former Soviet Union, Afghanistan and Northern Iraq have demonstrated that humanitarian disasters are not confined to 'the South' but may strike anywhere in the world. As a result, relief agencies have been tested in ways previously unimaginable. Aid workers have to be ever more adaptable in order to provide life-saving water supply and sanitation facilities in areas where freezing conditions occur.

This revised handbook is designed for aid workers working in cool temperate or cold regions. It is designed to provide specific supplementary information that can be used together with the information given in more general emergency manuals.

120pp. (250/176)   **2002**
Price: £19.95   **ISBN:** 0 906055 91 1
http://www.lboro.ac.uk/wedc/publications/oitc.htm

www.ingramcontent.com/pod-product-compliance
Lightning Source LLC
Chambersburg PA
CBHW051555030426
42334CB00034B/3445